THE NEXT CRASH

*How Short-Term Profit Seeking
Trumps Airline Safety*

AMY L. FRAHER

ILR PRESS
AN IMPRINT OF
CORNELL UNIVERSITY PRESS
ITHACA AND LONDON

First published 2014 by Cornell University Press
Printed in the United States of America

Library of Congress Cataloging-in-Publication Data

Fraher, Amy Louise, author.
    The next crash : how short-term profit seeking trumps airline safety /
Amy L. Fraher.
        pages cm
    Includes bibliographical references and index.
    ISBN 978-0-8014-5285-7 (cloth : alk. paper)
    1. Aeronautics—United States—Safety measures—Finance. 2. Aircraft
accidents—United States—Prevention—Finance. 3. Airlines—
Employees—Salaries, etc.—United States. 4. Airlines—United States—
Finance. I. Title.
    HE9803.A5F73   2014
    363.12'4—dc23   2013046809

Cornell University Press strives to use environmentally responsible
suppliers and materials to the fullest extent possible in the publishing
of its books. Such materials include vegetable-based, low-VOC inks
and acid-free papers that are recycled, totally chlorine-free, or partly
composed of nonwood fibers. For further information, visit our website
at www.cornellpress.cornell.edu.

Cloth printing   10 9 8 7 6 5 4 3 2 1

In memory of my brother Pete, an inspiration
January 19, 1961–June 15, 2013

CONTENTS

THE NEXT CRASH

Prologue: Falling

I remember how clear and blue the sky was as we climbed away from Chicago's O'Hare International Airport. I was a United pilot based in San Francisco flying my leg heading homeward. The crisp fall morning made me reminisce about Septembers from my New England childhood and anticipating the start of school. The captain reached over and tore off the paper message that spit out from the cockpit printer: "SECURITY BREACH. LAND ASAP. DON'T ALARM PASSENGERS." We weren't too surprised to receive the instructions. We had already heard several Delta airliners diverting. By the time it was our turn, air traffic controllers no longer sounded confused. Everyone was coming out of the sky. We assumed some late-running passenger must have skipped through the airport security checks and we'd be back flying shortly, once things got sorted out on the ground. We couldn't have been more wrong. The world was fragmenting.

I increased the range of my navigation screen and peered into the future, calculating our descent.

"Where would you like to land?" the captain asked.

"Looks like Omaha's best."

"Omaha it is then," he confirmed and set about communicating our request.

We landed, taxied to the gate, and parked, as ill informed about the developing events as we were when airborne. I opened the cockpit door and a passenger wandered up. He shared news headlines about some escalating crisis streaming across his pager. One story claimed an airliner had a navigation failure and had hit a skyscraper in New York.

"That's ridiculous," I thought. "What pilot would fly into a building on a morning so clear you could almost see the future from the flight deck at 35,000 feet?"

Nothing made sense.

The captain left the cockpit to investigate. I trailed behind slowly, only then realizing that our 298 passengers and eleven flight attendants had already quickly deplaned. Pausing in the vacant first-class cabin, I snapped my mobile phone open and speed-dialed home. My partner picked up on the first ring.

"Looks like I may be late landing," I said. "We've run into some security problem; don't know what's up. But, we should be back in the air soon."

"Don't you know what's happened?"

"Happened?"

"It's fallen!"

"Fallen—what's fallen?"

"Everything: the Twin Towers, New York, airplanes. People are jumping out of buildings!"

"What?"

"Are you all right?"

"Yes, yes."

"Thank God. Check the TV!"

I found a television in the ground crew lounge and joined a group of about fifty other aviation employees crammed into a room designed for about twenty. Pilots, flight attendants, mechanics, customer service reps, baggage handlers, dispatchers, and fuelers from a variety of companies— we were all in this together. The second building, the North Tower, of

New York's World Trade Center had just collapsed. The image played over and over on the television: first one tower, then the other, imploding in a heap of grey dust. One minute it was up, and the next it was down. Ashes to ashes, dust to dust. It was a beacon on the horizon, solid and steady, a place where people worked, dedicated their lives, provided a service, and shared an identity. And now it was hit and falling.

We were in that kind of nightmare place where something horrible is happening and you can't make it stop. Frightened yet fascinated, we kept watching. As if you'll be rewarded with clarity if you just stand watch long enough. We didn't know it then but we were watching the world change irreparably, right before our eyes.

This book, written more than a decade after that fateful day in September 2001, attempts to make sense of what happened next within America's airline industry. In particular, my aim is to reconceptualize the idea of risk and safety, drawing parallels between aviation and other risk management professions, particularly finance. The question motivating my analysis is simple: Has profit seeking been allowed to trump safety in the US commercial airline industry? If so, what are the repercussions for risk—should we expect another major airline crash sometime soon?

If this topic immediately makes you feel uneasy, that is good. Aviation safety is an area that should concern us all. Yet, for reasons discussed in the following chapters, safety has not often been the priority in aviation industry decision making. And perhaps most important for you or your family's next flight, air safety does not concern the right people—namely, airline executives, aviation industry regulators, politicians, watchdog groups, or even the flying public—in the right way often enough. I hope this book will help change that.

Almost two decades ago, light years in the evolution of the aviation industry, several excellent books provided a candid behind-the-scenes look at the long history of troubles within US aviation, noting various flaws within the airline industry.[1] Yet, these books became quickly outdated in the post-9/11 aviation business world, as bankruptcy, cost cutting, downsizing, merger, employee layoffs (called furloughs), and increased passenger fees with reduced customer service became the norm. Although none of these events are individually unusual in commercial aviation, the extent to which they have combined to leverage change during the past ten years has been unprecedented. However, few authors have tried to make sense of the impact of these drastic changes on airline employees and passenger safety until now.

During this same period social science researchers started examining the ways organizations evolved into what is now variously called the "new risk economy," "new capitalism," or "flexible capitalism."[2] The findings of these studies indicate that in many industries employers are providing less skill training, mentoring, job stability, community support, and career advancement while expecting more from employees in terms of experience, flexibility, and loyalty.[3] Some researchers have even claimed employment is now "dead" and that all workers today are essentially "self-employed."[4] Workers can no longer expect lifetime employment with one firm and must develop a variety of different skills—technical and psychological—to successfully negotiate the new risk economies' flexible market demands. In this book I look at the US airline industry as an addition to research on this "flexible economy" and find ample support for the new economy hypothesis that employers today are providing less while expecting more from America's workforce. However, my research also expands on this body of literature by evaluating the implications of new economy changes for workers in high-risk professions such as aviation, which have not been extensively examined.

Cutting across several business disciplines including corporate social responsibility, ethics, leadership, sustainability, and organization studies, I adopt a critical theory approach to question the wisdom of accepting the virtue of management as self-evident or unproblematic, and to challenge managers' single-minded pursuit of short-term profits above all else. Critical theory scholars have been criticized for a preoccupation with a cynical rhetoric over practical attempts to bring about real social change in the business world.[5] In this book I aim to bridge the gap between theory and practice by examining the airline worker-management relationship within the framework of the ethical responsibility of airlines, managers, government, and regulators to the wider community. This unique framework moves critical theory forward by providing a comprehensive analysis of *potentialities*, not just actualities, pushing critique beyond clever descriptions of existing airline management practices toward an exploration of what management could be.

Instead of seeing management failures as a result of poor behavior by individual managers, this socioanalytic approach draws our attention to how a particular system of government, business, and regulation can create opportunities for abuse. For instance, critical theory scholars have argued that as long as the market is the dominant mechanism for allocating resources, employee and community needs, interests, and knowledge will be subservient to it, further intensifying managers' focus on financial bottom lines and stockholder interests.[6] In this book I document the development of such dangerous dynamics in the US airline industry.

An economic war is occurring within the aviation industry in the post-9/11 period as managerial short-term profit seeking has been allowed to trump long-term safety concerns with little regulatory oversight. One way to redress this imbalance is to recognize the power of what Foucault called "subjugated knowledges," those bodies of knowledge that have been disqualified as inadequate, naïve, unqualified, low ranking, or unscientific.[7] By reconceptualizing the idea of risk and safety from the vantage point of the disenfranchised, I hope to shift the responsibility for safe flight operations away from employees—already stressed, fatigued, and working more while earning less—back to the airline industry, its regulators, and US society as a whole. As one pilot I interviewed succinctly noted, "The way the company puts pressure on the employees, it's just a matter of time [before there's an airline accident.] Something's got to give." Until the substance of these subjugated knowledges held by employees can be brought more into focus, questions about the escalating risks will remain in the shadows, and short-term profit seeking will continue to take precedence over safety in increasingly dangerous ways.

To examine this issue, I draw historical parallels with other industry crises. I show how airline executives' fixation on maximizing short-term profits at the expense of long-term safety—and government regulators' inability to stop them—has resulted in a period of arrogant optimism, willful blindness, and entitled insularity in commercial aviation, not unlike Wall Street in the years prior to the 2008 financial crisis. I show how industry risk management processes have not kept pace with the escalating risk in aviation, just as it didn't on Wall Street before the crash. And as several researchers warned about the looming US financial crisis, I identify similar hidden fractures in the aviation safety system as well. With no government intervention or regulatory supervision on the horizon, the only question left to ask is if Wall Street could crash, can't the airline industry crash too?

1

The (Not So) Secret Secrets

Awareness about what is happening in the post–September 11, 2001, airline industry comes to each of us in different ways with varying intensity. One thing is certain: aviation in the United States changed forever after 9/11. Only now, over a decade later, is it becoming apparent how much. And I don't just mean increased security measures during the flight check-in process. The entire aviation industry has changed radically over the past decade with serious risk and safety implications, and certain sectors continue to hope no one will "alarm the passengers."

We know *what* happened on 9/11. And we also know about the economic instability of the aviation industry that followed. But what is less frequently discussed is *why* that instability really occurred and where the decisions made to address it are taking us now. Commercial airline executives want us to believe that the terrorist attacks caused the post-9/11 aviation industry downturn thus creating the current hypercompetitive environment. They use that logic to justify charging fees for everything from soft drinks and pillows to ticket changes and checked baggage.

It's a lucrative strategy. In 2011, the top airlines at the time (United, Delta, American, Southwest, US Airways, and Alaska) generated $3.4 billion in revenue from checked bags, up from $464 million in 2007, the year most airlines began the practice. These airlines also collected $2.4 billion from passenger penalty fees for rebooking nonrefundable reservations. Add in other incidentals and we find passengers paid an astonishing $12.4 billion in extra fees in 2011 alone—and this revenue is not taxed like traditional airfares.[1]

Yet, well before that crisp fall day in New York, informed insiders considered the aviation industry overdue for an adjustment. September 11 simply handed the already struggling airlines a popularly accepted excuse to downsize and adopt other changes executives had long wanted to implement. Major airlines used the event as an excuse to slash jobs, eliminating over two hundred thousand employees in the post-9/11 period, all the while eliciting sympathy and government support as one of the most visible images of America's struggle against terrorism. As of 2010, airline employees continued to give up more than $12 billion a year in wages, benefits, pensions, and other work rules, while over 10,000 pilot jobs had disappeared at major air carriers.[2] (Table 1 reflects total layoffs and hiring 2000–2012.)

Like a clever magic trick, industry leaders used 9/11 as a foil, distracting the public by blaming the airlines' financial slump on war, recession, terrorism, and travel scares such as SARS (severe acute respiratory syndrome), while pointing to rising fuel costs, greedy employees, aggressive labor groups, and frugal consumers' bargain shopping online to explain airline insolvencies. Meanwhile, US air carriers quietly pocketed over $2 *trillion* in revenue between 2000 and 2012,[3] and airline executives earned millions of dollars for themselves (fig. 1). Consider Jeffrey A. Smisek, president and CEO of United Continental Holdings, the company created after the United-Continental merger in 2010. Number 123 on the list of America's highest-paid CEOs, Smisek earned $13.3 million in compensation in 2011, falling just behind Wall Street executives such as Jamie Dimon of JP Morgan Chase, Lloyd C. Blankfein of Goldman Sachs, and Vikram S. Pandit of Citigroup.[4]

You might think that *staying out of bankruptcy* was the primary job of an airline executive. However, in an odd twist of the bankruptcy process, on exiting Chapter 11 airline management teams typically keep between

TABLE 1. Total number of pilots per US airline, 2000–2012*

	2000	2001	2002	2003	2004	2005	2006	2007	2008	2009	2010	2011	2012	% Change
United	11,278	9,968	7,992	7,688	6,374	6,133	6,277	6,338	6,350	5,581	5,515	5,490	9,899	-12
Northwest	5,981	6,103	5,534	5,112	4,942	4,995	4,531	4,340	4,345	3,426	0	0	0	-100
Delta	9,123	8,103	8,074	7,155	6,786	6,181	5,706	5,904	6,391	6,581	10,701	10,708	10,606	16
US Airways	5,330	4,649	3,743	3,147	2,967	2,599	3,132	4,278	4,234	4,073	3,967	4,003	4,035	-24
American	10,408	10,586	12,297	10,857	9,929	9,074	8,572	8,343	8,306	8,092	7,934	8,029	7,737	-26
Continental	4,656	4,571	4,209	3,852	3,943	4,184	4,408	4,598	4,578	4,227	4,199	4,139	0	-100
Southwest	3,316	3,725	3,966	4,022	4,197	4,535	4,845	5,317	5,588	5,626	5,564	5,676	8,866	167
JetBlue	75	236	371	591	809	1,059	1,451	1,707	1,794	1,795	1,828	2,021	2,183	2,811
Total	50,167	47,941	46,186	42,424	39,947	38,760	38,922	40,825	41,586	39,401	39,708	40,066	43,326	-14

Source: "P10-Annual Employee Statistics by Labor Category," Research and Innovative Technology Administration, US Bureau of Transportation Statistics, http://www.rita.dot.gov/bts/sites/rita.dot.gov.bts/files/subject_areas/airline_information/number_of_employees/labor_category/index.html. Table created by the author.
* US Airways merged with America West in 2005; Delta acquired Northwest in 2008; United and Continental merged in 2010; Southwest acquired AirTran in 2011. Numbers reflect these changes.

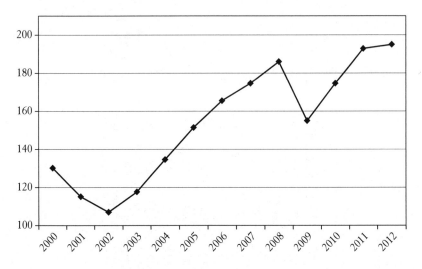

Figure 1. US airline revenue in billions of dollars, 2000–2012. *Source*: Data from http://www.transtats.bts.gov/Data_Elements_Financial.aspx?Data=7.

5 and 10 percent of the company's shares. CEOs often keep 1 percent just for themselves.[5] That means managers are handsomely rewarded for getting their company out of financial messes they created in the first place. It is a nice payoff for stiffing creditors, wiping out shareholders, furloughing employees, and alienating passengers. Over the last several decades, this is where airline CEOs have gotten rich. United's CEO Glenn Tilton received a pay package worth nearly $40 million in new shares and other compensation after the airline emerged from bankruptcy in 2005. Northwest's CEO Doug Steenland received a package worth some $26.6 million when the company emerged from Chapter 11 in 2007. And the process continues to this day, unregulated.[6]

In 2012, American Airlines and US Airways were negotiating a merger as well. Most industry analysts agree that American, the third-largest US airline, and US Airways, the fourth-largest, will eventually have to merge if they are to stand a chance of competing against the United-Continental and Delta-Northwest conglomerates. However, American's CEO, Tom Horton, and his management team will profit more if American emerges from bankruptcy first, earning them somewhere between $300 and $600 million. Meanwhile, US Airways' CEO Doug Parker's contract has a change-of-control provision that could earn him more than $20 million if his airline is bought by another company and he is forced out.[7]

During this same period, when airline executives like Tilton, Smisek, Steenland, and their management teams were collecting record compensation, thousands of their airlines' employees remained out of work. When challenged about this inequity, airline executives defended their managerial decisions and compensation strategies. Like the financial industry's defensiveness about Wall Street's executive bonuses paid just months after the $700 billion government bailout of the Street's "troubled assets" in 2008, airlines justified the post-9/11 executive rewards as appropriate and necessary to attract and retain top performers.[8] Are these high-priced, short-term managerial strategies—and the shady deals and organizational culture they foster—mere coincidence, or are there identifiable patterns between the business practices of these two boom-or-bust American industries?

Both finance and aviation have long histories of secret deals and political gamesmanship behind exorbitant financial wins and losses. As both industries became increasingly deregulated over the past few decades, a new type of manager took over the executive suites, and troubling evidence emerged of a managerial fixation on maximizing short-term profits for themselves at the expense of long-term company sustainability while disregarding the resultant systemic risks. The following chapters unpack the details of this confluence of events. For now, let us consider that if this pattern of risk taking brought Wall Street to the brink of collapse in 2008, might growing cracks in the airline industry related to self-serving risk taking be threatening air safety as well?

My review of government documents and accident reports, along with interviews with hundreds of aviation industry professionals, provides evidence that hidden fractures have been widening in the aviation industry in ways alarmingly resonant with patterns preceding the financial crisis of 2008.[9] Contrary to the Federal Aviation Administration's (FAA) claim that "this is the golden age of safety, the safest period in the safest mode, in the history of the world,"[10] we seem to be entering a period of unprecedented global risk. Perhaps US Airways Captain Chesley "Sully" Sullenberger, the pilot who landed his Airbus-turned-glider on the icy surface of the Hudson River, said it best when he spoke to Congress in 2009.[11] Voicing concerns held by most veteran airline employees, he testified, "While I love my profession, I do not like what has happened to it." US airline employees "have been hit by an economic tsunami." Citing bankruptcies, layoffs, pension loss, pay cuts, mergers, and "revolving door management teams who have used airline employees as an ATM" as causes for the turmoil, Captain Sullenberger confided that he was "deeply worried" about safety and the industry's future, claiming, "I do not know a single professional airline pilot who wants his or her children to follow in their footsteps." With airlines no longer able to "attract the best and the brightest" to aviation careers, he worried that "future pilots" will be "less experienced and less skilled" with "negative consequences to the flying public—and to our country." To avoid this, he insisted that "airline companies must refocus their attention—and their resources—on the recruitment and retention of highly experienced, well trained pilots," making that a priority "at least equal to their financial bottom line."[12]

Captain Sullenberger is not alone in expressing these concerns. The chaotic state of the post-9/11 aviation industry generated such widespread attention in Congress that the Government Accounting Office (GAO) was asked to investigate the implications of airline bankruptcies, mergers, loss of pension plans, and high fuel prices, and even consider re-regulating the struggling industry.[13] One study claimed that "the airline bankruptcy process is well developed and understood" and went on to document the liquidation of employee pension plans, offering examples of the significant loss of benefits senior airline employees, such as Captain Sullenberger, will experience when they retire. Yet it nonetheless contended there is "no evidence" that bankruptcy "harms the industry."[14] Another report noted, "The historically high number of airline bankruptcies and liquidations is a reflection of the industry's inherent instability."[15] However, the GAO failed to investigate the implications of this instability for employees or passengers. In fact, not one of the government's reports considered the impact of this tumultuous climate of outsourcing, mergers, downsizing, furloughs, and changing work rules on employees, their job performance, risk, or airline safety.

What do I mean when I talk about risk and safety? Risk is commonly understood as a situation involving exposure to danger, harm, or loss. And safety is the process of controlling situations to minimize exposure to these hazards. How can managing risk and safety be a profitable process? In the nineteenth century, commercial trade in risk emerged as a commodity much like the exchange of timber, cotton, and tobacco. Marine insurance became the first form of risk management when merchants insured their cargo against "perils of the sea" and insurers sold these policies to each other for financial gain.[16] Since then, shifting risk has become a lucrative business strategy.

As corporations began to amass extraordinary wealth, questions soon followed about whether industrial profit making should come from assuming risk, as with marine insurance, or from reducing it through better work practices.[17] In response, three risk-related roles emerged in the corporate industrial economy: the entrepreneurial "risk-maker" who jumpstarts the industrial process, the financial "risk-taker" who invests in corporations and their stock, and the managerial "risk-reducer" who rationally supervises economic production.[18] Over time, neoliberalism, and the increasingly deregulated marketplace associated with it, blurred the boundaries between these risk management roles, as executives, previously risk-reducers, now adopted risk-maker strategies throughout corporate America. I will return to this important managerial shift and its implications for risk and safety.

Obviously, no airline flight, business decision, or financial investment is 100 percent risk free. So what then are acceptable levels of risk? It depends. To determine which air safety regulations to adopt and which situations to risk, the FAA, nicknamed the "tombstone agency" for basing their decisions on body counts,[19] conducts a cost-benefit analysis. "The basic approach taken to value an avoided fatality," the FAA explained, "is to determine how much an individual or group of individuals is willing to pay for a small reduction in risk."[20] For instance, the FAA might weigh the risk of a fatal accident occurring every year by considering the loss of the aircraft ($100 million) and the death of its one hundred passengers, each life valued at $3 million ($300 million) versus the cost to airlines to fix a reoccurring mechanical flaw ($10 million) in every airplane of this type in service (1,000).[21] In this example, the aviation industry would accept the risk of $400 million—and, more important, the risk of an airplane crash annually and the death of one hundred people as a result of this mechanical failure—rather than adopt a regulation that forces airlines to fix the problem at a cost of $10 billion. This may sound reminiscent of the Ford Pinto fiasco from the 1970s.

At that time, in an effort to compete in the burgeoning yet lucrative small-car market, the Ford Motor Company introduced a new subcompact car called the Pinto. It was rushed to market to capitalize on American's new desire for cheap, fuel-efficient vehicles, "The Little Carefree Car," as the Pinto was advertised, became everything but untroubled. During preproduction crash tests, Ford engineers discovered that the car's fuel tank was vulnerable to explosion during rear-end collisions.[22] Yet Ford executives reportedly conducted a cost-benefit analysis, comparing the cost to reinforce the Pinto's rear end ($121 million) against the chance of collision and cost of lawsuits ($50 million).[23] They decided it was cheaper to accept the risk. For eight years Ford lobbied against increased safety standards and paid millions to crash victims out of court rather than fixing the $11 per-car problem.[24] Twenty-seven people died as a result.[25]

Although the Ford Pinto became a famous business school case study in shoddy ethics and helped spawn the field of corporate social responsibility, there is still more we can take away from the case than just a lesson in bad management. What this case, and others I discuss in this book, exemplify is how corporate leaders have quietly shifted their role from risk-reducers to risk-makers over the last few decades, forcing American consumers to become the ultimate risk-takers, in ways often unknown to them.

Are there safeguards within the system designed to address these concerns about escalating risk and diminishing safety? Aren't government regulators, airline management, employee labor unions, and consumer watchdog groups monitoring aviation industry developments and, perhaps most important, long-term passenger safety? The simple answer is that the required oversight is either not happening at all or not fast enough to keep pace with the rate of aviation industry changes over the past decade.

Like Wall Street before the crash, airlines have been free to pursue economically driven agendas with little regulation or incentive to consider the wider risks. In part, the reason is that cost-benefit analyses have become so prevalent and fatal aviation accidents seem to have become so rare. It is commonly believed that the chance of being killed on a commercial flight is about 8 million to 1—far safer than other forms of transportation.[26] For example, the US Bureau of Transportation Statistics' 2008 study (the most recent) reported fewer than 600 airline fatalities annually, while almost 38,000 people died in motor vehicles and nearly 800 on railroads.[27]

Massachusetts Institute of Technology professor Arnold Barnett has made a career out of consulting to airlines and studying aviation fatalities. He uses applied probabilistic and statistical modeling, a risk assessment method similarly adopted by Wall Street quantitative analysts, or "quants," before the 2008 financial industry crash.[28] How this occurred on Wall Street will be discussed further in chapter 5. Through these mathematical models Barnett and his team of aviation quants concluded that the chance of dying in a US airline jet crash is 1 in 22.8 million commercial flights.[29] "A traveler would have to fly every day for more than 64,000 years before dying in an accident," he contends.[30] "Fatal accidents are on the verge of extinction."[31]

Yet, fatality data, like cost-benefit analyses, can be deceiving as a measure of overall risk and safety. Captain Sullenberger notes, "It's important not to define safety as the absence of accidents,"[32] and most pilots I interviewed for this book agreed. They worried that the apparent rarity of aviation deaths has caused passengers to become indifferent, regulators lackadaisical, and airlines complacent about air safety. Like another magic trick, contradictory evidence is there to see for those who know where to look. In fact, 70 percent of the pilots I surveyed believe post-9/11 cost cutting has made it likely that a major airline accident will occur in the coming years. It is not a matter of *if*—only a matter of *when* (fig. 2).

Nonetheless, in 2013 the front page of the *New York Times* proclaimed that "flying on a commercial jetliner has never been safer."[33] What has led to this disparity of opinion? Captain Sullenberger has noted how airline employees have, in some ways, contributed to this illusion, a victim of their own success. "We make it look too easy," he argued. When "it's possible to go several calendar years without a single fatality" in a jet crash at a major US airline, the public starts to see airlines as "ultrasafe," and it becomes "easy to forget what's really at stake" when flying on a commercial

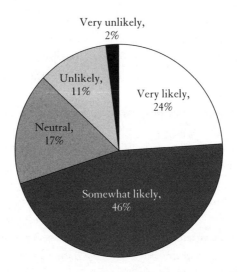

Figure 2. US airline pilots' rating of likeliness of airline accident. *Source*: "How likely do you feel it is that a major airline accident will occur in the coming years due to post-9/11 airline cost cutting?" Author's survey data, no. 10.

flight.[34] Echoing pilots' concerns, Mike Ambrose, director of the European Regions Airline Association, expressed alarm as well. Today's airline managers have no experience with aviation accidents, he argued. They "tend to believe this level of safety is a given, so will more easily pass responsibility for safety down the authority chain," making it less of a financial and managerial priority.[35]

Former inspector general of the US Department of Transportation (DOT) Mary Schiavo agrees, noting how aviation industry leaders have become adept at manipulating the illusion of safety without making any substantive changes:

> When a plane goes down in flames and dozens or hundreds of lives are lost, what the public most wants is reassurance—reassurance that the accident was a fluke, that flying is statistically the safest way to travel and that someone is watching over aviation to guarantee it is safe. FAA officials and members of Congress automatically take to the airwaves, vying to outdo themselves with sound bites about oversight and safety. . . . [However] once the media scrutiny passes, the safety problem will be gone too.[36]

In addition, the random nature of accidents and the way federal agencies quantify safety makes the apparently low aviation fatality rate, particularly when compared with other modes of transportation, attributable to luck and data manipulation.

For instance, aviation quants' statistical models often only consider fatal *jet* crashes, ignoring all other kinds of aviation accidents such as general aviation aircraft, cargo carriers, and turbo-propeller (turboprop) airplanes. This oversight is particularly problematic because regional air carriers and their turboprops now provide over half of domestic air service in the United States.[37] Eliminating their operations from the mathematical model significantly skews the findings. When challenged about the selective nature of this data set, aviation quants admit the occurrence of just one accident would sway their results. For example, they concede including Air France Flight 447, which crashed into the Atlantic Ocean in 2009 killing all 216 passengers and 12 aircrew, in the data would drop fatality statistics from 1 in 22.8 million to about 1 in 14 million flights—a 37 percent decline.[38]

Other experts have voiced similar concerns about over-relying on statistical modeling. John Breit, former head of market-risk oversight at Merrill Lynch and one of the first to build value-at-risk (VaR) financial models for Wall Street, notes that mathematical models like these often disguise risk, not reveal it. Instead of fixating on statistics, Breit recommends that risk managers develop what spies call *humint*—"human intelligence from flesh and blood sources"—a network of frontline people who will report when things don't seem right before a major problem occurs.[39]

With so many questions surrounding the reliability of applied probabilistic and statistical modeling to assess real-world risk, whether in finance or aviation, why then do these quantitative models remain attractive? As Breit observes, their popularity "is all in the interests of senior management and regulators to avoid blame. They may not think they can prevent the next crisis, but they can blame the statistics" for informing their decisions after the fact.[40]

Besides disguising risk and creating a false sense of security, there is a third problem with aviation quants' probabilistic and statistical modeling risk assessment methods. Researchers who study organizational decision making agree that disasters rarely spontaneously occur out of nowhere, as mathematical models imply.[41] Instead, problems often "incubate,"[42] sometimes for years, as organizations slowly "drift towards failure,"[43] until one day factors align in a "window of accident opportunity."[44] These disasters are so inevitable, and the warning signs that precede them are often so clear, scholars have taken to calling them "normal accidents,"[45] not because of their frequency, but because they are the normal consequence of increasingly complex operating systems that challenge human sense making in unanticipated ways.[46] Yet, they are nonetheless disasters that, with a little bit of awareness and imagination, we could have seen coming.

In their thought-provoking book *Predictable Surprises: The Disasters You Should Have Seen Coming and How to Prevent Them*, Max Bazerman and Michael Watkins offered several generalizable characteristics as signs of impending disaster.[47] First, leaders are aware that there is a problem and many people recognize the problem is escalating, yet fixing the problem would incur significant short-term costs with questionable long-term return on this investment. Next, since there is a natural human tendency to maintain the status quo, resistance to change is allowed to dominate. Finally, this resistance is fueled by a small yet vocal minority who benefit from inaction and are motivated to subvert leadership efforts for their own private benefit. As a result of these pressures, decision makers are reluctant to risk taking action in the present in order to prevent a potential disaster in the future, particularly if they are unlikely to receive credit for averting it and have mathematical models to back them up.[48]

The history of aviation disasters is replete with examples of this type of flawed thinking. For instance, in the early 1990s, safety analysts predicted that even if aviation industry accident rates remained constant, the anticipated 3–4 percent annual industry growth would result in a near doubling of US air crashes by the turn of the twenty-first century. Alarmed by these statistics and prompted by two seemingly mysterious 1996 aviation accidents and the corresponding 340 fatalities—the midair explosion of TWA Flight 800 and the inflight fire aboard ValuJet Flight 592—President Bill Clinton created the White House Commission on Aviation Safety and Security led by Vice President Al Gore.[49]

Initially, the commission recognized that there were escalating problems in the US commercial airline industry and held both airline executives and the FAA responsible for repairing the broken aviation system. They laudably recommended a reduction in accidents by a "factor of five within a decade" and a re-engineering of the FAA's regulatory and certification programs.[50] That was, until resistance to change was allowed to dominate, just as the Bazerman and Watkins model predicted. The airlines flexed their political clout, lobbyists mobilized, the FAA stonewalled, and the price of change became too high in the government's cost-benefit analysis. Politicians, reluctant to risk a decline in popularity or donations during an election year over a questionable long-term gain on issues they would likely not get credit for, waffled on key points.

As a result, the final report moved from a tough call to action for the aviation industry as a whole to a watered-down version condoning business as usual. Airline executives, who presumably had the most to gain by improving air safety, did everything possible to block meaningful reform, and in doing so denied the very real possibility that a predictable surprise was likely to occur. Since then predictable surprises have occurred in the form of several aviation accidents and near misses that airlines would rather not discuss (detailed in chapters 5 and 6).

One shining moment on Gore's White House Commission was when Commissioner M. Victoria Cummock stubbornly refused to endorse the committee's final report because it "contains no specific call to action, no commitments to address aviation safety and security system-wide," and "no deadlines." She suggested "that all recommendations be re-written for specific actions by specific agencies," otherwise, "once again, we will allow the airlines to lead and the government to follow." In conclusion, she stated, "I cannot sign a report that blatantly allows the American flying public to be placed regularly at 'unnecessary risk.' "[51]

As validation of Commissioner Cummock's concerns, one predictable surprise that might have been averted had her recommendations regarding a systemwide commitment to improving airline safety and security been adopted was the terrorist event of 9/11. Instead, airlines were once again allowed to prioritize short-term profits at the expense of long-term safety, disregarding the resultant systemic risks.

Who should we believe? Is the US airline industry heading for a predictable surprise, or is this the golden age of safety and stability in which fatal aviation accidents and other dangerous situations are on the verge of extinction? The spectrum of expert opinion makes the issue of air safety confusing and assessing real risks difficult. Yet an opportunity to explore this question in the post-9/11 period came about when the National Aeronautics and Space Administration (NASA) sponsored a study called the National Aviation Operations Monitoring System (NAOMS), which examined everyday aviation operations *before* an accident occurs for clues to systemic vulnerabilities.

Over 24,000 pilots had been interviewed between 2001 and 2004—almost one third of the US commercial airline pilot population—when the study was suddenly terminated.[52] The data remained unused for two years until an anonymous NASA whistleblower informed the Associated Press, which filed a Freedom of Information Act request. Initially denied access because, NASA noted, the data "could materially affect the public confidence in, and the commercial welfare of, the air carriers," a Congressional inquiry finally forced release of the data in 2007.[53] Yet the data produced was in a format that made it nearly impossible for outsiders to analyze. When asked about this, NASA administrator Michael Griffin replied, "We were asked to release the data and I said that we would, and I've done that."[54]

What was so troubling in the study's findings that NASA risked accusations it was prioritizing airlines' financial interests over public safety concerns in order to hide it? A review of the NAOMS data produced some clues. Numerous inconsistencies with other governmental statistical reports emerged, potentially tarnishing the FAA's "golden age of safety" image and aviation quants' predictions that accidents are on the verge of extinction. For instance, NAOMS data showed four times the number of engine failures and twice the number of bird strikes and near midair collisions than did other government monitoring systems, which called into question the ways aviation safety was measured. When pressed about these inconsistencies, Griffin criticized the NAOMS "reporting mechanism," calling the project "poorly organized" and the data "not properly peer reviewed" and likening it to "hangar talk."[55]

NAOMS researchers Jon Krosnick, Stanford University professor, and Robert Dodd, principal investigator, defended their work. Their defense, the $11.5 million NASA spent sponsoring this study, and the high response rate from pilots raises suspicions about the motivations behind NASA's abrupt decision to abandon the project. As Congressman Brad

Miller noted, "If 80% of the pilots [asked agreed] to sit still for a half-hour survey, voluntarily, my conclusion is the pilots had something they wanted others to know about."[56] Why don't some people want to hear what they had to say?

The NOAMS study was not the only inquiry into aviation safety issues that required whistleblowers to force government to take action over the past decade. Two FAA aviation safety inspectors testified before the 2008 House Committee on Transportation and Infrastructure on the regulatory relationship between the FAA and the airline industry; they claimed that the FAA knowingly allowed Southwest Airlines to operate unsafe aircraft over a period of several years.[57] The inspectors tried to raise warnings for years about this problem, yet they were repeatedly undermined by FAA managers in their efforts to increase surveillance of airline maintenance.[58]

The committee found that these were common employee complaints at the FAA. Several aviation safety inspectors reported "that they found it difficult to bring enforcement action against airlines because FAA management appeared to be 'too close to airline management.'" They reported feeling "pressure from management to not identify too many problems with an airline" or else they might face "retribution."[59] A typical confession was, "I often don't even bother" bringing airline violations forward "because I know FAA management won't do anything with it."[60] As a result, the committee found "extensive evidence," that "points toward a systemic pattern of FAA failure to exercise the required regulatory oversight" over US airlines.[61]

Although these results were identified in 2008, little seems to have changed since then. Similar to criticisms of Wall Street before the financial crisis, many aviation insiders believe the government's regulatory system, established over five decades ago, is just too antiquated to keep up with today's technologically complex, globalized airline industry. Of the pilots I interviewed, only 5 percent reported aviation regulators as "competent" in supervising safety in the US commercial airline industry; 66 percent rated regulators as either "incompetent" or "very incompetent" (fig. 3). Similarly, Stuart Matthews, president of Flight Safety Foundation, succinctly noted, "The FAA was simply never created to deal with the environment that has been produced by deregulation of the air transport industry."[62] And, in many ways, regulators agree.

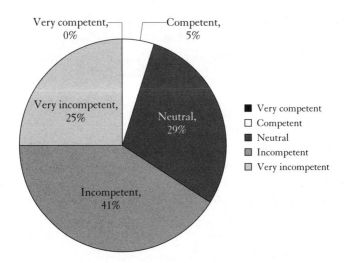

Figure 3. US airline pilots' rating of aviation industry regulators. *Source*: "How competent are regulators at supervising safety in the US commercial airline industry?" Author's survey data, no. 15.

A 2005 internal FAA management memo entitled "A Time for Change" expressed with concern how the FAA had "retreated from the proper exertion of our influence and authority" and relaxed "into a level of coziness" with airlines, settling "for winks, nods, verbals, and emails" instead of proper business protocol.[63] Yet, with only about 3,600 aviation-safety inspectors, the FAA knows its personnel is inadequate to oversee all aspects of flight operations and aircraft maintenance under its jurisdiction. To offset this shortage, the FAA developed "partnership programs" in the 1990s to encourage a more collaborative relationship with airlines as "customers." Although civil-penalty programs were a priority in the past, and often resulted in substantial fines and negative airline publicity, the FAA revised its focus, instituting several "voluntary programs" to encourage airlines, pilots, and mechanics to "self-disclose" noncompliance in a collaborative effort to share important safety information.[64]

This collaborative approach sounds good in theory, but not everyone is convinced this type of self-monitoring regulatory strategy can work. It didn't work on Wall Street before the 2008 crash. Prior to the 1990s, the FAA was a "cop on the beat," inspecting "everything from the nuts and bolts in your tool kit to the paperwork in the cockpit" and handing out hefty penalties to those who broke the rules.[65] After 9/11, critics noted, the FAA's more collaborative approach "went too far" in "coddling the airlines" and drifting too far "toward over-closeness and coziness between regulator and regulated."[66] The history of the Boeing 787 Dreamliner is an example of the risks of this cozy relationship.

Although the Dreamliner was initially touted as a revolution in aerospace design and manufacturing, production of the 787 quickly became an engineering nightmare. The project was fraught with delays and overruns, and delivery only occurred in 2011—three years behind schedule and billions of dollars over budget—the worst production record in Boeing's history.[67] Much of the 787's problems were a direct result of the complexity of its new, more collaborative manufacturing and certification process. In order to save money, only 40 percent of the plane was built by Boeing in house; the rest was outsourced to over fifty different subcontractors around the world, which created ample opportunity for errors.[68] When mechanics finally assembled the first plane in 2007, they found a gap of nearly half an inch between the cockpit section and the body of the airplane.[69] This was just the beginning of the problems.

A little over a year after release, the Dreamliner was grounded again when battery fires erupted in two planes. In one case, the fire burned so intensely it took Boston firefighters forty minutes to put the blaze out.[70] Although the danger inherent in using lithium batteries in airplanes was well known, in the spirit of collaboration, the FAA let Boeing develop its own inspection protocol, establish the safety standards, perform the tests, and certificate its own work.[71]

The final frightening fact is that only three months after the grounding, the FAA recertified the 787 for flight carrying the same lithium batteries that had ignited without ever determining the root cause of the battery fires. Japanese pilots, who flew twenty-seven of the fifty-seven Dreamliners then in service, worried that Boeing hadn't done enough to address the danger. "Boeing says that any battery fire will now go out on its own, so there's no safety issue," Japanese pilots' union spokesperson Toshikazu Nagasawa said. He added, "But that's on paper. No pilot would ever want to keep flying with a fire on board."[72] Yet, regulators and airline executives in Japan and the US seem unconcerned. Once again, short-term profit seeking has trumped employees' safety concerns and the best interests of the flying public.

Meanwhile, Congress has largely stayed on the periphery of the 787 safety debate. This unusual bipartisan silence reflects Boeing's political clout, a position sustained by hefty political campaign contributions and $83 million spent on lobbying between 2008 and 2013.[73] The bottom line is industry regulators have put aviation industry leaders in control of air safety while employees and passengers are strapped in for the ride.

2

THE ROOTS OF TURBULENCE

Even before there was a commercial airline industry, the fledgling field of aviation was already a risky and competitive business where major players, struggling to outdo one another, were not beyond pilfering a profitable idea. For instance, while most any schoolchild can credit Orville and Wilbur Wright for the invention of powered flight in 1903, it is more accurate to say that the Ohio bicycle manufacturers synthesized the best aspects of many inventors' experimentation and innovation—such as Sir George Cayley, Otto Lilienthal, and Percy Pilcher—to build their Wright *Flyer*.[1]

In the early 1800s, Sir George Cayley built a "flying parachute," itself a knockoff of Chinese kites built around 1,000 BC, to study lift, drag, and flight controllability, while other inventors such as Samuel Henson were still fascinated with steam power. Henson proposed an "aerial steam carriage" that included many elements of modern-day airplanes. Yet, the steam engine was too heavy to get airborne. Several other researchers, such as machine gun inventor Sir Hiram Maxim, focused on this power issue as well. "Give us a motor," Maxim wrote, "and we will very soon give you a successful flying machine."[2] The pilot was already often an afterthought for these businessmen, as little consideration was given to how someone might actually control the aircraft once it became airborne.

In the 1890s, Otto Lilienthal, a German engineer, completed over two thousand hang glider flights, advancing understanding of wing design and shifting the question about controllability back to humans. Although he unfortunately died in a glider crash just a few years later, he had earned an international reputation as "the flying man." One of Lilienthal's most influential contributions to aviation research was his belief that "proper insight into the practice of flying" could only be achieved through "actual flying experiments," which involved centralizing the pilot's role in the emerging field, a protocol that the Wright brothers adopted to test their designs.[3] Lilienthal's disciple Percy Pilcher was the first pilot to develop a petroleum, not steam, powered engine and attach it to glider wings—ultimately the same successful design used in the Wright *Flyer*. Unfortunately, Pilcher was also killed when his aircraft crashed during a demonstration flight.

On the eve of the Spanish-American War in 1898, the US government paid nonpilot Samuel Langley, a leading scientist and astrophysicist, $50,000 or about $1.3 million in today's dollars to develop a flying machine.[4] Design setbacks, budget overruns, and a final failed flight attempt led many US government leaders to conclude that powered flight was simply not possible. Yet, just nine days later the Wright brothers, relative unknowns at the time, succeeded in achieving powered flight on December 17, 1903. Scientists like Langley and engineers like Maxim imagined a flying machine to be stable, like a car, with flight achieved through power, mathematical equations, and physics. However, pilot-inventors such as Lilienthal, Pilcher, and the Wrights envisioned flying to be more like riding a bicycle—a constant adjustment of lift and thrust balancing weight and drag—more art than science. Right from the start these pilot-inventors brought a unique perspective, as they considered not only wing structure and engine power but also human factors and controllability in their aircraft design.

The power struggle between pilot influence and airplane controllability remain contested issues even today at airlines and manufacturers, as designers such as Boeing and Airbus adopt different engineering approaches in aircraft development. Nevertheless, the elusive premise behind the Wrights' successful design, which they called "wing warping," still remains central in the aileron design of most airplanes today. In 1906, the Wrights received a patent for "wing warping," and the design could not be copied without paying a royalty.[5]

In hindsight, the Wrights' invention marked an exciting historical development in aviation. Yet, at the time, enthusiasm for their achievement was low in the United States. Most Americans saw little use for airplanes, and government was reluctant to get involved. Seeing wealthy businessmen offering prize money for record-setting flights,[6] the general public tended to dismiss aviation as a rich man's sport and pilots as either reckless glory seekers or flying fools, addicted to risk. America's love-hate relationship with aviation has persisted ever since.

To promote their aircraft, the Wright brothers organized a touring exhibition team, and Wilbur left for France where he gave their first public demonstration flight in 1908. Unlike Americans, the French were enthralled with aviation, which catapulted the brothers to a level of fame they never imagined. Songs, poems, and plays were written about them; women proposed marriage; and a frying pan Wilbur supposedly cooked with was displayed at the Louvre.[7] Back home in Dayton, the Wrights established a consortium of wealthy business leaders and built a factory to manufacture their plane, with most orders coming from Europe. Yet, the brothers soon lost their early aviation industry lead by focusing more on legal action against competitors for patent infringement than long-term development and promotion of their product.

Setting records and thrilling spectators came at a steep price. Although the Wrights had always emphasized safety in their own flying, others were not so disciplined. Five of the original nine members of the Wright exhibition team died in aviation crashes.[8] By 1913, nearly 350 aviation fatalities had occurred, a rate of about one death per three thousand flights.[9] The reasons were both individual and systemic. Wood, wire, and fabric aircraft were underpowered and structurally fragile, with flawed control systems. There were no operating manuals and little understanding of performance limitations or aerodynamics. Therefore, it was easy for pilots, who were all relative novices, to unwittingly exceed aircraft limitations, which led to structural damage.

An underlying factor contributing to all of these failures was that no regulatory body existed to approve aircraft design, supervise manufacturing, or monitor operations. It was often only after several crashes, and corresponding fatalities, that deficiencies were identified, for example, when the US Army investigated crashes of the Wright Model B and Model C aircraft. A safety board concluded that cockpit control sticks were difficult to move, flight control surfaces were too small, and the engine's rear location endangered pilots in the event of a crash. Although the military eventually banned the airplane from service, by then ten airmen had already lost their lives.[10] This became a trend that exists to this day: regulators often only react after several accidents and numerous fatalities establish a pattern deemed worth investigating.

While the US government was apathetic toward aviation, Germany and France sped ahead, providing well-built aircraft and fearless pilots backed by their governments' eager encouragement and financial support. By 1913, a cumulative $86 million had been invested in aviation worldwide: Germany was first, dedicating $28 million, and France was a close second with $22 million. The United States was a dismal fourteenth, spending only $435,000 in support of aviation. Without active government support, the United States trailed Europe in aviation development for more than a decade.[11]

Worn down by lawsuits and stricken by typhoid, Wilbur died in 1912, leaving Orville to carry on their legacy alone.[12] Now that the patent suits had been adjudicated in their favor, the Wright Company had an opportunity to help America seize the aviation lead again and steer industry developments for years to come. Yet Orville, a reluctant businessman, soon tired of the cutthroat environment and chose to settle for royalty payments and short-term gains instead. In 1915, he sold the company to New York financiers for $1.5 million and retired from airplane manufacturing. The next major advances in aircraft design were all be pioneered by others.[13]

What is important to note about this historic beginning is how individual innovations coalesced into industry developments that fostered competition, attracting investors and financial backing, with no government regulation. Initially, operators' input and issues concerning controllability were an afterthought. However, once industry leaders recognized that flight was more art than science, previous obstacles were overcome. As it does on Wall Street, money drove technological developments that pushed the industry in new and unpredictable directions—with little attention to risks, so that government entities were challenged to catch up after the fact. In effect, a pattern was already emerging in America's aviation industry in which market forces, innovation, and investment were far more influential in guiding industry developments than long-term planning, federal regulation, or safety concerns. This pattern persists to this day in the US aviation industry.

Ironically, similar questions concerning controllability, risk, and the role of government were also being quietly debated within the US financial industry prior to the Great Depression.[14] Given what we know about how these three factors contributed to the 2008 implosion of the US financial sector, it is worth reviewing this history for other parallel trends that may prove helpful in identifying problems in the airline industry.

Like aviation, Wall Street had inauspicious beginnings in early America, albeit several hundred years earlier. It is hard to even recognize today's multibillion dollar, technologically advanced, quantitatively driven financial industry as it was in its formative years. Merchants and traders would gather to buy and sell shares and loans in lower Manhattan in New York City along a wall built in 1653 to protect early settlers from Indian attack. Auctioneers set the price, and dealers traded among themselves in coffee shops and street corners with no regulatory supervision. The result was that auctioneers often rigged the price to their own advantage rather than providing fair prices for their customers, who had no way to research prospective investments.[15] This method of exchange continued for over a hundred years until 1792 when dealers finally agreed it was time to standardize their operation. Twenty-four stock brokers met under a tree at 68 Wall Street and instituted the Buttonwood Agreement, which created an early predecessor to today's New York Stock Exchange.[16] Similar to the early period of aviation, these early years were largely self-regulated with negotiations outside government's direct control.

As the financial sector matured in the 1800s and banks steadily increased in power and influence, a trend emerged in which the commercial banking sector made enormous profits, often at the expense of the still-maturing US government. For example, by backing bonds supporting the War of 1812 and the Civil War in the 1860s, rich merchants used the banking system to create a virtual monopoly, underwriting the nation's armed conflicts for personal gain. Prominent figures like Andrew Carnegie, John D. Rockefeller, and J. P. Morgan dominated, working the system to their advantage. Others, like Jay Gould and Jay Cooke became legendary robber barons, adept at manipulating the market. Short selling became a particularly favorite mode of predatory speculation.

Typically investors buy stock in a company for the long term, believing its price will rise over time and they will profit. In a short sale, the investor is betting against the company, anticipating a decrease in share price. Robber barons used short selling as a way to pounce on distressed companies, often spreading false information in order to depress the market and increase their gains. These types of deceptions were commonplace, as a gambling atmosphere underpinned with predatory motivations dominated the financial marketplace. Although traders were considered to be gentlemen, they often only honored agreements when it suited them, and investors had little recourse. Stories abound about traders who went on vacation, assured their interests would be looked after by colleagues, only to find their positions worthless on their return. The problem was the financial sector was developing much faster than any regulatory apparatus, which challenged the government to constantly play catch-up, a pattern that besets aviation as well. With government leaders mired in debates over slavery, states' rights, and manifest destiny, there was little energy for establishing regulatory guidance in the financial sector. Banks were allowed to make money most any way they deemed fit as long as they did not create a scandal that embarrassed politicians,[17] an approach similar to the FAA's laissez-faire regulatory strategies in aviation today. Unfortunately, as the 2008 financial crisis shows, such passive regulatory approaches eventually fail as loopholes become exploited for personal gain.

Even before the Crash of 1929, stock market crashes in 1857, 1869, 1873, and 1893 were already demonstrating how vulnerable the financial sector was to manipulation. Yet, what is important to note is how Wall Street came to its own rescue during these industry downturns. The stronger financial firms bailed out the weaker ones without government intervention or taxpayer handouts. During the panic of 1907, for instance, wealthy businessmen J. P. Morgan and John D. Rockefeller rescued several banks and corporations and even the city of New York in order to prevent a financial industry implosion.[18] Similarly, before airline industry deregulation in 1978, airlines worked much more collaboratively to help one another manage the financial challenges brought on by labor union strikes. In 1958 six of the nation's largest airlines signed an agreement known as the "mutual aid pact" as a way for struck airlines to recoup their loss of income with assistance from nonaffected airlines that benefitted from an increase in revenue during the labor action at another airline.[19] This pattern of banks and airlines policing and protecting one's own during hard times stands in stark contrast to both Wall Street and airline industry behaviors in the post-9/11 period, where self-sufficiency has faded in favor of taxpayer bailouts and bankruptcy court protection. How did the ethos of these industries change so dramatically over time?

Transportation and finance have a long complicated history together in the United States. First shipping and canals, and then railroads, offered astronomical financial gains for some investors, huge losses for others, and tempting territory for corrupt politicians. In the late 1800s, several government officials used insider knowledge to take advantage of investment opportunities in transportation at critical times. For example, Senator Kimble of the New York state legislature pushed a bill through that predictably caused railroad stocks to fall, which led to his gains through short selling.[20] Others, such as Rep. Russell Sage of New York, Rep. Oakes Ames of Massachusetts, Sen. James W. Patterson of New Hampshire, Rep. James Brooks of New York, and even President Ulysses Grant's vice president, Schuyler Colfax, also attempted to profit through deviant market manipulation strategies that would be considered illegal today. Although the congressmen were censured and Colfax was not renominated, no one was ever prosecuted because no laws prohibited insider trading yet. It wasn't until after the stock market crash and the 1930s that insider trading laws were passed by Congress.

Another early financial industry strategy, later successfully adopted by airline executives, was first originated by Cornelius "Commodore" Vanderbilt, a robber baron in the shipping business. Like other robber barons, Vanderbilt came from a poor family and had little formal education. As a young man, he borrowed a small sum of money from his family to start a ferry service from Staten Island to New York City, and within ten years his company dominated shipping on the Hudson River. His most successful tactic was to charge low fares to customers, underbid competitors, thus putting them out of business, and then drive customer prices back up. Nearly all US airlines have employed this tactic in recent years. Vanderbilt's strategies were so efficient he reportedly made sixty thousand dollars a month just from businesses paying him *not to compete* in their segments of the shipping industry. Moving on to railroads, Vanderbilt used similar strategies and accumulated a massive amount of money. He died the richest man in America in 1877, worth over $100 million, about $143 billion in today's dollars.[21]

Not everyone was pleased with this incredible concentration of wealth and power in the hands of a few, often ruthless and self-serving, business-men. Yet, similar to the situation today, the government was reluctant to intervene. Telegraphs and railroads gave way to telephones, electric com-panies, and automobiles as key industries. Small local businesses were con-solidated into larger companies that sold their products nationwide in the single-minded perspective that bigger was always better. Better for robber barons it would turn out but not always better for the general public. With few regulations governing activities, bankers used their financial acumen and insider knowledge to force business deals, keeping a piece for them-selves. Once again, it was all perfectly legal.

By the 1890s, a new form of politics was emerging in which organized groups formulated explicit political demands and found sympathetic chan-nels in Washington willing to apply legislative pressure. We now call this lobbying by special interest groups. While self-interest has always had a long history of influence in politics, prior to this period lobbying occurred largely underground as it carried a stigma of being unethical.[22] Overtime this image changed as lobbyists influenced politicians, testified to congres-sional committees, and eventually took their causes directly to the Ameri-can people causing alarm that their methods of mass persuasion created propaganda that often influenced public opinion through misinformation and deception.[23] Nonetheless, by 2012 lobbying had grown to a very visible $3.31 billion industry employing over 12,000 lobbyists.[24]

Another significant change in the late 1800s was the way in which com-panies, previously owned and operated by generations of families, were now run. Prior to the mid-1800s, owners managed and managers owned US companies with very few exceptions. However, after that, many com-panies were no longer sole proprietorships or partnerships and were in-stead publically traded stock companies run by a class of manager who were often not related by blood or marriage to the founding family. Under this system of "managerial capitalism" corporations grew ever larger, re-quiring cash infusions and credit to expand, which made the real benefi-ciaries professional managers and their bankers who consolidated smaller companies into large conglomerates.[25]

During this entrepreneurial period, modern investment banking began to form, emerging as a major industry in its own right. But capital was still limited, that is until investment bankers figured out how to sell stocks and bonds and extend credit directly to the general public through consumer banks, earning themselves a tidy fee on every sale.[26] The character of Wall Street evolved in response to this large influx of cash into a curious amalgam of utilitarianism, which emphasized capital's role in stimulating economic growth and meeting social goals, and social Darwinism, which held that only the fittest survive.[27] Yet without regulatory restraints, the survivalist side began to dominate just like in aviation today. Since minimal information was available about company performance, investors had to simply trust bankers that the deal was a good investment. Similarly, passengers today must trust that airline executives understand the risks of their managerial decisions for air safety.

With so much blind faith, it is easy to see how things got out of balance in both industries. For example, in 1882 Rockefeller converted his Standard Oil alliance of forty loosely connected companies into the Standard Oil Trust, centralizing power under one head office. Few other companies could compete with the resultant level of economies of scale, and the structure of many industries became oligopolistic, just like the airline industry is today.[28] In the 1980s, airline executives such as Frank Lorenzo adopted similar strategies, aggressively acquiring smaller airlines, dominating the market through holding companies, and strong-arming anyone who stood in the way. Within a decade, Lorenzo controlled almost 20 percent of the US airline industry and had amassed an extensive amount of personal wealth.[29]

Like all wars, World War I provided opportunities for legitimate entrepreneurship as well as exploitation and irreversibly changed the course of history. In the development of the aviation industry, the battlefield provided a research and training ground for new equipment and personnel that proved particularly influential. However, progress was initially slow. It was unclear, aside from aerial observation, what military use small single-engine wood-and-fabric airplanes could offer. Individual pilots prowled the skies in search of an unsuspecting enemy to pounce upon, trying everything from handguns and grenades to grappling hooks and sideways mounted rifles for their assaults. Tactics changed in 1915 when Anthony Fokker invented the machine gun synchronizer, which enabled pilots to shoot through the arc of their spinning propeller without damage. Technological innovations like this not only improved airplane performance but also irrevocably changed the role of the pilot. Aviators became fighter pilots as they flew combat aircraft for the first time. Similarly, computers, improved avionics, and advances in navigation equipment on today's flight decks have changed commercial airline pilots into resource managers, in some ways overshadowing and potentially devaluing their actual flying skills and decision-making capabilities.

Since the United States did not officially enter World War I until 1917, many eager American men who dreamed of flying joined the British Royal Flying Corps or the French Air Force Lafayette Escadrille in order to serve. Fledgling pilots were given a brief introduction of about ten flight hours and then shipped to the front to hone their skills through trial and error. Clearly, this was not the best learning environment. Life expectancy for a British Royal Air Force pilot in France in 1916 was only about three weeks. By 1917, it was down to two. As a result, nearly fifty thousand airmen perished during World War I. To succeed as a pilot, you had to be courageous, smart, and dedicated to the profession. The stress and fatigue of flying three or four combat missions per day with death all around was intense. Like their colleagues in the trenches it was not uncommon for them to suffer from shell shock, or post-traumatic stress disorder as it is now called. Some historians claimed this was one reason British commanders opposed providing parachutes—they thought it might encourage overstressed pilots to give up and jump out.[30]

A number of female pilots volunteered for military service as well, but only a few were permitted to serve, and not on the frontlines. Typically women flew as flight instructors for male cadets, test pilots for manufacturers, or exhibition pilots for fund-raising drives. These accomplishments earned them genuine, but distant, respect from the men, many of whom were fearful of the competition for scarce pilot seats and suspicious of the growing suffrage movement.[31]

By war's end, the airplane had evolved from an observation platform with questionable utility to a full-blown military asset. Squadrons flew in formation and developed combat tactics for in-flight attacks while large all-metal multiengine bombers provided long-distance flight and cargo capability, which paved the way for commercial airliner development after the war. These technological achievements continued to change the pilot's role as well. Exciting stories of death-defying bravery in aerial combat, some true and some inflated, made their way stateside, impressing Americans with aviation's military value. Yet, it still remained difficult for most people to see any commercial potential in aviation.[32]

Most pilots left the military after World War I, but there was little opportunity for steady civilian employment flying. Crop dusting, skywriting, aerial photography, and, for some lucky airmen, Hollywood stunts in war movies provided some income. Others toured the country as "gypsy fliers," or "barnstormers," presumably because they stormed into small towns, demonstrating low-level maneuvering skills to avoid farm structures and then landing in fields. Acting as their own mechanics, flight planners, dispatchers, weathermen, and air traffic controllers, these pilots sold rides and performed at air shows, fairgrounds, or wherever they could attract an audience. Like the early years in the financial sector, people could basically do whatever they liked in aviation. There were neither licensing criteria nor a supervisory agency to enforce them.

Without clear regulatory guidance, barnstormers were free to improvise and they developed an astonishing repertoire of aerobatics and in-flight tricks such as parachuting, midair transfers, wing walking, automobile-to-airplane transfers, and trapeze hanging, to name a few. The show often concluded with a staged in-flight slip-and-fall or crash landing to liven things up. And small town Americans, many of whom had never before seen an airplane close up, were thrilled.[33] The appearance of a barnstormer overhead was akin to a national holiday, and a town would often shut down to enjoy the show. Although barnstormers helped increase aviation awareness in the United States, these stunts often reinforced the public's belief that flying was dangerous, airplanes unsafe, and pilots risk takers.

While some aviators prospered, for most pilots, barnstorming was not as glamorous as it appeared. With low pay and a nomadic lifestyle, many pilots struggled to stay financially afloat, sleeping under their planes and bartering for food. Fatigue, hunger, and exposure to the elements became real challenges. It was even more difficult for women pilots, sidelined during the war, to catch up and compete with the large number of government-trained military pilots who were barnstorming after the war. Nevertheless, defying overwhelming odds, sexism, and in some cases racism, several women barnstormers made their mark as well.

The general public's demand for more extreme stunts created risky competitions in which pilots upstaged one another as they attempted increasingly foolhardy maneuvers for the crowd's entertainment. Unfortunately, many female barnstormers followed their male counterparts' right into an early grave.[34] Like the increasing risks in aviation today and need for greater safety measures, it was clear to many people, both inside and outside the field, that federal aviation regulation was long overdue. It was time for the US government to get involved. Yet, as with the financial sector, effective regulation of aviation was difficult to institute.

Although small town America was captivated with barnstormers and intrigued by the complex mix of risk and romance of flight, interest in commercial air travel still lagged in the United States. Aviation's dangerous reputation and the open cockpit flight experience, compared with the comfort and efficiency of railway travel, hindered US airline development, which had already begun in other countries.[35] In Europe, where several major cities were separated by water and most railroads, bridges, and roads were damaged by the war, aviation became a logical alternative to other modes of transportation. As a result, Europe became a natural incubator for commercial aviation.

Unlike the situation in the United States, European governments were keen aviation supporters. France, Germany, and then Great Britain all took an early interest in civil aviation, providing federal subsidies to support commercial development.[36] While American pilots were still barnstorming, European aviators were trailblazing routes to their nations' distant colonies, mapping the way for airmail, cargo, and passenger services to follow. French pilots flew to West Africa; Dutch aviators mapped routes to Indonesia; British airmen navigated to Australia; and German pilots established networks connecting Europe to China and Russia, overflying dangerously inhospitable areas of Siberia. These flights were not without their own unique risks. Pilots were shot at by camel-riding nomads, attacked by rebels, and threatened by natives with spears, all astonished by the sight of unfamiliar flying machines.[37]

In the United States, things developed differently without direct government support. Now that World War I proved aviation's military potential, the postal service was finally able to garner enough support to propose the use of aviation for their own service. In 1918, Congress appropriated $100,000 for an experimental airmail route between New York and Washington, DC. Yet, completing regularly scheduled flights in single-engine, open cockpit airplanes in all weather conditions with minimal instrumentation and little navigation guidance presented new, unanticipated risks. This sort of flying had never been done before in the United States. Pilots were poorly trained, airplanes ill equipped, airports inadequate, and airways—a sort of highway in the sky for pilots to fly along—nonexistent. As a result, an airmail pilot's life expectancy was only about four years at the outset of the program.[38]

However, much was riding on the success of this airmail experiment, and Assistant Postmaster General Otto Praeger set a personal goal to beat the railroads, which had previously enjoyed uncontested dominance in transporting the mail. Unfamiliar with aviation, Praeger pushed the inexperienced pilots to fly in most weather conditions with a "mail must go through" attitude, which ultimately proved disastrous. During the three years of his tenure (1918–21), one hundred and two crashes occurred, resulting in twenty-seven fatalities—a rate of one death about every 277 flights, or almost every thirty-nine days—a severe price paid for short-term thinking and poor leadership.[39] This would not be the last time professional pilots were pushed to fly by aggressive executives, unfamiliar with the challenges and limitations of commercial flight.

In 1919, airmail pilots confronted Praeger with a strike—the first pilot strike in history—protesting this pressure to fly. The two sides compromised after it was agreed that postal managers in New York or Chicago could not adequately judge the weather conditions at an airmail outstation and therefore the airfield manager would henceforth decide if it was safe to take off.[40] In 1921, the incoming Warren Harding administration ushered in new attitudes toward aviation safety. Funds were appropriated to upgrade airmail aircraft, install landing lights, improve airports, and illuminate airways. By the end of 1925, a lighted airway spanned the nation from New York to San Francisco, supporting cross-country airmail flying at night for the first time. Criteria were initiated that included a qualifying examination, five hundred flight hours, and regular physical examinations for pilots to be eligible to fly the mail. Aircraft maintenance was improved as well with regular airplane inspections and scheduled engine overhauls by experienced mechanics. These operational changes contributed to an extraordinary improvement in air safety, and airmail fatalities decreased by a factor of twelve.[41] This marks the first clear example of how industry's philosophical change about air safety coupled with government's proactive support and funding can directly reduce fatalities and risk.

As air safety improved, several air-minded businessmen attempted to establish scheduled airline service in the United States for the first time. The most popular used flying boats to shuttle wealthy passengers between coastal cities and tourist areas: St. Petersburg to Tampa, Key West to Havana, Miami to West Palm Beach, Seattle to Victoria, New York to Atlantic City, and New York to Newport, Rhode Island. Yet, flights were still seen as hazardous, and costs were prohibitive. No airline lasted more than one or two tourist seasons.[42]

In the early 1920s, the United States remained one of the few nations in the world with no aviation policy or clear sense of the role of state or federal government in industry regulation. Although President Calvin Coolidge was neither an aviation enthusiast nor a supporter of regulating American business, he nonetheless recognized that the aviation industry could no longer go unmonitored. However, the way forward was unclear. Federal politicians were polemical, state governments were territorial, and aircraft manufacturers were suspicious after years of patent fights harkening back to the Wright brothers. Even the few airlines that existed at the time were unable to agree on a common course of action. To sort things out, President Coolidge appointed Wall Street banker Dwight Morrow to chair a board of prominent businessmen, politicians, and military officers who would examine relevant aviation issues and make policy recommendations.

At the time of accepting this position, Morrow confessed to knowing little about aviation. In the coming chapters we will find Morrow was not the only political leader in aviation history unfamiliar with the intricacies of aircraft operations to nonetheless drive development of aviation policy. However, Morrow set about earnestly conducting his investigation, and the resulting nonpartisan report was just the sort of straightforward evaluation the United States needed to finally commit government's full support to civil aviation development.[43] As a result, the US government passed two pieces of aviation legislation in short succession. The Contract Airmail Act, or Kelly act, in 1925 was the first major legislative step toward creation of a US airline industry. It authorized the Post Office to hire private contractors to fly the mail. Then the Air Commerce Act of 1926 created the first federal aviation regulatory body to promote and supervise development of commercial aviation. It licensed pilots and mechanics, certified the airworthiness of airplanes, developed airport and navigational facilities, and established air traffic regulations—all for the first time in the United

States. When the commerce act passed, a patchwork of twenty-six different state aviation laws were nullified.[44] The federal government had finally begun catching up with its regulatory responsibilities.

Yet, US government leaders were reluctant to directly subsidize the burgeoning commercial aviation industry, as many European countries had done. Instead, they intended this new legislation to simply stabilize civil aviation temporarily—with limited government assistance—until private investors could be attracted to support and expand commercial air service. Unfortunately, this strategy backfired. Nearly a decade after this legislation was implemented airmail contractors still shunned passengers, happily flying mail in inexpensive war surplus planes and relying almost exclusively on Post Office subsidies to survive. Exploiting loopholes in the government's accounting system, contractors made money regardless of the actual demand for airmail service.

It was a lucrative business. The Post Office paid three dollars per pound, or nineteen cents per ounce to carry a letter. Yet, it only cost five cents an ounce to mail one. Enterprising aviation executives quickly discovered if they invested five cents mailing a letter, they could make fourteen delivering it. At those rates, a 150 pound passenger would have to pay over $450 for a ticket, or $5,500 in today's dollars, to make such transport worthwhile. That was not likely.[45] Some contractors sent bags of mail to themselves or bulky Christmas cards, stuffed with blank paper, to add weight. Registered letters, required to be in padlocked bags, were best; the Post Office paid for the weight of all of it. The most devious contractors topped off the plane's baggage compartment with postage-paid lead bars, bricks, telephone books, and even cast iron stoves.[46]

In an eerie case that foreshadowed airline executives' post-9/11 aviation industry strategies, none of the government regulators seemed to catch on to these shenanigans. The commercial aviation industry was already showing signs of the gamesmanship and short-term profit-seeking strategies prominent throughout Wall Street's history and which have become so pervasive in post-9/11 aviation in the United States. Just like today, there were neither repercussions for exploitation of the rules nor incentives to encourage better practices.

Fourteen years after the Wright brothers first flew, not a lot had changed in US commercial aviation. The luckiest companies flew airmail, capitalizing on government subsidies, and pilots eked out a living in their small, open-cockpit single-engine planes made of wood, wire, and fabric. It was difficult to see how a reliable passenger airline service would ever emerge in the United States. That was until 1927.

It all began with a French immigrant in New York City and a twenty-five-year-old farm boy from Minnesota. Raymond Orteig immigrated to New York City in 1912, working first as a bus boy and café manager and finally acquiring two profitable Manhattan hotels.[47] Intrigued by flying stories told by World War I aces, Orteig dreamed of linking his two favorite cities by air, New York and Paris. In 1919, he offered a $25,000 prize for the first nonstop airplane flight between them. Several aviators from both sides of the Atlantic attempted the feat, paying for it with their lives. For eight years the prize went unclaimed until technological developments finally enabled the manufacture of a plane capable of safely overcoming the obstacles presented by such a long-distance flight.

In 1927, US airmail pilot and army reservist, Charles Lindbergh conquered the challenge. Flying over 3,600 miles in thirty-three-and-a-half hours, he circled the Eiffel Tower and then landed in Paris to claim the prize money. Amelia Earhart followed in 1932 as the first woman to complete the achievement. These flights, and the quiet, confident courage of the pilots who completed them, created a paradigm shift in the United States. Lindbergh, Earhart, and other record setters, showed what a well-built aircraft in the hands of an experienced, professional pilot who understood how to fly it could accomplish.

Through the action of these pilots, Americans finally began to see the prospects of commercial air travel, and they wanted to get airborne in record numbers. Aircraft sales tripled between 1927 and 1929 as dozens of airlines sprang up, eager to carry them.[48] However, few airline managers had a solid business plan, and most air carriers lost money by perpetuating their reliance on airmail subsidies. Nevertheless, it was a turning point in American aviation history. Anyone with an airplane could start an airline, and in a country the size of the United States, there seemed to be plenty of open sky for everybody.[49]

The Roaring Twenties were in full swing. It was an era of widespread optimism, economic growth, business innovation, and increasing affluence. A few critics worried that stocks were dangerously overpriced, investor margins high, and portfolios undiversified and overly speculative.

However, most Americans chose to ignore these signs and rode the waves of optimism and prosperity.

Modern technology made everything seem possible—electricity, telephone, telegraph, automobiles, steel, chemicals, oil, paper, consumer goods, electronics, moving pictures, and radio were all growth areas—and aviation was primed for expansion as well. Manufacturers like Henry Ford, who had already perfected mass production of automobiles, saw how large multiengine bombers developed during World War I could easily be adapted to carry passengers. And airline executives like Clement Melville Keys saw the market for long-distance passenger air service.

Although railways were widespread and trains relatively comfortable, it took over seventy-two hours to travel between New York and Los Angeles. Keys bet he could cut travel time in half using airplanes. To help him accomplish this goal, he recruited Charles Lindbergh who had just completed a Guggenheim-sponsored air tour visiting eighty-two cities in forty-eight states, flying over 22,000 miles and 260 hours. Nearly thirty million people came out to greet him. Yet, this was no joy ride for Lindbergh. Every flight was made with the purpose of furthering his knowledge of regional weather, obstacles to flight, airport availability, navigation, fuel management, and flight planning.[50] No one had ever done this before. Charles Lindbergh had become the bold young face of American aviation, eager to expand the commercial market and improve its image as a safe industry.

In 1928, Keyes launched Transcontinental Air Transport (TAT), the first US airline established to fly passengers, not airmail, long distance. Unsurprisingly, Keys picked Lindbergh as his technical consultant. For $250,000 and 25,000 shares in the business, Lindbergh both designed TAT's transcontinental network and marketed the concept to wealthy businessmen. From then on TAT became known as "the Lindbergh Line." Customers travelled in modern Ford Tri-Motor airplanes by day, then, because night flights were still unsafe, they continued the trip overnight in sleeping trains. This approach cut travel time down to forty-eight hours but cost almost four hundred dollars for a one-way ticket, an exorbitant price at the time.[51]

For Lindbergh and Keys, no detail was too insignificant. Airways were lit, and weather and radio stations were established en route. Airplanes were designed with exacting specifications, equipped with three engines and modern instrumentation for flight safety and kitchens, reading lights, and velvet curtains for passenger comfort. Railway stations were improved and new air terminals built so that passengers could wait in comfort; $1.5 million was spent on ground-based improvements alone. TAT even awarded each passenger a solid-gold Tiffany fountain pen as a keepsake of their transcontinental trip. When service began in 1929, a thousand people applied for tickets on the first scheduled flight, and Lindbergh piloted the West Coast leg himself, heading east from Los Angeles.[52] It seemed to be a glorious time in commercial airline history, but like the post-9/11 image of the golden age of safety, appearances can be deceiving.

In hindsight, it's not surprising that the unbridled optimism of the Roaring Twenties resulted in a crash—several crashes, in fact—by the 1930s. Eleven less-experienced pilots attempted to match Lindbergh's and Earhart's feat by flying across the Atlantic Ocean. Three of the flights crashed, killing four people.[53]

About eight weeks after Lindbergh's inaugural airline flight, a TAT plane nicknamed *City of San Francisco*, which departed from Albuquerque heading west for Los Angeles crashed as well. After takeoff, the weather turned dark and ominous and the pilots diverted north of course, trying to stay clear of the building clouds. It's unclear exactly what happened next; perhaps they were attempting to turn back for landing. But Mount Taylor, standing over 11,000 feet high, loomed in their flight path. The aircraft struck the tree-covered slope and was demolished on impact, killing everyone on board. In the days before radar and air traffic control, the *City of San Francisco* seemed to just disappear. It took nearly four days to find what was left of the bodies and wreckage. There was simply no process in place yet to effectively guide aircraft in inclement weather, track their flight path, locate a crash site, or investigate an accident. Radar, cockpit voice recorders, flight data recorders, and accident-analysis techniques were still decades away.

Just weeks after the *City of San Francisco* accident, the US stock market crashed, too, creating the worst financial disaster in US history. Conventionally considered to have started on Black Thursday, October 24, 1929, the selling panic did not end until 1932. By then, stocks had lost nearly 90 percent of their value. Just like responses to the 2008 credit crisis, most Americans rightly blamed the 1929 crash and the Great Depression that followed on lax regulations and greedy bankers. In 1932, the United States Senate Committee on Banking and Currency conducted an inquiry called the Pecora hearings and determined that the government's poor supervision of the financial industry allowed banks to take on increasingly risky stock speculation and push unsophisticated consumers into buying overpriced investments.[54] In the coming chapters, I discuss how lax aviation regulation and risky airline executive decisions have put a naïve flying public in jeopardy as well.

Despite Lindbergh's charisma and the efforts of Keys to usher in an era of long-distance passenger air travel that would rival travel by railroad, TAT crashed as well, losing $2.75 million in a little over a year. As the effects of the Depression deepened, there was no longer much interest in long-distance flights when they cost twice as much as railroad travel while only saving twenty-four hours over train service. Although TAT survived long enough to merge with Western Air Express, becoming Transcontinental & Western Air and eventually Trans World Airways (TWA), many people at the time wondered if its demise marked the end of long-distance passenger air service forever.

TAT's struggles to make a profit provided the evidence airmail contractors sought to continue justifying their prioritization of airmail over expanding into passenger air service. Like TAT, some airlines attempted to attract passengers by creating an illusion of modernity and sophistication. Yet, the only luxury they actually provided was a high ticket price that few people could afford. Most commercial aircraft were neither fast nor comfortable: vibration was intense, engines noisy, toilets crude, and heating unreliable. It was not uncommon for bad weather or mechanical problems to force pilots to make an emergency landing in a cow pasture or remote airstrip, stranding passengers short of their final destination. All this and a fatality rate 1,500 times that of railroads and 900 times that of buses made it difficult to convince people to fly. But then, in 1930, the airline industry stumbled on a way to help change its image and improve passengers' flight experience. Once again it had to do with employees.

The change began when a young woman pilot and nurse from Iowa, Ellen Church, approached Boeing Transport, the predecessor to United Airlines, about a flying job. Although Boeing would not hire a woman pilot, she nonetheless persuaded them to employ her and seven other women as in-flight "stewardesses." These sexy young nurses in uniform, trained to face emergencies calmly, served food and coffee on elegant china, pampering the predominantly male passengers with pillows and blankets while pointing out landmarks along the flight path. Since air sickness was common, some airlines advertised "windows which can be open or shut at pleasure," a function that allowed passengers to lean out and throw up.[55] In this environment of coddling by good-looking unmarried women with medical training, businessmen felt reassured that flying was safe and worth the ticket price. Not unlike the influence of Lindberg, Earhart, and other competent pilots who helped change the public's perception of the risks of flight, stewardesses also vastly improved the image of air travel.

Female stewardesses quickly replaced many airlines' male stewards called "couriers", improving the industry's appeal by creating an image of luxury, glamour, and adventure with a hint of sexual innuendo. Yet for some air carriers employment decisions came down to economics.[56] Unlike women—who were subject to height, weight, and age restrictions, and fired if they married or had children—men had no employment regulations and so typically held their airline jobs longer, providing a better return on the airline's $1,000 training investment. It was not until the 1970s that women's age limit of thirty-five was eliminated, the 1980s for women's no-marriage rule to be abolished, and the 1990s for women's size restrictions to be declared discriminatory.[57]

However, as an indication of the depth of loyalty to their profession, stewardesses endured these practices for over forty years. This type of employee dedication to an aviation career was not uncommon, even during the tumultuous years of the post-9/11 period. Consider Robert Reardon. At eighty-seven he is the oldest flight attendant at Delta Airlines, having begun his aviation career in 1951. Or United's Ron Akana, who at eighty-three has worked as a flight attendant for sixty-three years, logging some 20 million miles along the way. Although no one tracks seniority across airlines, Akana is widely believed to be the longest-serving flight attendant in the United States, and most likely the longest-serving employee.[58] However, these flight attendants have seen a lot of changes and not necessarily for the better. After adjusting for inflation, the flight attendant median hourly wage dropped by 26 percent between 1980 and 2007, while that of all US workers rose by 13 percent during the same period.[59] Of the approximately 110,000 flight attendants employed by US carriers, over 40 percent are now fifty or older, while less than 18 percent are thirty-four or younger—down from 78 percent in 1980.[60] All of these factors have been exacerbated by post-9/11 restructuring as hiring stagnated, wages tumbled, and pensions vaporized at most major airlines.

In 1929, a new Postmaster General, Walter Folger Brown, took office vowing to stop the airmail abuses allowed by his predecessor. His goal was to foster development of a commercial airline industry infrastructure that could thrive without government subsidies.[61] Yet Brown was concerned that without guidance the nation's air transportation network might evolve in the same corrupt and inefficient manner that US railroads had sixty years earlier. The key to avoiding this, he thought, was to use his political influence and financial clout through airmail contracts to encourage a select group of larger air carriers to develop a nationwide interconnected network of routes. Already displaying an industry predilection for bigger is better, Brown observed that "there was no sense in taking the government's money and dishing it out to every little fellow that was flying around."[62] His vision was to build a commercial airline industry that would be self-sustaining. However in actualizing this vision we find many of the roots of problems encountered in the post-9/11 period.

Drafting new legislation, most notably the Airmail Act of 1930 also known as the McNary-Watres act, Brown pushed Congress to support his network vision and institute new airmail compensation methods, closing previous loopholes. Instead of paying contractors per pound, for instance, the Post Office would now compensate according to cargo space available. In a manner similar to today's aviation industry shift toward regional jets, this new government regulation and the space-available method of compensation encouraged contractors to buy new planes in order to receive the greatest subsidies and then add passenger service to help fill the aircraft.

Although Brown's strategy worked, ending previous corrupt profiteering practices, it created other opportunities for abuse. When awarding contracts, Brown had "near dictatorial powers to bypass low bids and force [airline] consolidations and mergers."[63] And he was not reluctant to use this power. In 1930, Brown invited sixteen airlines to a closed-door meeting, known as the infamous "spoils conference," where he hand-picked several to receive noncompetitive ten-year airmail contracts.[64] The victors were Transcontinental & Western Air, American Airways, Eastern Air Transport, Northwest Airways, and Boeing Air Transport. Most major US airlines today have roots in this early secret selection and contracting process. In exchange for helping him develop a nationwide airway route structure, Brown practically assured his chosen airlines a regional monopoly supported by governmental airmail subsidies for the next decade. Yet, in a strangely magnanimous gesture, he also ensured that the smaller air carriers that were left out of the bidding process would at least receive a fair price for their airmail routes when they lost their contracts to his primary operators.[65]

For smaller air carriers, this was not good enough, and they were justifiably outraged by the Post Office's behavior. Several attempted to challenge the growing industry monopolies, their love of aviation too strong to allow Brown's bigger-is-better philosophy to prevail. These included such men as Tom and Paul Braniff of Braniff Airways, Walter Varney of Continental Airlines, and Alfred Frank of National Parks Airways. These independent-minded aviation pioneers not only had the guts to challenge Brown and the airmail system but they had political clout in Washington too.[66]

In 1934, a nationwide scandal erupted when Sen. Hugo L. Black of Alabama uncovered evidence of collusion and fraud in the government's airmail contracting process and accused Brown of circumventing established methods of competitive bidding. In yet another situation that foreshadowed today's airline industry patterns, according to Black, "the control of American aviation had been ruthlessly taken away from the men who could fly and bestowed upon bankers, brokers, promoters and politicians sitting in their inner offices allotting among themselves the taxpayer's money."[67] Black called revelations of the Congressional investigation that followed a "dismally familiar picture" of big business corruption and included "immense salaries, bonuses, and speculative profits" for airline executives, "dubious relations" between the industry and government regulators, suspicious noncompetitive bidding processes, and "covert destruction of official records."[68] The Congressional inquiry concluded that Brown's airmail contracting was "an exceptionally blatant case" of "an industry using government to exploit the public" and regulators allowing them to get away with it.[69] A similar charge might well be leveled at the airline industry today.

In other examples of suspicious business practices, aviation holding companies strategically invested just a few hundred dollars in their own stock—right before a big deal was struck—then converted that investment into millions when the contract was signed. This insider trading was pervasive. For instance, Fred Rentschler and his colleagues bought stock in their own company, Pratt & Whitney, for twenty cents a share and then approved an 80-to-1 stock split just before the company merged with United Aircraft and Transport. After the merger, they exchanged their Pratt shares for United stock, which traded as high as $160, allowing Rentschler to turn his initial $253 investment into over $35 million. Charles Deeds, the chairman's son, parlayed a $40 outlay into $5.6 million. Similarly, William Boeing purchased stock in his company, Boeing Aircraft and Transport, for six cents a share, investing $259, and then sold those shares for $5.3 million. And, as with examples previously discussed, industry regulators never seemed to catch on.[70]

This pattern of behavior found in the history of both aviation and the financial sector and continuing to the present day prompts the following question: How is it greedy executives are able to continue to exploit the cracks between weak government regulations, apathetic enforcement agencies, and naïve consumers with few repercussions? Was there no one who attempted to rein in these excesses at some point in an effort to institute a sense of ethics and professional responsibility?

Outraged by the aviation industry's exploitation of government's regulations, newly inaugurated President Franklin D. Roosevelt seized the opportunity to make good on his campaign pledge of a "new deal for the American people" and cancelled Brown's questionable airmail contracts in 1934. After consulting with military leaders, Roosevelt directed the Army Air Corps to take over flying the mail.[71] Yet this decision proved disastrous, as overzealous post–World War I generals, more familiar with horses than airplanes, had little knowledge of aviation operations or any sense of the mission they were committing their pilots to accomplish. This will not be the last example we find of uninformed policy decisions directly increasing the risk of frontline flight operations. As one might expect, air safety predictably suffered.

Airmail contractors and their pilots and planes had come a long way in the five years since the Kelly act was passed. Airlines now had experienced commercial pilots with thousands of flight hours and who were familiar with night and instrument conditions. They flew modern airplanes with the latest instrumentation, lighting systems, radios, and navigation aids. Airline captains typically had about six thousand flight hours and copilots a minimum of one thousand. In contrast, the army had young, inexperienced pilots with just a few hundred flight hours flying small open-cockpit airplanes with no instrumentation that were built for combat operations in daylight and good weather.[72] Before the army even began their assignment, two planes crashed in training as military pilots attempted to familiar-ize themselves with the challenging airmail routes. Within the first few months there were sixty-six fatal accidents, and costs quadrupled, forcing the president to rapidly return airmail service to more-experienced private contractors.

However, this time, Roosevelt promised, there would be a transparent bidding process with airmail contracts going to the lowest bidder based on three eligibility criteria: First, any airline that had previously held an air-mail contract awarded through Brown's secret selection process could not bid. Second, any airline executive involved in Brown's closed-door meet-ings was barred from the aviation industry for life. And third, no aircraft manufacturer could also operate as an airline. Gone were the days when an aircraft manufacturer like Boeing or Pratt & Whitney could also run an airline, securing the plane builder a guaranteed market for its aircraft at whatever price it chose to demand.[73]

Yet in what had already developed into a pattern in both the financial and aviation industries—finding loopholes to circumvent government's attempts at regulation—airlines quickly strategized to work around the restrictions. Existing airlines simply changed their names, and manu-facturers spun off an airline subsidiary. For instance, American Airways changed their name to American Air Lines, Transcontinental & Western Air added "Inc.," Eastern Air Transport became Eastern Air Lines, North-west Airways changed to Northwest Airlines, and manufacturer Boeing spun off United Air Lines. All received new airmail contracts. Newcom-ers Braniff and Delta Air Lines also won out. Propped up by the stability of government airmail contracts once again, these seven air carriers faced minimal regional competition for the next fifty years.

Some people claimed President Roosevelt's response to the airmail fiasco was excessive, the "opening shot in a larger battle" about government's role in regulating businesses across the board that still rages in Congress today.[74] Like airmail contractors, railroads, shipping companies, and bank-ers, and utility companies in the 1920s and 1930s had also been exploiting loopholes in the federal and state regulatory system. Rapid technologi-cal advances and explosive growth in the power industry left government agencies unable to effectively monitor utilities, and a cozy relationship de-veloped between regulators and the purportedly regulated.[75] An analogous situation prevails in the aviation industry and Wall Street today.

Roosevelt saw these corporate excesses as a disturbing trend, part of a larger, more complex social issue with moral, economic, and political implications. He was committed to using his governmental power to rein in what many perceived to be the exploitation of consumers and bilking of taxpayers. Calling for more "truth telling" in business, Roosevelt said that "government cannot prevent some individuals from making errors in judgment," but government could prevent businesses from fooling "sensible people through misstatements," manipulating markets, and "withholding of information."[76] He blamed these abuses on government's laissez-faire leadership and its reluctance to regulate. Not unlike criticisms of President Barack Obama's efforts to regulate the financial sector after the 2008 credit crisis, Roosevelt's critics similarly attacked his efforts as "socialism," claiming that federal regulation would lower efficiency, increase costs, squelch innovation, and scare off investors. Yet, these feared consequences never became a reality.

Regulation of the growing aviation industry was similarly sporadic and it was taking its toll on public safety as airlines now carried nearly a million passengers annually.[77] In 1934, the Bureau of Air Commerce (BAC) was established to provide stability and encourage airlines to collaborate in creation of an air traffic control (ATC) network. In 1935, the first of several air traffic control centers was established, staffed by the airlines themselves not by federal employees as they are today. In an unprecedented move, airlines recognized the need to increase safety and hastened to take action ahead of government intervention. Although their action was commendable, the BAC nonetheless took over the nation's ATC system, intricately linking the federal government and taxpayer dollars with air safety and airline operations in a complex relationship that still exists today.[78]

In addition to ATC development, the BAC was charged with accident analysis. Yet, in this task, they were not unbiased either. Between 1932 and 1936, air passenger fatalities more than doubled to practically one death every twenty-eight days.[79] However, BAC accident reports rarely uncovered any systemic or organizational flaws. In its first one hundred investigations, the BAC blamed individual pilots, or pilots and weather together, in over half the crashes and found no cause of accident in nearly a quarter of the other cases. No airline, aircraft manufacturer, aviation regulator, or any government entity was ever found to be at fault.[80]

With so many responsibilities, the BAC was admittedly having difficulty keeping up, just like government regulators today. The BAC had just sixty aviation inspectors to supervise 14,000 commercial pilots, 24,000 student pilots, 8,000 aircraft, and 2,500 mechanics nationwide and no airplanes to help shorten their travel between locales.[81] In addition, two general categories of aviation companies had emerged with distinctly different operations but no clear regulatory standards: larger airmail contractors flew people, property, and mail over established routes while smaller fixed base operators provided smaller airport services, flight training, crop dusting, and air taxis. The distinction between these two separate areas of the aviation industry—commercial operators such as airlines and general aviation operators such as airport flight schools—remains blurred even today. Ideally, airlines would take a more proactive interest in the basic training of aspiring civilian pilots. Unfortunately, this responsibility is typically left to small airport flight schools or professional training programs whose flight instructors do not often have significant airline industry experience. It is assumed that pilots will eventually pick up the requisite commercial knowledge and professionalism along the way. Yet, we know from post-9/11 accidents of regional airlines like Colgan Air, Comair Airways, Corporate Airlines, and Pinnacle Airlines (discussed in detail in chapter 6) this does not always happen.

To add to the confusion, three different agencies held overlapping jurisdiction over these diverse operations: the Post Office, Commerce Department, and Interstate Commerce Commission. It was a regulatory nightmare. The final blow came in 1937 when five airliners crashed in a two-week period, killing forty-one people. Most disturbing was that these crashes were not in older, obsolete aircraft. They involved airliners thought to be part of a new generation of sophisticated airplanes equipped with the most modern safety devices available, flying on the most highly developed airways. Once again, it became apparent that government regulatory agencies had not kept pace with the explosive growth in an industry they were tasked to supervise.

Congress attempted to address this confusion with the Civil Aeronautics Act of 1938, which created the Civil Aeronautics Authority, placing the regulatory functions of all civil aviation and air transportation within one federal administrative agency for the first time. Through three semiautonomous subsystems, the Civil Aeronautics Authority would: investigate accidents; regulate air traffic, navigation, and mail; and assign airline routes, schedules, and fares. Although it was a start, and a positive indication that the federal government had begun to recognize the need for more proactive regulation, conflicting lines of authority and competing tasks made it far from perfect.

For example, one of the most confusing aspects of the Civil Aeronautics Authority's new charter was Congress's direction to encourage development of civil aeronautics while also improving industry relations and promoting safety.[82] This direction to both "promote" while also "regulating" air safety created overly complicated relations between regulators and the regulated in ways that had previously challenged the financial and utility industry. One would have thought government leaders would have learned from their previous regulatory mistakes. Yet the approach nonetheless persisted, undermining regulators' authority and ability to do their job successfully right from the start.[83] The aviation and financial industry history is replete with ways the political system undermined the very tasks its regulatory bodies were purportedly designed to accomplish.

Perhaps recognizing some of this regulatory confusion, President Roosevelt signed new legislation just two years later establishing an independent civil aeronautics body to regulate aviation-related commerce and safety. The law split the Civil Aeronautics Authority into two new agencies: the Civil Aeronautics Administration (CAA) and the Civil Aeronautics Board (CAB). The CAA was responsible for air traffic control, safety programs, and airway development. The CAB was assigned supervision of postal contracts, safety rule making, accident investigation, and economic regulation of the airlines. This division of duties proved to be better suited to the industry challenges, creating a formidable political alliance among Congress, the CAB, and the airlines that lasted for twenty years.

It was no secret in the 1920s and 1930s that most European governments saw air power as essential to their nations' sovereignty. To protect their interests, many countries sponsored pilot training for their youth, hoping to improve the aviation skills of their enlistment pools. Although Germany was specifically prohibited from assembling military forces after World War I by the Treaty of Versailles, Adolf Hitler argued that Germany was training pilots for peaceful purposes such as civilian airlines. In reality, the government-backed program was a military flight school preparing pilots for service in the Luftwaffe, Germany's air force. Many countries, including the United States, were alarmed by Hitler's behavior and eager to take action as they recognized the pivotal role air power would play in any future war.[84] Yet Germany already had an early lead. Aviation training was mandatory for all boys; the Hitler Youth studied aeronautics in school and practiced flying with gliders, and by the age of seventeen thousands of boys and girls were slated for aviation careers. Through this process, the Nazis produced 25,000 pilots, mechanics, and aeronautical engineers annually.[85]

Although it was clear at the outset of World War II that the rest of the world was woefully behind Germany in its aviation preparedness, there was nonetheless mixed responses in the United States about providing federal funds for aviation training. Isolationists feared pilot training would appear overly aggressive and militaristic, raising doubts about America's neutrality. Other critics saw it as yet another New Deal pork barrel and a waste of tax dollars. And some thought introducing aviation to young people turned schools into vocational adjuncts for the armed forces. Even the US military was ambivalent, suspicious about the quality of a pilot-training program run by civilians.

Yet President Roosevelt persevered, using a clause in the Civil Aeronautics Act to authorize funding of a trial program called the Civilian Pilot Training Program. The goal of the program was to provide a pool of well-trained civilian pilots from all walks of life—men, women, white, black, rich, and poor—who could support aviation operations in the event of war, improving military readiness. A secondary purpose was to develop a generation of air-minded young people for future employment in the commercial airline industry and boost civil aviation at regional airports. The government paid for ground school and up to fifty hours of flight training at select facilities around the country. At the program's peak, over two thousand educational institutions participated nationwide, training nearly four hundred thousand pilots to fly between 1939 and 1944. Small-plane manufacturers hoped these pilots would create a postwar demand for recreational flying and envisioned cheap, easy-to-operate personal planes becoming as common as automobiles.[86] Obviously, this vision never came to fruition.

Another solution to the pilot shortage during World War II was found in the establishment of the Women Airforce Service Pilots (WASP) program.[87] A pioneering organization of female pilots, the WASPs flew support missions for the US Army, freeing male pilots for combat duty. Twenty-five thousand women applied to join, but only about a thousand were selected and trained. Flying every type of aircraft in the military inventory, these dedicated women ferried aircraft, provided flight instruction, towed gliders, and dragged targets. Although their safety record exceeded that of their male peers, the program disbanded in 1945, and only a few of the women found flying jobs after the war. Piloting for commercial airlines remained a male bastion until the 1970s.[88]

In addition to women, African American men were recruited as military pilots for the first time during World War II. Many of the applicants had begun training in the Civilian Pilot Training Program at the Tuskegee Institute and therefore became known as Tuskegee Airmen. The military was still segregated at the time, so Congress forced the Army Air Corps to form all-black training and combat units. Despite the War Department's initial reluctance, the 332nd Fighter Group and the 477th Bombardment Group were established, and aircrews flew with distinction under the name of "Red Tails," amassing a near-perfect safety record.

Another form of civilian pilot training took root during World War II in Tracy, California, where the Boeing School of Aeronautics trained civilian pilots for employment with United Air Lines. Between 1940 and the end of 1941, when the pilot shortage became most acute, the school trained 120 young airmen for six months in ground school and flight maneuvers, preparing them to become United pilots. After the Pearl Harbor attack, the West Coast was considered too vulnerable for civilian training, and the school moved to Cheyenne, Wyoming, and then later to Denver, which became the United Air Lines Training Center that is still in existence today. The young student pilots who trained in Tracy later became United's senior captains, colloquially known as "Tracy Aces."[89] The point here is that through examples like the Civilian Pilot Training Program, Women Airforce Service Pilots, Tuskegee Airmen, and United's Tracy Aces we find evidence of a historical precedent for safe, reputable civilian pilot-training programs supported by the government or airlines themselves.

After World War II, many aviation supporters argued that these civilian pilot-training programs should continue indefinitely and even be expanded. They believed the war had shown the need for a ready reserve of trained airmen to deter aggressor nations and that it was in the country's best interest to standardize training and provide a solid foundation of aviation skills to ensure commercial air safety. In addition, the government-backed programs leveled the playing field, allowing women and minorities the opportunity to enter aviation, a profession that had been largely dominated by wealthy white men.

The issue became hotly debated in Congress, and although the Civilian Pilot Training Program was extended for two more years, no funds were ever appropriated. The program silently died in 1946, a victim of postwar belt tightening.[90] The long-term impact of this, and the resultant effect on flight-training standardization and air safety, is evaluated further in later chapters. For now, it is important to emphasize that through the loss of these programs young people aspiring to become pilots were largely left to their own devises to learn the basics and build the required flight time. Two options emerged that are still in place today: joining the military to gain flight experience, if possible, or paying for training through airport flight schools at a cost that can easily approach sixty thousand dollars.[91]

Although during World War II the US government impounded half the nation's commercial airliners and recruited nearly all available pilots, airlines still managed to grow during the war years. The aerospace industry manufactured record numbers of aircraft, and airlines capitalized on returning military veterans flight training, enticing them into professional piloting careers. After the war, millions of Americans who were introduced to air travel through their military service were eager to fly, creating an expanding market. Nearly sixteen times as many passengers flew commercially after the war as flew before it.[92] A 1953 study found that airplanes had surpassed trains and buses as the preferred means of passenger transportation for trips of over two hundred miles.[93]

Thanks to technologies tested during war, manufacturers developed new generations of jet aircraft after the war. However, the air traffic infrastructure still was not ready to support it. Commercial jetliners could carry a hundred passengers at five hundred miles per hour, but not a single US airport was fully prepared to accommodate jet service. Airport runways, taxiways, and terminals needed expansion, and with radar emerging slowly, air traffic control services were still quite limited. The skies seemed more crowded than ever, and few safety procedures were in place to help. Although the CAA and CAB were trying to keep up—in a pattern common in both finance and aviation—the industry was evolving at a speed and complexity beyond the regulatory capacities of established agencies.

In the 1950s, once a plane departed the airport area, it entered uncontrolled airspace in which each pilot was responsible to "see-and-be-seen" to avoid midair collision. No external air traffic control guidance or traffic separation was available. Although aircraft were usually assigned a specific altitude, pilots were authorized to modify their course at will to take advantage of favorable winds, avoid bad weather, or fly more directly toward their destination. With no radar to follow their flight progress, commercial airliners would report their position via radio to dispatchers who would track their progress on paper or chalkboards. It was an archaic, unreliable process.

The result was that, although ATC might know of airplanes flying in a common geographical vicinity, controllers had no responsibility for traffic separation or obligation to alert pilots about a potential midair collision. Like a boat on the open ocean, responsibility for collision avoidance rested solely on the operators themselves. One crash in particular gained the nation's attention, highlighting the growing risks of this unregulated environment.

On the morning of June 30, 1956, two modern airliners departed within minutes of each other on regularly scheduled flights from Los Angeles International Airport, both heading east. TWA Flight 2 to Kansas City took off first carrying seventy people, and United Flight 718 to Chicago followed carrying fifty-eight.[94] After takeoff, both planes were vectored along a similar flight path by ATC and directed to climb visually through a cloud layer as they exited controlled airspace. As TWA Flight 2 approached Las Vegas pilots reported their position, estimating their next checkpoint "Painted Desert" at 10:31 a.m. Meanwhile United Flight 718 checked in about one hundred miles in trail, estimating their next checkpoint "Painted Desert" at 10:31 a.m. as well.

Although ATC knew of these airliners converging flight paths for almost twenty minutes, no one alerted the aircrews until a garbled radio transmission was heard at 10:31 a.m.: "United 718 . . . ah. . . . We're going in."[95] The TWA aircraft was found on the west side of the Grand Canyon with a short wreckage path, indicating the aircraft hit the ground inverted and at a steep angle. Although most of the United aircraft was found about a mile to the northeast, several pieces of its left wing were discovered intertwined with the wreckage at the TWA crash site, suggesting the planes had become entangled in flight.

The CAB determined that the probable cause of the midair collision was a combination of limited visibility due to cloud build up and the pilots' preoccupation with providing a scenic view of the Grand Canyon for passenger entertainment. With 128 fatalities, this crash was the deadliest aviation disaster of that era and caused much concern about air safety and the lack of effective regulations. Once again government agencies were caught having to catch up with industry developments after a fatal crash. People wondered if this sort of collision could occur with relatively slow-moving propeller airplanes in the middle of the Arizona desert, what was going to happen when jet airliners would soon crowd the skies over the nation's busiest cities. America did not have to wait long to find out.

US air traffic doubled after World War II, and by 1956, there had been six airline midair collisions, five involving military aircraft, resulting in three hundred deaths.[96] In one example, a United Airlines passenger flight established on a major commercial airway in Nevada collided head-on with an Air Force fighter jet executing a tactical maneuver. Despite clear skies, excellent visibility, and aircraft communicating with their respective ATC, neither flight was aware of the other's location. With a closure rate of over seven hundred miles per hour, both aircraft lost control and crashed into the desert southwest of Las Vegas. There were no survivors.

The CAB's investigation faulted both military and civilian aviation authorities for not taking action to reduce collision risks. Evidence emerged that airline crews had complained for over a year before this crash about the potential for a midair collision at this exact location between civil and military aircraft operating on separate radio frequencies—but to no avail. Once again, it took an accident to get regulators' attention. This tendency to disregard pilots' safety concerns until an actual accident occurs is a troubling but common pattern that still exists in aviation today; it's a practice that needs to come to an end.

Just a month later, a Capital Airlines passenger plane collided with an Air National Guard Lockheed T-33 in clear weather over Brunswick, Maryland, killing eleven more people. The faster, more powerful military plane had overtaken the slower airliner at eight thousand feet without apparently realizing it, and then proceeded to gradually turn right into the passenger plane.

These accidents highlighted some of the imperfections in air traffic regulations, dramatizing the CAA and CAB's inability to keep up with the explosive postwar aviation industry developments. It also shows ways that aircrew concerns voiced *before* an accident occurs rarely get the attention they deserve until after the next crash. It was time to end the see-and-be-seen rule, increase the use of radar for traffic avoidance, expand air traffic control responsibilities, and incorporate a unified method of airspace control for both civil and military flights. However, as previously discussed, the US government's approach has historically included a general reluctance to invest in aviation and apprehension about its role as industry regulator. Just like today, government leaders in the post–World War II period wagered that private investors, market forces, and airline competition would keep the skies safe. It was and is a risky bet.

3

Riding the Jet Stream

In 1958 the era of commercial jet service began in the United States, changing most everything in the aviation industry. Like the sleek, sexy jetliner itself, air carriers finally began living up to the glamorous image of modern air travel they had been trying to sell for decades. Besides the increased speed, travel distance, and reliability of jet aircraft, the comfort, romance, and intrigue of jet travel permeated American culture as well. *The Jetsons*, an animated television sitcom about a futuristic family reliant on jet cars, robots, and other automations, ran in prime time from 1962 to 1963; *Lost in Space*, a television show about earthlings coping with space colony life on a distant planet, headlined from 1965 to 1968; and the TV series *Star Trek* with its spaceship *Enterprise* crew began their intergalactic adventures in 1966, so far spawning twelve movies, six television series, numerous games, and even a Las Vegas theme show.

Back on Earth, The Beatles rode their own rocket ship to fame, first landing in America in 1964. In a famous photo of the era, the Fab Four are exiting an airliner, strolling down the plane's metal air stairs like

descending deities to greet thousands of screaming fans; Pan Am's cur-
vaceous 707 and blue-globe logo figures prominently in the background.
The band left London early that morning and arrived in New York the
same afternoon, adding to the out-of-this-world feel of both jet travel and
the "Beatle invasion." Fans could not get enough of The Beatles, and pas
sengers similarly flocked to commercial air travel in record numbers. After
decades of questionable financial support and fickle interest, Americans
had finally fallen in love with aviation. By the end of the 1960s, 1.3 billion
people had flown, and major airlines expanded dramatically as a result.[1]

Yet, behind the scenes, nagging safety issues centered on inefficient air
traffic control systems, and antiquated regulations continued to plague
operations. Concerned by the number of recent midair collisions, several
of which took place over densely populated urban areas including New
York City, the danger of which was compounded by the speed, size, and
passenger capacity of modern jetliners, Dwight D. Eisenhower, America's
first pilot president, took action. In 1958, he signed the Federal Aviation
Act into law, which revised aviation regulations that had remained largely
unchanged since the Civil Aeronautics Act of 1938, and created a new independent air safety watchdog body, the Federal Aviation Agency (predecessor to today's FAA) to replace the CAA.

A few years later Eisenhower established the Department of Transportation (DOT) and the National Transportation Safety Board (NTSB),
and restructured the FAA and thirty other previously scattered federal
elements relating to transportation under DOT jurisdiction. Apparently
conceding that the government had, at times, contributed to aviation's
regulatory confusion, Eisenhower developed this structure in order to join
at a "Cabinet level the presently fragmented Federal functions regarding
transportation activities."[2] As a result of this new arrangement, a federal
aviation triumvirate emerged that remained in place for almost two decades: the FAA promoted and regulated aviation while monitoring safety;
the NTSB investigated accidents; and the CAB continued to supervise all
aspects of airline operations from flight scheduling to fiscal management.

Yet, over time, the CAB's tasks became increasingly convoluted and
overly bureaucratic, harkening back to Postmaster General Brown's airmail
fiasco. Although Congress explicitly intended the CAB to create a competitive airline industry by helping to guide sound growth in the emerging
air transportation industry, over time something went desperately wrong.[3]

To control schedules, the CAB assigned specific routes to hand-picked air carriers—most with origins in the early airmail days—then limited the power of charter operations and regional airlines to compete. To control finances, the CAB assured select airlines "just and reasonable" profitability based on a simple formula: air carriers reported their operating costs, and the CAB calculated fares assuming a load factor of 55 percent and then added a 12 percent profit. To control competition, the CAB reviewed the details of all new air carrier applications, no matter how trivial.

However, the CAB was more than just fiscally conservative and overly bureaucratic. Its level of invasiveness bordered on the absurd. Airlines required CAB approval on even the smallest details, from employee uniforms to the price of drinks.[4] Clearly, the federal agency was not created to provide this level of regulatory scrutiny, nor was it warranted, and the slow-moving CAB got bogged down, unable to keep up with the needs of the quickly evolving post–World War II airline industry. Like Postmaster General Brown's airmail policies that affected all aviation, in the 1970s the regulatory pendulum had once again swung too far in the overly bureaucratic and highly regulated direction. Brown had good reason to tighten the regulatory reins in the 1930s. His goal was to stop previous subsidy abuses and use airmail to foster development of a nationwide network of routes and a self-sustaining commercial airline industry. It was a well-intentioned plan, but it was flawed in its execution. In the case of the CAB in the 1970s, it is unclear exactly why this gradual over-regulation occurred. The CAB's goal was to create a competitive airline industry by helping to guide sound growth—a nearly impossible task for government administrators unfamiliar with the intricacies of airline operations. It was a bad public policy that continued to get worse because the people involved knew little about the industry they were regulating.

Almost immediately after the CAB was established problems arose. It became clear, for example, that it was both impractical and inequitable to require all sizes of air carrier to navigate the expensive and time-consuming process of obtaining a Certificate of Public Convenience and Necessity required for commercial operators. Yet, Congress foresaw this issue and gave the CAB authority to make certain exceptions for a category of "non-scheduled" air carriers. For years there was not much interest in this classification, but after World War II and the explosive growth in air travel, hundreds of "irregular" air carriers commenced service, exploiting regulatory loopholes. At its peak in 1951, irregular air carriers constituted 7.5 percent of passenger service and 21 percent of cargo transport, operating largely without oversight. It took nearly a decade for the slow-moving CAB to catch up and rein in this practice, which contributed further to the impression that regulators were perpetually chasing the industry they were tasked to lead—just like in the banking and finance industry.[5]

In an effort to offset this image, the CAB sought to develop a mystique that their regulatory decision-making process was rational, scientific, and nonpolitical, and that their findings were based on industry-specific data unavailable to other sources. They created this image through elaborately staged governmental hearings on nearly every aspect of commercial airline operations, no matter how picayune.[6] Hearings were ostentatious in their choreography, yet predictably scripted in their outcome, with decisions often made arbitrarily—the answer was almost always "no." Of the seventy-nine new air carrier applications filed between 1950 and 1974, not one was authorized. And between 1969 and 1974, not one new route was assigned.[7] John E. Robson, chairman of the CAB from 1975 to 1977, described the process as being like a Hollywood movie set, the "regulatory equivalent of the 'kabuki dance.'"[8]

With little incentive to seek more efficient ways to run their air carriers, airline executives instead spent their energy and resources mastering the intricacies of the absurd regulatory system that yoked them. During this process a complex paradox emerged in which airlines complained about the CAB's tedious oversight, while at the same time aviation managers found the system addictively easy to work within. Unlike today's challenging marketplace, airline executives did not need to manage company finances or make route and fare decisions in order to compete. Through the CAB, the government managed these things for them. And while airline executives were denied the ability to reap the millions of dollars in personal profits they earn today, they were nevertheless protected from significant corporate losses as well.

In fact, things seemed to be going so well within the US airline industry in the 1960s that a sense of excessive optimism settled in, not unlike that in the financial sector during the Roaring Twenties. Aerospace manufacturers designed larger, faster aircraft with little thought to the repercussions, and eager airline executives purchased even more jetliners, betting on the appeal of the industry's latest technology to attract a steady increase in eager travelers. And if they didn't, it didn't matter anyway. The airlines were protected by the CAB. In 1969, the largest civilian airplane in the world was built, the Boeing 747, and along with it came new aviation terms like "wide-body" and "jumbo jet." Fifty thousand Boeing employees, nicknamed "the Incredibles," made aviation history when they built the first one in just sixteen months.[9] The 747 was the world's first double-decker, four-engine jetliner and was capable of carrying almost five hundred people at 640 miles per hour, an amazing feat at the time.

However, things did not initially turn out so well for this new generation of behemoths. Some passengers did not enjoy the feeling of being herded onboard en masse like cattle, and there were infrastructure obstacles as well. Many airports, runways, and taxiways were not equipped to accommodate the size and weight of the jumbo jet, and terminals could not load passengers efficiently. The 1973 economic recession, combined with the Middle East oil crisis, rising fuel costs, and an increasing prevalence of airline hijackings, resulted in air travel plummeting. Jumbo jets, expected to be a sensation, were flying half full. It seemed that, for a variety of reasons, technological developments had preceded market demand.

It was something like the later US automobile manufacturers' fixation on producing ever larger sport-utility vehicles until the Great Recession of 2008 made consumers want cheaper, greener, more fuel-efficient vehicles.[10] This misreading of the environment nearly put General Motors and Chrysler out of business until the US government stepped in with a $15 billion federal bailout in 2009.[11] By the mid-1970s, the situation looked dire for aviation as well. Yet air carriers, controlled by CAB policies, were unable to quickly modify services, eliminate unpopular routes, or adjust airfares. Hamstrung, airlines struggled to turn a profit. Unsurprisingly, the government was forced to intervene, and the CAB once again helped prop up US air carriers. In an intervention eerily prescient of the 2008 Troubled Asset Relief Program (TARP) in which the US government bolstered select Wall Street firms, the CAB helped handpicked airlines increase passenger load factors and improve profitability by reducing flights on a number of major routes.

In another time and place this secret, collective agreement to reduce market supply to drive up demand might be called anticompetitive price-fixing and deemed illegal under antitrust laws. But the CAB apparently saw no problem. There were other instances of persistent, unsanctioned collusion among major airlines that the CAB conveniently overlooked as well. Once again, the relationship between regulators and regulated had become overly cozy.[12] The problem was not regulation per se, but rather the combination of the overly broad scope of the CAB's regulatory reach and the controlling nature of the administrators tasked to lead it.

Considering the aviation history we have discussed, it remains mysterious how the US government—apathetic for years about supporting aviation industry developments or regulating commercial flight in the early twentieth century—got so deeply intertwined in the day-to-day business of airline operations in the post–World War II period. To examine the roots of this seemingly contradictory occurrence, we need to revisit the implications of Postmaster General Brown's spoils conference in the 1930s and once again consider parallels between aviation and Wall Street history.

As discussed in the previous chapter, once President Roosevelt nullified Brown's preferential airmail contracts in 1934, the stipulations of the new bidding process required that contracting be open and competitive and that awards be given to the lowest bidder.[13] Although these criteria were intended to create a more equitable selection process, they nonetheless opened up other areas ripe for exploitation. Once again, airline executives were eager to game the regulatory system, often offering bids that were absurdly low to undercut rivals and drive out the competition in order to expand their own nationwide network. Thus began the first in a long series of airline price wars, reminiscent of Commodore Vanderbilt's strategies in the shipping and rail industries, a strategy that continues to the present day. Economies of scale help here because, just like today, large airlines can tolerate financial losses on select competitive routes because they earn huge profits via monopolies on others.

For example, in 1938 Eastern Air Lines CEO Eddie Rickenbacker was intent on diversifying his airline's predominately East Coast service area by expanding westward. His goal was the creation of a transcontinental route across the southern states. Tackling Braniff Airways head-to-head in a struggle over their home turf in Texas, Eastern won the Houston–San Antonio airmail contract by bidding "zero cents" per mile.[14] "That's illegal," Braniff Airways founder Tom Braniff declared. "The hell it is!" Rickenbacker shot back.[15] At the time, fearing worse to come, Edgar Gorrell, president of the Air Transportation Association, noted that without government intervention "there is nothing to prevent the entire air-carrier system from crashing to earth under the impact of cut-throat and destructive practices."[16]

Congress met to discuss the evolving situation, and a government committee concluded that the aviation industry suffered from "the wrong sort of competition,"[17] a charge that could be leveled at airlines today. Yet, it was unclear what, if anything, should be done about it. Before the CAB was established, air carriers seemed trapped in a conundrum not unlike the later challenges of the post-9/11 period: airline executives believed that they could not afford to stay competitive and buy new planes with the latest technologies while simultaneously paying employees well and maintaining high levels of customer service. Delta Airlines founder C. E. Woolman summed up executives' worries best when he observed in 1956, "We are buying airplanes that haven't been fully designed, with millions of dollars we don't have. We're going to operate them off airports that are too small, in an air traffic control system that is too slow, and we must fill them with more passengers than we have ever carried before."[18] Yet, in reality, with commercial aviation expanding rapidly and so many markets still untapped, there was plenty of business for everyone. It was all a matter of perspective.

Fearing the worst for his airline, Tom Braniff appealed to politicians and supporters back in Texas urging them to invalidate Eastern's new airmail contracts. But Eddie Rickenbacker had a different market vision. Speaking to local community leaders, he boldly guaranteed that even with Eastern entering the Texas market as a new competitor Braniff would not lose. There is "definitely enough business for both of us," Rickenbacker predicted.[19] Many perceived Rickenbacker's strategy to be a risky bet, given the competitive spirit of the time. However, within a year passenger traffic for both airlines had more than doubled.

The main reason behind this development was Eastern employees' enthusiastic salesmanship of air transportation, attracting people away from railroads that had previously enjoyed a three-to-one advantage over air travel. Just as pilots like Lindbergh and Earhart and flight attendants like Ellen Church helped change the image of air safety, so too did customer service representatives at Eastern spread the word about the safety, affordability, and convenience of air travel. This airline strategy of creating a new aviation market by attracting travelers away from various modes of ground transportation has been successfully implemented by Southwest

Airlines in the recent past as well. Rather than viewing competition as stealing customers from rival airlines, as most did, this strategy encouraged development of new, previously unexploited markets.

We have come to a historical turning point that helps explain the mystery about how the US government, after years of apathy, got so deeply intertwined in the day-to-day business of airline operations. For most airline executives in the 1930s the solution to the emerging hypercompetitive environment was not to engage with the managerial challenge, like Rickenbacker did, but rather to try to get the federal government even more involved in regulating their business. This behavior may seem contradictory. Yet, in many ways it is surprisingly similar to ideas expressed by some Wall Street executives after the 2008 financial industry crash.

For example, Morgan Stanley CEO John J. Mack suggested to Congress in 2009 that "regulators have to be much more involved" in monitoring the financial industry's competitive practices because "we cannot control ourselves."[20] Similarly, early airline executives pleaded for federal intervention to protect the aviation industry from its own predatory behaviors because they did not think they could control themselves. Thus, in the 1930s, US airlines asked the government to do what Federal Reserve Chairman William McChesney Martin saw as one of its main tasks, that is, to be willing to "take away the punch bowl just as the party gets going."[21] This, therefore, became a pivotal moment in the history of airline regulation.

The timing of airline executives' request for government to "take away the punch bowl" in the 1930s and tighten regulatory oversight over the increasingly competitive aviation marketplace could not have been more auspicious. As part of his New Deal agenda, President Roosevelt was already in the midst of increasing the regulation of businesses on a scale never before seen in the United States. After the death of a popular US senator from New Mexico in a commercial airline crash, Congress was more than happy to increase supervision of aviation as well.

The senator, Bronson Cutting, was on a TWA flight caught in dense fog over Missouri. The pilots circled for more than an hour while looking for some way to land safely. With their radio dead and fuel almost gone, the captain finally dove into the cloud deck in a desperate attempt to locate the runway. The aircraft struck a fence and flipped over, killing five of the eight persons on board.[22] On receiving news of Senator Cutting's death, people in Washington wept openly, and a Congressional recess was declared. Once back in session, Congress gave the airlines exactly what their CEOs thought they needed—increased supervision by a government agency—and the CAB took control of commercial aviation, guiding US airlines for the next forty years.[23]

Other areas of government increased regulation as well. After the stock market crash of 1929, Congressional inquiries revealed a shocking range of shady commercial practices. It had become apparent that the growth of American business and influence of industry lobbyists had created a bigness that had become difficult to regulate, and the resultant concentrated economic power had run rampant. In response to the crisis, Americans demanded reform. A new philosophy of government emerged in this New Deal era, and similar legislation was passed in other industries such as the Emergency Railroad Transportation Act of 1933, the Motor Carrier Act of 1935 for trucking, and the Natural Gas Act of 1938 for interstate pipelines.[24]

Another important landmark, the Banking Act of 1933, commonly known as the Glass-Steagall Act, was adopted, establishing the Securities and Exchange Commission (SEC) and separating commercial banks, which take customer deposits and provide loans, from investment banks, which invest, speculate, acquire, and trade. After the devastating stock market crash of 1929 and subsequent depression, a disgraced and humbled Wall Street could not prevent the integration of tighter standards of industry control. Yet they never fully accepted the level of regulatory supervision Washington finally introduced. During this process, Wall Street came to be seen as a malevolent force that placed the country at risk rather than the creator of wealth and cornerstone of American capitalism that financiers decidedly preferred.[25]

In retaliation, over the next sixty-six years, Wall Street firms attempted to create ingenious methods to work around restrictions and exploit regulatory loopholes, just like aviation executives have been doing since 9/11. Their political lobbying efforts finally paid off in 1999 when President Bill Clinton repealed the Glass-Steagall Act, removing the divide between commercial and investment banks and thus returning them to their pre-1929 state. In addition, the Commodity Futures Modernization Act was passed, which exempted all derivatives, including the now notorious credit-default swaps, from federal regulation. Banks were emboldened to loosen mortgage application processes and increase dubious lending. We now know that these three events—loophole exploitation, regulation repeal with a corresponding reduction in supervision, and increasingly risky decision-making by industry leaders—directly contributed to the 2008 financial industry crash and the so-called Great Recession that followed.[26] We will find these same three factors pervasive in the airline industry today.

However, not everyone was a supporter of these regulatory changes. For example, one of the leading voices of dissent, Sen. Byron L. Dorgan, warned in 1999, "We have now decided in the name of modernization to forget the lessons of the past, of safety and of soundness." He noted, "We will look back in ten years' time and say we should not have done this, but we did because we forgot the lessons of the past, and that that which is true in the 1930s is true in 2010."[27] The same problem of the difficulty of regulating very large corporations, the concentration of economic power in the hands of a few firms, and forgetting the lessons of the past can be said to exist in the US airline industry today. To fully appreciate this, we need to return to aviation history and explore the character of the airline pioneers who built this industry.

Like Wall Street firms, the ruthless competition between airlines in the early days of industry development was largely instigated by the character and personalities of airline executives of the time. As Rickenbacker had shown in Texas in the 1930s, there was plenty of sky for everyone if managers and employees worked together. Yet Robert Crandall, CEO of American Airlines from 1985 to 1998, noted that commercial aviation has nonetheless always been "intensely, vigorously, bitterly, savagely competitive."[28] Similarly, Gordon Bethune, CEO of Continental from 1994 to 2004, summed his job up this way: "[People] don't realize that while you're sitting here talking, someone is fucking you. Changing a fare, changing a flight, moving something. There's no autopilot, and that's why I've seen a lot of guys come and go [as airline executives in this industry]."[29]

As a result of this competitive environment, both finance and airlines have tended to attract a certain type of individual to the higher echelons of the executive offices. In the formative years, aviation leaders were colorful characters who balanced their competitive nature and capitalistic yearnings with a love for aviation, a commitment to building America's air transportation infrastructure, and a genuine fondness for their employees and their community—men like Pat Patterson of United Airlines, C. E. Woolman of Delta, Eddie Rickenbacker of Eastern Airlines, Jack

Frye of TWA, and C. R. Smith of American Airlines. These were not just businessmen, they were airline industry leaders. Although aggressive and ambitious, these aviation pioneers nevertheless had a long-term vision for their airlines and a personal commitment to building a safe airline industry in the United States. Most were pilots themselves who took their airlines from open-cockpit airmail planes to international jetliner service over the decades that spanned their careers.

Consider William "Pat" Patterson, for example, the president of United Airlines for thirty-two years (1934–66). As a boy, Pat tired of school and quit at any early age to get a job. Demonstrating initiative and a keen work ethic, he answered a newspaper ad for employment at Wells Fargo bank and made his way from office boy to teller and eventually to loan officer.[30] It was while working there that he became an early airline enthusiast when he authorized a risky loan to Pacific Air Transport, a company that was eventually sold to Boeing. Patterson's boss did not share Pat's aviation enthusiasm and was concerned about the loan, so he advised him to "stick close to those flying machine men until we get our money back."[31] And stick by them he did, eventually moving to United Airlines as general manager, then vice president. After President Roosevelt cancelled the airmail contracts in 1934, United's leadership was forced out and Patterson moved up to become company president. A firm believer in face-to-face contact and honest communication, Pat was renowned for his open-door policies and mastery of "management by walking around." Employees loved him, and passengers began to as well. Patterson expanded flight attendant service and improved passenger meals, installing the first inflight kitchens on board aircraft. Always dedicated to safety, he pushed for development of autopilots, onboard weather radar, and four-engine airliners providing greater reliability. Then, in a spirit of collaboration, he openly shared his technological developments with his competition, saying, "Safety is not something to be patented for anybody's exclusive use."[32]

On his retirement Patterson summed up his lengthy airline career: "I was engaged in what I believe to be the most thrilling industry in the world—aviation. My heart still leaps [when I see a] plane soaring gracefully through the sky. Our great airlines awe me. Yet I know they were not produced in a day or a decade." Urging long-term planning, he concluded, by saying that for an idea to have "real worth" it has to be "something that will endure."[33]

In a similar career trajectory, Collett Everman "C. E." Woolman was the principal founder of Delta Air Lines and served in various leadership roles for nearly thirty-six years. Woolman was a modest, genial man with a passion for aviation, a high sense of integrity, and a stubborn resistance to failure. After earning his agricultural engineering degree and pilot's license, he developed some of the first aerial crop-dusting operations in the United States. In 1929 he expanded into passenger service, naming his airline after the Mississippi Delta area his crop dusters served.

Although the media frequently referred to Woolman as a stern patriarch, he had a genuine concern for his workers, believing "if you take care of your employees, they will take care of your customers."[34] He was famous for urging Delta employees to "put ourselves on the other side of the counter" and remember "we have a responsibility over and above the price of a ticket." Woolman's daughter recalled when she was young "sometimes I'd wake up on a cot in the hall" because "Daddy had brought home" a stranded passenger to "put in my bed."[35]

Perhaps even more important than his awareness of the interrelated importance of both employee and customer satisfaction to an airline's success, Woolman had a clear sense of the limits of cost cutting. "There's more to flying than just buying a ticket," he was known to say. "It is never sufficient to just transport people," he said, we must do it "with the highest respect and safety." Although he retired decades ago, Woolman's memory lives on with Delta employees who dedicated their new dining center to him in 2009, calling it the Woolman Café. His portrait, which was presented to Woolman "on behalf of the pilots of Delta Air Lines, our wives and children, in appreciation for what you have done for us and permitted us to do for ourselves," still hangs at the airline's Atlanta headquarters.[36] Like Patterson, Woolman recognized the long-term implications of his managerial decisions on employees, customers, and the safety of air travel.

Similarly, Edward Vernon "Eddie" Rickenbacker, a World War I fighter ace, Medal of Honor recipient, race car driver, and automotive designer, recalled how he left the automotive industry to work in aviation because he believed in this "great industry" and wanted to "serve my country and civilization." Pursuing his dream, Rickenbacker purchased Eastern Air Lines from General Motors with a certified check for $3.5 million in 1938, an advance from the investment bank Kuhn, Loeb and Company. "Eastern Air Lines was everything," he said. "It was my life, its employees were my personal friends and my personal concern." Although he continued piloting and subsequently completed several record-setting flights, Rickenbacker recalled his main "interest was in building an air-transport system of major proportions to serve the American people."[37]

Initially, employee morale was low at Eastern, yet Rickenbacker wrote in his autobiography that knew he "was not going to understand the problems, much less solve them, from a desk in New York." So he took to the airways, traveling at night and working by day at various out stations, loading bags, servicing aircraft, helping customers, and meeting employees. "Associating with the pilots was one of the greatest fringe benefits for me as an airline operator," he said. "I soon came to know every pilot by his first name." Pay was a system-wide concern, so Rickenbacker froze his own salary at fifty thousand dollars in order be able to raise compensation for his employees. Interested in promoting career advancement, Rickenbacker encouraged copilots to upgrade to captain after three years because "their individual contentment with their jobs" was "a positive asset for the company." He added, "One of the greatest safety devices in the world is a free state of mind, a happy state of mind, on the part of those at the [flight] controls."[38]

Rickenbacker pushed Eastern to become one of the most profitable airlines in the post–World War II era. He created a niche with his hunch that New Yorkers would rather fly to Florida than go by railroad. Like Patterson and Woolman, Rickenbacker believed that by talking with employees, listening to their problems and suggestions, he would discover solutions to the airline's real challenges. And, similar to other early airline leaders, he spent his twenty-five-year career at one airline fulfilling a long-term vision of building a safe air transportation system for the American people.

William John "Jack" Frye was born in 1904 and raised on his family's Texas ranch. But it was not long before he tired of the rural life and headed to California with stars in his eyes. Meeting up with barnstormers in Southern California, Frye began to fly and quickly established a reputation as an excellent pilot, flight instructor, and movie stunt pilot. In 1927, Frye founded Standard Airlines with some friends and inaugurated regular air service between Los Angeles and Phoenix-Tucson—a bold move given they had no airmail contracts to subsidize their income.

Three years later, Standard Airlines was taken over by Western Air Express, allowing Frye to turn his original $50,000 investment in the airline into $2.5 million in Western Air Express shares and have a seat on their board of directors and a position as chief of operations.[39] Shortly thereafter, Transcontinental & Western Air was born from a shotgun wedding between Western Air Express and Lindbergh and Keys' Transcontinental Air Transport, a marriage arranged by Postmaster General Brown at the infamous spoils conference. Since both Western Air Express and Transcontinental Air Transport had been run by high-profile aviation pioneers like Lindbergh and Frye, Transcontinental & Western Air quickly gained a reputation as "the pilot's airline." And the air carrier was keen to exploit this image, for example, calling their cross-country service the "Lindbergh Route."[40]

Frye was convinced that the key to airline success was passenger comfort. So he teamed up with Lindbergh and high-altitude navy test pilot Captain D. W. "Tommy" Tomlinson to help aircraft manufacturer Donald Douglas design some of the first pressurized airliners. Their goal was to fly over weather not through it, as aircraft then did, finding smoother air at higher altitudes in a pressurized airplane. By chance, during their research they discovered the jet stream, which enabled pilots to use the earth's natural hundred-mile-per-hour tailwind to expedite flights.[41] Although Frye remained an active pilot, setting records with Howard Hughes, like the other early pioneers he was committed to long-term airline industry developments as well. In 1934 he became president of Transcontinental & Western Air, and under his thirteen years of leadership the airline grew from eight hundred employees to seventeen thousand and became an industry leader in aviation research. Unfortunately and ironically, Frye was killed in an automobile accident in Arizona in 1959 at just fifty-four years of age.[42]

The final example of an early airline executive is Cyrus Rowlett "C. R." Smith. A gruff, hard-drinking Texas businessman, Smith was president of American Airlines for thirty-five years.[43] A living legend at American, even C. R.'s competition admired his business acumen. "There's no man in the industry I respect more," United's Pat Patterson recalled, "and you usually don't say nice things about competitors."[44] An accountant by training, C. R. first worked for a utility company and then for Southern Air Transport. Although he learned to fly, he admittedly was not a very good pilot, so he stuck with the business side of aviation operations and was eventually named vice president. He ran the airline so well it was acquired by Aviation Corporation in 1929. It eventually became American Air Lines with C. R. as the first president in 1934. A hardworking do-it-yourself kind of boss, Smith answered his own phone and typed his own letters. Fond of communicating via personal memos, he also enjoyed close relationships with both executives and employees. On weekends he would fly around the country on American flights, meeting employees, asking for input, checking on service, and sampling food, all the while scribbling notes to himself on scraps of paper.

A man's man in a rough and tumble industry, Smith peppered his dialogue with profanity and took action with deliberate assertiveness backed up by shrewd calculation. In a corporate world often bogged down by bureaucracy, C. R. acted with bewildering speed, sometimes ordering millions of dollars' worth of aircraft during a seemingly short, casual conversation. As Convair president Jack Nash put it at the time, "C. R. is one of the few businessmen left in America with whom you can close a $100 million deal on his word alone."[45]

As a generation, these airline executives were dedicated men with a high sense of integrity, a passion for aviation as a unique business enterprise, and a long-term vision of building a safe and prosperous airline industry for America. Most took their airlines from canvas-winged, open-cockpit airmail flights in the 1930s to jetliners providing coast-to-coast and international passenger air service in the 1960s. Many did not possess high levels of formal education, but each amassed a significant amount of aviation industry knowledge over their tenure. All were people savvy and street smart. Typically, these men spent their entire careers—often spanning thirty to forty years—at one air carrier, becoming intimately involved with both employees and the inner workings of the business of aviation. Many were pilots themselves and took pride in fostering a familylike work environment, often knowing employees by name, which generated deep-seated loyalties to the company and industry. As a result, generations of airline employees could be found within the ranks of their respective airlines: fathers and sons, husbands and wives, brother and sisters. Several of these pioneers worked collaboratively with pilots, aircraft designers, and plane manufacturers to improve airliner designs and enhance safety and passenger comfort for the industry as a whole.

The character of these airline pioneers was so influential, in many cases aspects of their personalities can still be found in the DNA of the airlines they served today. Pat Patterson made the word "integrity" synonymous with United Airlines. It was the first airline to adopt an employee team-building program, which they called "crew resource management" and to protect a captain's authority to make decisions without fear of reprisal. Delta's C. E. Woolman personified southern hospitality He was the only airline CEO who refused to have an unlisted telephone number: he *wanted* customers to call him directly to provide feedback. Jack Frye combined his Southern California career, record-setting flights, aviation research, and connection with famous pilots such as Charles Lindbergh and Howard Hughes to foster a glamorous Hollywood feel for the (now defunct) international carrier TWA. And C. R. Smith's policies and professionalism, which developed American into the "businessman's airline," can still be seen in the airline's emphasis on efficiency and good service.[46]

However influential these men were, they were not perfect. Most had detractors, some had enemies, and many struggled with labor groups. All dealt with strikes during their tenure.[47] Yet, fundamentally, each one was personally dedicated to their airline as a community and to its employees and customers. Their singular goal was to improve the air travel experience in America. Most did not grow rich by managing their airline; their reward was a job well done and the satisfaction of helping to develop a safe industry they felt passionate about. It was a labor of love that was contagious, permeating employee work groups within their organizations. There is still evidence of their influence on the walls of their airlines' work spaces in commemorative plaques, paintings, and photographs. Yet, by the 1970s these early airline pioneers were all gone and a new generation of executives entered the aviation industry. These were a different breed of men, motivated by different ambitions, operating in a different time. These airline industry leaders did not share the same passion for aviation, love for employees, or dedication to building a safe airline industry for America.

4

A New Solution: Deregulation

With the US government controlling nearly every aspect of airline industry operations through the CAB in the post–World War II period, one of the only ways air carriers could compete for passenger loyalty was by providing a level of customer service difficult to comprehend in today's austere travel environment.[1] Airline "fare wars" of the 1930s, before the CAB took over, gave way to wide-body "lounge wars" of the 1960s as air carriers battled it out over the best in-flight experience. Mimicking ocean liners' premier services, airlines offered chef-prepared meals and fine wines served in fancy restaurant style and famous performers to provide live entertainment in nightclub-like piano lounges.[2] To ensure the right image was projected, airlines developed employee training and incentive programs encouraging all workers to see themselves as part of a "service organization."[3] In compensation, everyone from baggage handlers and mechanics to aircraft cleaners and gate agents were airline employees with full travel and retirement benefits, not hourly workers from an outsourced subcontractor as most are today.[4]

In the days before bag-check fees, body scans, and Transportation Security Administration (TSA) checkpoints, an airline flight was an exciting event. Friends and family often accompanied passengers directly to the gate, and people sometimes went to the airport just to watch the planes and travelers. Airlines recognized that this was a prime opportunity to showcase the pride and professionalism of their company brand, which could send an important message about air safety to passengers on board and others watching from the terminal. To help develop these "brand" personalities, airlines sought ways to cultivate loyalty and instill in employees a sense of being part of an elite corporate family. As previously mentioned, generations of family members often would all work for the same airline. Both airlines and labor unions helped foster this image, supporting social events, picnics, Christmas parties, credit unions, athletic teams, and special travel-award programs. Monthly newsletters included employee photos; recognitions of engagements, marriages, and births; and company sports team results. Articles emphasized the fun and excitement of being an airline employee and taking advantage of exotic vacations using the air carrier's pass privileges to travel on company aircraft.[5] Little of this familylike feeling remains today. In sharp contrast to these previous generations, 92 percent of the pilots surveyed for this book would not recommend an airline career to a young person today.

Unlike air travel today, during this period, a commercial airline flight was a celebration to be remembered, not a bus ride to be endured. Airlines provided food and beverages free of charge and handed out passenger gift bags containing logo-emblazoned memorabilia to commemorate the occasion. Children would get toys and pilot wings and a tour of the cockpit; a couple on their honeymoon would be given a bottle of champagne. Yet, in order to pay for these services, airfares were high, well beyond the budget of average Americans. To increase affordability, Pan Am started a "Fly Now, Pay Later" marketing program with installment payments, just like buying a car, and other air carriers followed.[6]

This lack of access to air service for average Americans in the 1960s and 1970s is a surprising contrast to the flying experience of travelers today, who can often fly for just a few hundred dollars, significantly less money than it costs to drive the same distance. As a result of this increased affordability, a recent Gallup poll reported that 83 percent of Americans have now flown on a commercial airliner.[7] Considering that the National

Institute of Mental Health estimates that 6.5 percent of Americans have aviophobia, a fear of flying so severe it keeps them grounded, the Gallup results support that nearly every citizen who would like to fly does so in the United States today.[8] What events led to this drastic increase in accessibility and corresponding decrease in customer service?

The story begins with an influential professor of economics at Cornell University named Alfred E. Kahn. Academics like Kahn had made theoretical arguments in their books and scholarly articles for years that government regulators like the CAB stifle innovation, increase inefficiency, and contribute to higher consumer costs.[9] However, it was not until the 1970s, when problems with the highly regulated national rail system resulted in one of the largest taxpayer bailouts in history, that the federal government was ready to commit to a new plan: a strategy called *deregulation*.[10]

Like Gerald Ford before him, President Jimmy Carter embraced deregulation as a way to stimulate growth in a stagnant economy. In this environment, Kahn's regulatory theories garnered significant bipartisan support and spurred a broad movement toward smaller government, freer markets, and wider consumer choices.[11] To get the reform movement going, Kahn needed to bolster his theories about deregulation with a high-profile real world success story to help President Carter sell the broader concept to the American people.

Kahn proposed starting with telecommunications, an industry he had some experience with, and suggested that Carter appoint him as chairmen of the Federal Communications Commission (FCC). Yet others thought the lagging airline industry might be a better test case. When approached about chairing the CAB instead of the FCC, Kahn, known for his quick wit and sarcasm, stated he would rather switch places with the current FCC chairman because, whoever he is, he "can't possibly know less than I do about the airline industry."[12] He readily confessed, "I can't tell one plane from the other. To me, they're all just marginal costs with wings."[13] He added, "I don't think it's my highest aspiration to make it possible for people to jet all over the world."[14]

Nevertheless, despite having little passion for aviation, no knowledge of the intricacies of airline operations, and sparse consideration of the risk or long-term safety implications of sudden aviation regulatory change, Kahn succumbed to political persuasion and agreed to chair the CAB. Like Dwight Morrow in the 1920s and Postmaster General Brown in the 1930s,

inexperienced government officials were once again driving federal aviation policy in the 1970s, having an impact on an industry in which they had
no specific knowledge, expertise, or even any particular interest. Thus, the
airline industry became the first test cell in Kahn's deregulation "labora-
tory," in which he experimented with the basic concepts of his political
economy theories.[15] Kahn's personal goal in leading the CAB, he said, was
to make it so that "there would be no such agency when I was through." In
1978, he accomplished this when the Airline Deregulation Act was passed,
eliminating government control over commercial aviation and disbanding
the CAB.

As one might imagine, airline managers were skeptical about Kahn's
theories of deregulation, suspicious of government leaders, and fearful
about the looming market uncertainty. Most took a hard-line stance against
deregulation and were angered by academic ideologues, economic theorists,
and political pundits who were using their industry for professional posturing. They viewed deregulation as political gamesmanship cleverly masquer-
ading as free enterprise and regulatory reform, and with good reason.

Although airline executives agreed that reforms were needed, they were
opposed to the free-for-all Kahn's deregulation theories implied. In their
opinion, the airline system wasn't broken, so why change it. As one manager explained, "the types of changes we feel are worthy of consideration
are those that would tend to improve the present system, and not destroy
it."[16] For them, it seemed only a matter of time before government would
be forced to step in again, this time with even more reactive and invasive
levels of regulation.[17] For instance, Delta Airlines' CEO W. T. Beebe predicted: "Once the public is faced with the chaos, disruption of service, economic demoralization of carriers, and concentration of service in the hands
of the remaining few air carriers . . . a demand would arise that the government take restorative action."[18] American Airlines CEO Robert Crandall
was perhaps the most graphic in voicing his concerns when he addressed a
Senate lawyer in 1977: "You fucking academic eggheads! You don't know
shit. You can't deregulate this industry. You're going to wreck it. You don't
know a goddamn thing!"[19]

So why, then, despite widespread opposition from aviation industry leaders, did US politicians give Kahn the chance to apply his economic theories to a real industry with no reliable way to predict the outcome? The

answer to this question begins with reconsidering the creation of the overly bureaucratic CAB in the first place, a government regulatory entity that grew increasingly out of step with the world around it. By the mid-1970s, man had walked on the moon, 747 jumbo jets had been flying for half a decade, and aerospace manufacturers had achieved their dream of supersonic passenger transportation with the launch of the Concorde. The airline industry was growing so quickly, it seemed only a matter of time before commercial space travel on rocket ships would become routine for passengers as well—just like it was on television.

However, at the same time that these technological achievements were occurring, the human side was lagging behind—the sociopolitical advancements that also needed to occur were absent. As Kahn's predecessor, CAB chairmen John E. Robson, put it, "By 1975, the airline industry was like a forty-year-old still living at home with his parents."[20] For some people, like Robson, it had become apparent that the regulatory philosophies of the prewar days were now passé and it was time for the airline industry to find its wings. Yet, unlike the Tea Party's opposition to government in the 2000s, this movement toward less government regulation actually started under the leadership of left-leaning individuals.

Politicians such as Senator Ted Kennedy and consumer advocates such as Ralph Nader became mobilized in the 1970s to change an American culture full of ethical lapses represented by events such as the Ford Pinto fiasco and political scandals like Watergate. Enraged by airliners flying half-full on taxpayer-financed subsidies, these social reformists were intent on flattening class divides and widening consumer access to air travel by reducing airfares.[21] In fact, this one point—prioritizing cheap airfares—became a government fixation for the next forty years, investigated as recently as 2013 when the Government Accounting Office ensured that the proposed merger between American Airlines and US Airways would not raise ticket prices.[22] As such, we come to a historical turning point in the late 1970s when, like the early days of aviation, the airline industry regulatory pendulum swung almost entirely away from government intervention toward an ideology of free market supply and demand on the flawed assumption it will improve customer service and accessibility. This development moved air travel away from the postwar model of luxurious ocean liners in the sky to one of transcontinental bus lines and the sparse accompaniments that we find after 9/11.[23] What caused this radical shift?

This new egalitarian airline model emerged based on the pre-deregulation success of two spunky start-up airlines, first Pacific Southwest Airlines in California and then later Southwest Airlines in Texas. Operating on shoe-string budgets, these low-frills airlines skirted the CAB's bogged down federal regulatory process by only flying within their respective states. In both cases, they offered safe, reliable service on a par with the larger inter-state airlines yet at about half the price, allowing them to gain consider-able advantage over other air carriers within their markets.[24] Advocates of airline deregulation like Alfred Kahn, Ted Kennedy, Ralph Nader, and some in the media admired these discount carriers, touted their signifi-cantly lower cost basis, and erroneously envisioned that all airlines could, and should, emulate this low-frills model.

It was here in the 1970s and 1980s, long before 9/11, with policymakers who were admittedly unfamiliar with airline operations, that we find the roots of today's austere air travel experience. Since this era, the entire US airline industry has been chasing after this Greyhound bus model, attempt-ing with very limited success to move toward a low-cost, low-fare egalitar-ian operating environment that academics, politicians, and deregulation supporters envisioned over thirty years ago. This flawed vision has taken a toll on airline employees and led to greater risk and air safety issues, which all passengers should be concerned about. As one United Airlines captain I interviewed explained, talking about all carriers, "Everybody wants their $99 ticket now. But when the shit hits the fan, they want to open up the cockpit door and see somebody with grey hair—they want to see Captain Sully sitting there. You don't get Captain Sully for $99 bucks. . . . For $99 they get crappy service, they get crappy maintenance, and they get crappy pilots."

How universal is this captain's opinion? Seventy-three percent of the pilots I interviewed basically agreed, reporting that they had witnessed questionable safety practices at their airline due to post-9/11 company cost-cutting measures; 29 percent saw this on a daily basis (fig. 4). Yet the Government Accounting Office has never investigated these widespread concerns. In fact, the GAO's 2013 study of the impact of airline merger mania only mentions the effects on employees once in its thirty-one pages.[25]

After the Airline Deregulation Act was passed the philosophy of smaller government and bigger airlines pursued by Postmaster General Brown

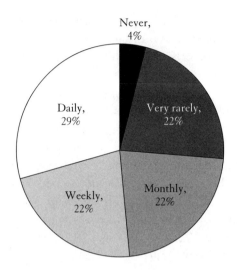

Figure 4. US airline pilots' observation of questionable safety practices. *Source*: "How often did you witness questionable safety practices at your airline due to post-9/11 company cost cutting measures?" Author's survey data, no. 12.

gained renewed popularity. In 1981 President Ronald Reagan took office. Although it had only been three years since the act was passed and it was still unclear if Kahn's experiment was successful or not, Reagan nonetheless pursued deregulation in other industries. The president characterized his economic philosophy, later termed "Reaganomics," as merely a return to free-enterprise principles.[26] Yet, far from increasing aviation industry competition, the Reagan administration's approval of nearly every airline merger application put 92 percent of the market share in just eight "too big to fail" air carriers that often enjoyed a near-monopoly on their routes, which allowed them to charge high airfares as there was little competition.[27]

Reagan also became one of the biggest union busters in aviation history, encouraging labor-management discord and establishing a troubling precedent that still has impact today. It all started in 1981 when about 13,000 of the nation's 17,500 federal air traffic controllers walked off the job, demanding an increase in wages and safer work rules due to the high-stress nature of their profession. Although newly elected President Reagan considered himself a working-class hero and had significant labor union experience, having served as president of the Screen Actors Guild and as spokesperson for workers at General Electric, he had a different solution in mind in this case.[28]

Ever the showman, Reagan seized the opportunity to make a stand, supporting big business and getting tough on labor. Invoking the Labor Management Relations Act of 1947 (the Taft-Hartley act), which prohibited federal-employee strikes, Reagan ordered striking controllers back to work, and when they refused, he fired 11,345 union members and hired permanent replacement workers.[29] The strategy succeeded largely because of behind-the-scenes work by J. Lynn Helms, head of the FAA, who, knowing the strike was imminent, negotiated a collaborative agreement for airlines to cut back flights and the Pentagon to temporarily provide military controllers.[30]

Although the strike-busting plan worked flawlessly in the short term, it took years for air service to return to prestrike levels of operational efficiency. Many labor scholars consider the unsuccessful strike of the federal air traffic controllers as the single most significant factor in hastening the decline of organized labor in the United States in the late twentieth century.[31] Particularly influential was encouragement by a sitting US president to hire thousands of replacement workers to cross union picket lines. Because of Reagan's legitimization of use of replacement workers, companies across a range of industries felt empowered to engage in a managerial practice once considered extreme and destructive.[32] The same could be said of airline executives' tactics after 9/11, when they collectively exploited sympathetic government leaders, bankruptcy protection, pension default, employee furloughs, and work outsourcing in unprecedented ways.

Yet Wall Street loved it. Federal Reserve Chairman Alan Greenspan deemed Reagan's aggressive posturing and firing of striking workers the most defining domestic initiative of his presidency, broadening the rights of employers to hire and fire workers at their discretion.[33] And reverberations are still being experienced today.[34] Because of Reagan's tactics, an air traffic control employment bubble was created when the FAA was forced to hire thousands of workers, all approximately the same age, to replace striking controllers. As a result, many of the country's 15,000 controllers are now approaching the mandatory retirement age of fifty-six en masse, and their young replacements will likely form another generational bubble.

Since it can take over three years to train a new air traffic controller, this influx of new employees raises serious concerns about controller experience, skill levels, and air safety, just as it did after the 1981 strike. The problem has become so serious that Congress asked the GAO to study the issue in 2002,[35] and the office identified serious gaps in controller coverage, questionable hiring practices, and poor training, raising safety concerns.[36] Questions about competency, supervision, and safety became particularly problematic in 2011 when six controllers were caught napping on the job—and not just briefly nodding off at their workstations. One controller had gathered cushions, pillows, and blankets from a nearby break room in order to make a bed on the floor.[37] "We have come to a crossroads," said the president of the National Air Traffic Controllers Association, Patrick Forrey. "We have so few veteran controllers left that we cannot safely handle the volume of aircraft. [People] are fatigued, and when you are fatigued you make mistakes."[38]

Airline deregulation was intended to make the aviation industry a free market in which increased competition from new airlines would force older established air carriers, termed "trunk" carriers, to remove inefficiencies and improve services while decreasing passenger airfares, improving air travel for Americans. During the first few years of deregulation, there were several new airline upstarts entering service, challenging the main air carriers. Airfares did decrease, and airlines were making money. However, by the mid-1980s all airlines were struggling with rising fuel costs that ate into cash reserves, high interest rates that made it expensive to borrow to buy new equipment, and an economic recession that decreased passenger demand.[39] Most new carriers disappeared in this hyper-competitive market, and the trunk carriers dwindled as well. In 1978, there were eleven trunk carriers: American, Braniff, Continental, Delta, Eastern, National, Northwest, PanAm, TWA, United, and Western. By 1991, there were just five of the original carriers and in 2013, only American, Delta, and United remained, each airline having about one-third of the market share.

These major airlines increased their competitive edge in two ways in the era after deregulation. First, by dominating a geographical region using a new route system called the "hub-and-spoke," airlines funneled passengers between smaller airports along "spokes" of a wheel to a major airport "hub." For instance, Delta dominated in Atlanta, American in Dallas, and United in Chicago, building fortress-like route structures that were extremely difficult for other airlines to penetrate. Thus, a hub such as United's Denver International Airport could connect with twenty cities to the northeast and twenty to the southwest, providing one-stop service to 440 city pairs.[40] Second, airlines created built-in loyalty through newly

inaugurated "frequent flyer" programs that encouraged customers to accumulate miles on just one carrier. As a result of these two strategies, passengers intending to travel to one of a trunk carrier's city pairs had almost
no choice but to fly on that dominant airline and pay whatever airfare was
demanded—hardly the free market competition that was predicted by deregulation theorists.

Although frequent flyer programs and the hub-and-spoke system were
profitable for air carriers, these strategies came with "baggage" for both customers and airline employees. Changing airplanes at airline hubs was often
a time-consuming inconvenience for passengers, checked luggage was
more likely to get lost, and people missed connecting flights. In chapter 7
I discuss the implications for airline employees and air safety, as hubs became the perfect place to park both airplanes and aircrews between flights.
Once again we find that seemingly innocuous industry changes have un-
expected reverberations throughout the entire aviation system. Following
Postmaster General Brown's bigger-is-better philosophy, major airlines
used their extensive networks to profit by reducing airfares on competitive
routes, undercutting rivals and forcing them out of business, while making
up for these losses by charging other passengers higher airfares on different routes. By the 1990s, like Wall Street's "too big to fail" banks in the
2008 financial crisis, the airline industry had quickly become the oligopolistic market place critics of deregulation had warned about. Too much
power was now in the hands of too few airlines with too little regulatory
oversight. By early 2001, the aviation industry was already in a tailspin.

In addition bankruptcy laws, developed to help sound companies with-
stand temporary market setbacks without being forced by creditors to liquidate, now enabled the weakest air carriers to set the market pace for
stronger airlines. This occurred because, under the protection of a federal
judge, airlines were allowed to continue to operate, retaining their aircraft
and valuable infrastructure assets such as landing slots and terminal gates,
while cancelling union contracts, slashing employee wages, defaulting on
pension plans, and withholding payments to creditors. Without these overhead expenses, bankrupt airlines could afford to drop airfares to drive out
competitors and then pump airfares back up uncontested, just like Commodore Vanderbilt in the mid-1800s.[41] During bankruptcy, the work rules
labor unions carefully negotiated over years of contract talks with airline
management were eliminated in months and employees were powerless

to intervene because terms of the Railway Labor Act prevented strikes or other job action. Nearly every major airline adopted this strategy in the post-9/11 period. United Airlines, for example, exploited the advantages of bankruptcy protection for over three years, a historically unprecedented timeframe by a major US airline. Only the low-frill air carrier America West spent more time in bankruptcy between 1991 and 1994.

A third innovation of the post-deregulation era that helped major airlines grow and profit, but often inconvenienced passengers and adversely effected employees, was the emergence of commuter airlines. Prior to deregulation, the CAB limited the power of regional airlines. But, after 1978, major airlines outsourced much of their "spoke" flying to smaller regional commuter airlines. The strategy proved so profitable that both major and commuter airlines were eager to strike deals with virtually any carrier without much thought to the implications for employees, passengers, or air safety. As one commuter airline president described it, "We were like lemmings going over the cliff."[42]

Although many commuter operators had been around for a while, government regulators tended to dismiss these "scheduled air taxi operators," as they were originally known, considering them small and inconsequential. Therefore, regulatory supervision was sparse and often half-hearted.[43] This lackadaisical oversight by regulators and opportunist attitudes of airline executives foreshadowed problems such as those of regional operators like Colgan Air and Pinnacle Airlines, which grew very quickly in this fertile environment by exploiting inexperienced pilots and bargain-hunting customers, addressed in later chapters. Before 9/11, labor unions controlled the outsourcing of major airline flying to regional carriers by negotiating side letters of agreement which were collective bargaining agreements that stipulated under what limited conditions outsourcing could be done. Unions used this strategy to protect the interests of higher paid major airline employees. However, when nearly every US air carrier entered bankruptcy in the post-9/11 period, all side letter agreements were voided, and executives outsourced major airline flying to regional air carriers without restriction. Once again, we can see how air safety problems today actually have roots in managerial strategies developed decades ago, just like the 2008 financial crisis had its origins in policies instituted in earlier years.

One of the biggest boons for commuter carriers—and biggest areas of concern for air safety—during the period after deregulation was a controversial part of the Airline Deregulation Act called the Essential Air Service (EAS) clause. The EAS clause, included at the behest of politicians representing smaller communities fearful of losing commercial service, subsidized airlines for ten years to guarantee flight connections to larger airports. Nearly all of these EAS flights were provided by regional commuter airlines.[44] It was at this historical turning point that regional air carriers and major airlines became fused through code sharing in computerized reservation systems in ways that make it difficult for customers to know which air carrier they are actually flying on.

Interestingly, in this era of so-called deregulation, EAS subsidies have been renewed by Congress every year since 1978. This "selective regulation" cost taxpayers $143 million for fiscal year 2012 alone, even though only 153 rural communities receive service, and prompts the question: Has airline deregulation become just a clever cover for union busting and employee exploitation?[45] Consider the Jonesboro to Memphis route for which taxpayers chipped in $801 per passenger per flight to subsidize air service. On the Kingman to Phoenix route taxpayers contributed $651, and Decatur to Chicago cost taxpayers $628 for every passenger.[46] Political posturing and lobbyist influence aside, it seems difficult to justify this extensive taxpayer expenditure, especially since many of these subsidized airports are within driving distance of an unsubsidized airport. In 2011, one study found that using scheduled bus service would lower taxpayers' costs by 68 percent, and in most cases the bus trip was even shorter than the airplane flight, averaging just 43 minutes.[47] Yet, because of politics and airline lobbying, EAS subsidies show no sign of diminishing any time soon.

Another boon for commuter airlines was an EAS provision for low-interest aircraft loans. With government's backing, commuter airlines expanded rapidly, and by the mid-1980s, 240 commuter airlines were flying about fifteen million passengers—a 34 percent increase in just a few years' time.[48] Yet, concerns emerged about risk and air safety even then. Commuter airlines reported an accident rate six times higher than that of major air carriers, leading NTSB chairman James B. King to investigate. He reported that his safety board had uncovered "examples of sleazy to nonexistent maintenance, weight and balance problems, and inadequate training for pilots." And, he added, accident patterns revealed a reoccurring theme of "deficient management and disregard for federal safety regulations."[49] Yet, little has been done to address these concerns, in part because there is no regulatory influence or public pressure to change. As long as major airlines keep outsourcing, regional airlines will continue expanding, hiring low-time (inexperienced) pilots, and passengers may fly on questionably safe airlines when they thought they bought a ticket on a major air carrier.

With so many government subsidies and such strong political influence still affecting the US airline industry, one might wonder how the industry can even be considered deregulated at all. Since 9/11, the federal government provided airlines with $7.4 billion in direct assistance and authorized $1.6 billion in loan guarantees to six airlines (Aloha, World, Frontier, US Airways, ATA, and America West).[50] The post-9/11 bankruptcy filings of American, Delta, Northwest, United, and US Airways are particularly emblematic of the industry's reliance on government interventions to stay solvent, even during this so-called deregulated period. Among the largest bankruptcies in US history, these private companies left government programs and taxpayers footing the bill for their managerial inefficiencies with little regard for workers' interests.[51]

For instance, when United and US Airways emerged from bankruptcy, $9.7 billion in debt was shifted to the government-backed Pension Benefit Guarantee Corporation, causing employees to lose a staggering $5.3 billion in earned retirement benefits.[52] United's $6.6 billion default was the largest in US history to date,[53] and all three United employee unions— pilots, flight attendants, and mechanics—prepared to strike in protest.[54] The pension plans of Delta and Northwest were similarly underfunded by a combined $16.3 billion. If these airlines terminate their plans, employees will lose over $5 billion in earned benefits.[55]

A large part of United's problem began in the 1980s and 1990s when managers shifted their investment strategies from buying safe long-term bonds with employees' pension payments to a more aggressive approach. Typical in this casino-like era, United's portfolio included a volatile mix of real estate and private equities along with about 60 percent stocks, many of which burst with the tech bubble, and 30 percent high-yield bonds in companies that eventually went bankrupt, such as Adelphia and Bethlehem Steel.[56] It was a managerial gamble that failed; now airline employees and taxpayers are footing the bill.

In 2012, American Airlines executives similarly argued a need to default on pensions in order to stay competitive with other airlines. However, the federal government signaled it would fight this action. Joshua Gotbaum, director of the Pension Benefit Guarantee Corporation, said the agency was already operating with a $23 billion deficit and it was unable to shoulder an additional $9 billion loss if American terminated its four employee pension plans, adversely affecting about 130,000 employees.[57] American executives looked to Capitol Hill for support. However, the airline had already received $2.1 billion in relief from Congress over the last six years under the condition that it would keep its pension plan going. Another concern voiced by American executives was that their pilots had the right to take their pensions as a single lump payment on retirement. With the airline industry in such dire straits and 5,207 American pilots eligible for retirement, executives fear the lump-sum payout could hit their pension plan like a bank run and cripple airline operations as senior pilots exit en masse. As a result, the senior vice president of human resources, Jeffrey J. Brundage, said that continuing to offer this retirement option "is a risk that the company simply cannot afford to take."[58] Yet, lawmakers were unsympathetic this time and instead felt that the airline was reneging on its side of the pension bargain.[59]

Somewhere in this story something does not add up. One has to wonder why airline executives are more concerned about using bankruptcy court to dodge their fiscal responsibilities to employees and finagling government bailouts from their bad managerial decisions than worrying about why a large percentage of their most experienced pilots are eager to abandon their company as soon as possible. Meanwhile, the same airline executives who are reluctant to pay employees the pensions they earned over decades of loyal service do not mind paying high-priced consultants and financial advisers like McKinsey & Company, Bain & Company, and Perella Weinberg Partners exorbitant fees for their short-term services. And bankruptcy judges do not object. For instance, Bain & Company received $525,000 a month to advise American about their restructuring during bankruptcy.[60]

Much of the gamesmanship that I am highlighting here can be attributed to airline executives' efforts to compete in the deregulated environment. As Kahn and his supporters envisioned, the airline industry became much more competitive as low-frills air carriers like Southwest thrived using a simple business model of flying one type of aircraft on short-haul, point-to-point routes while many previous behemoths died on the funeral pyre of the hub-and-spoke system that required a variety of aircraft to meet the demands of its complex networks. Even Kahn noted, "I have to concede that the competition that deregulation brought certainly was terribly, terribly hard on the airlines and their unions."[61] In response to this challenge, the airline industry attracted a new kind of leader.

By the 1980s all of the early airline pioneers such as Pat Patterson, C. E. Woolman, Eddie Rickenbacker, Jack Frye, and C. R. Smith were gone, and a new generation of managers had moved into the executive suites. These were a different breed of men, motivated by different ambitions, operating in a different time. Unlike the previous service-oriented generation of airline executives who had a high sense of integrity, passion for aviation, fondness for employees, and long-term vision of building a safe airline industry for America, these new CEOs were often young professional managers who were educated at business schools and who had little loyalty to any particular industry or any one company. Their goal was to earn money, power, and prestige for themselves as fast as possible before moving on to their next business venture.

In this era, previously accepted ideals of respect, professionalism, learning the ropes, and gradually moving up the corporate ladder over a lifetime career no longer applied. These new executives often lacked airline industry knowledge yet were impatient to rise fast nonetheless. Most had no particular passion for aviation as a unique business enterprise and little concern for the safe, long-term development of the industry itself. To them the aviation industry lessons of the past, often written in blood, were irrelevant.[62]

Perhaps in the era after deregulation there was some justification for not looking back to history for answers. The industry had been turned on its head. Yet in aviation, arrogance and ignorance can be a dangerous mixture, and veteran employees, especially pilots, bristled at this insulated managerial approach. Just as airplanes were "marginal costs with wings" for Kahn,[63] so were airline employees just a statistic to be manipulated. Many new managers were not shy about articulating their belief that airline employees were "overpaid and underworked." Frank Lorenzo, renowned as the worst of this new breed, provides a classic example. When asked if he understood that if flight attendants accepted the pay cuts he was demanding from them many, as single parents, might lose their homes and families, Lorenzo replied: "Quite frankly, I don't believe flight attendants ought to make enough money so they can own houses. Maybe they should find another job that pays better."[64]

Predictably, these new airline executives clashed with employees and labor unions, creating a hostile work environment rife with strikes and job actions, including slow-downs and sick-outs. There had been airline strikes before, of course. But nothing in airline labor union history approached the venom and devastation that occurred after deregulation.[65] Strikes occurred at Continental in 1980 and then again in 1983, at United in 1985, TWA in 1986, Eastern in 1989, USAir in 1993, Northwest in 1982 and 1998 and again in 2005, and American in 1994 and 1997.[66] Although nearly all airlines struggled, Braniff International Airways became one of the first deregulation causalities among the major air carriers.

Of the major airlines, Braniff took off into the deregulated environment at full throttle. Originally founded by brothers Tom and Paul Braniff in 1930 to shuttle Texas oilmen around the southwestern states, Braniff Airways got its first big break as a result of the reallocation of routes after Postmaster General Brown's airmail scandal. It then steadily expanded. By 1965, both founding brothers had died and Harding L. Lawrence was appointed as Braniff's president. Although Lawrence had served as vice president at Continental Airlines, some people thought his promotion to Braniff president was beyond his leadership abilities, particularly as the airline headed into the uncharted waters of deregulation.[67] Yet, he prevailed.

Lawrence's vision for Braniff's growth was surpassed only by his personal ambition to run a megacarrier. To achieve his goal, he snatched up every available route, profitable or not, and unabashedly predicted: Braniff will be either "as big as United or gone."[68] He hired a New York advertising agency to give Braniff a sexy international image, expanded the fleet to include 747s painted by famous artists like Alexander Calder, reconfigured cabins with bright colors and fanciful designs, outfitted employees with uniforms designed by Halston, and provided passengers with meals by French chefs. Similarly, Lawrence spared no expense developing Braniff's massive corporate headquarters outside Dallas, which included a hotel on a lake, swimming pools, and tennis courts.[69]

Yet, the glamorous modern image of success at Braniff far outpaced its actual profitability. Upside down in debt and with no way out, Lawrence finally resigned, letting others sort out the airline's final days. In 1982,

Braniff abruptly quit flying, ending fifty-four years of air service and leaving employees and union leaders as bewildered as the passengers who were still holding tickets on grounded flights. It may seem that these were the risks of the deregulated marketplace, just as Alfred Kahn had envisioned. Yet, there are other lessons to be learned from Braniff's demise, lessons relevant to understanding the post-9/11 airline industry as well.

When establishing Braniff's board of directors, Lawrence selected friends and colleagues more recognized for their class and style than industry acumen. Unsurprisingly, they offered little credible guidance. Similarly, Lawrence surrounded himself with inferior "empty suit" managers who were "confused, ill-trained" and working in a "disastrously ineffective" environment, as one union leader recalled. Although Lawrence was "brilliant, astute, and completely open about where he wanted to take Braniff," the issue was that "the vast majority of our middle management were idiots."[70]

The biggest problem, several people noted, was Lawrence's failure to communicate with his employees. Information did not flow up, or down, the company hierarchy. Some people believed the managers took a perverse pleasure in ignoring employee input and that the lack of company information shared with employees was intentionally designed to keep them from recognizing Braniff's dire fiscal state. As a result, the demise of Braniff became a symbol of the growing disconnect between airline executives' priorities and the needs of employees and passengers, a chasm that has only widened over the past thirty years.

It may seem difficult to comprehend how just one airline could have such a widespread impact on the industry's management-employee relations, but the demise of Braniff was a benchmark in airline history. Because of Braniff, employees and unions began to develop their own sources of information, tracking their own financial data, and conducting their own corporate analyses of their airline's health. Many unions subsequently demanded that their own representatives sit on the airline's board of directors to observe firsthand the company's decision-making processes.

Although labor and management have always had a tenuous relationship, the demise of Braniff marked the beginning of a long, slow, continuous decline in trust between airline employees and executives. This change in industry ethos was caused, in part, by the new hypercompetitive deregulated airline marketplace but mostly by the personalities of the men this environment attracted. As one senior Boeing executive observed about the deregulated era, "The only guys who'll survive are those who eat raw meat."[71] Perhaps the most emblematic of this new breed of carnivores was CEO Francisco "Frank" Lorenzo.

In contrast to early airline pioneers like Pat Patterson and C. E. Woolman, who had loyal and lengthy tenure at just one airline, Frank Lorenzo managed five different air carriers over an eighteen-year career, earning the honor of becoming the most universally hated executive in the history of commercial aviation. If Braniff represented the prototypical deregulated airline gone awry, Lorenzo was the prototypical CEO running amuck. His maniacal ego and ruthless nature earned him such labels as "corporate raider," "robber baron," and "financial manipulator." He was so paranoid, flight attendants reported, that he would not even drink a soda on one of his own airliners if someone else had opened the can.[72] He drove Continental into bankruptcy, Eastern out of business, and was trying to start a new airline when he was finally banned from ever working in the US airline industry again.[73]

Like the early airline pioneers, Lorenzo came from a simple background and was eager to rise above his roots. However, this is where the similarities ended. Lorenzo earned college degrees from Columbia University and Harvard Business School, where he was nicknamed "Frankie Smooth Talk," and for good reason: he could talk the talk, but not walk the walk.[74] Widely recognized for his aggressive negotiation style and adroit ability to pull off highly complex financial transactions, he conquered one airline after another. Yet, Lorenzo's downfall was his inability to actually manage the airlines he acquired. Labor unions hated him, employees distrusted him, middle managers abandoned him, and the companies in his charge floundered because of it.[75] As one Eastern pilot recalled, Lorenzo "shakes your hand and smiles, and then as you walk away, he slaps you."[76]

Lorenzo's rise, and fall, was meteoric. Within just a few years of college graduation, Lorenzo acquired Texas International Airlines, a struggling air carrier on the verge of bankruptcy. He turned it around, in part, by aggressively acquiring other companies. Like a shark, Lorenzo thrived in the churning, unpredictable waters of the deregulated environment. "I'm a symbol of change," he told *Barron's* magazine in a 1983 interview. "The name of the game is to take risks."[77] Yet, with Lorenzo, the risks were always at other peoples' expense. In 1978, he became the first airline executive to attempt a hostile takeover by purchasing a struggling airline's lagging stock; he did this first against National Airlines, and then later TWA.[78] Although he failed to accomplish his intended coup, he nonetheless made $48 million from National stock and $50 million from TWA stock in the process.[79]

Time and time again, Frankie Smooth Talk proved to be a talented dealmaker but a weak executive, who lacked the managerial acumen to run the organizations he purchased. One of his favorite tactics was union busting. While airlines such as American and United sought to work with labor leaders, Lorenzo saw unions as a major obstacle to implementing his draconian cost-cutting measures and adopted a confrontational approach to employee negotiations.[80] Recognizing that unions would resist his aggressive strategies, in 1980, in an attempt to sidestep his labor problems he, founded his own low-frills airline without unions, New York Air. That same year he went after Continental, which was vulnerable because its stock was worth less than its assets. Yet his antiunion stance preceded him, and Continental's CEO Alvin Feldman fought the hostile takeover, convinced that Lorenzo intended to dismantle the airline, sell off its assets, and fire the workers. After a year of resistance, the takeover nonetheless seemed imminent. However, rather than give in to Lorenzo, Feldman committed suicide by shooting himself in the head in his Continental office at the Los Angeles International Airport.[81]

In 1981, the deal went through anyway with the blessing of President Reagan, and Lorenzo established a ruthless professional pattern at Continental that he would later repeat at other airlines. Pitting unions against each other, he whip-sawed employee groups creating suspicion and discontent. No matter what employees gave up, no sacrifice was ever enough.[82] He immediately announced a 50 percent across-the-board pay cut and then antagonized labor groups by outsourcing their work, leading to a strike that lasted 716 days—the longest in aviation history.[83] In a move commonplace today but unheard of at the time, Lorenzo intentionally sent Continental into bankruptcy in 1983 in order to circumvent union work rules, cancel employee contracts, and be able to hire low-cost replacement workers. No major company had attempted this strategy before.[84] It was a gamble, but with Reagan's recent success fighting federal air traffic controllers it was a safely calculated risk, one that paid off for Lorenzo.

Demoralized Continental employees, who had witnessed firsthand the demise of Braniff, feared for their jobs and slowly crossed the picket lines, drifting back to work. The process was accelerated by Lorenzo himself, who, armed with personal data and family information, called pilots at home to express concern about their financial and familial challenges. People with credit problems, money issues, or rocky marriages were particularly susceptible to this type of coercion. As one pilot recalled, Lorenzo made it seem like he really cared and needed that one particular pilot back at work. It was hard to resist: "Frank's a savvy guy, and he can be really slick."[85] Within a few months, about a third had returned to work, joining Lorenzo's replacement workers and accepting the drastic reduction in pay and benefits. It was enough to keep Continental flying.

In retaliation, striking employees confronted returning workers as they crossed the picket line, spitting on them and cursing. A rotting, bloody elk was thrown through the home window of one pilot who had returned to work, and Texas police apprehended two striking pilots carrying pipe bombs and a map, en route to the homes of other strikebreakers. Yet, for all the bravado, by Christmas of 1983 nearly all labor groups had acquiesced to Lorenzo's demands. Other airline executives, watching from afar, now followed Lorenzo's lead and demanded similar concessions from employees, triggering a wave of labor strife throughout the industry. Pilots at other airlines scorned Continental strikebreakers as "scabs", often refusing to talk to them or to recognize their jump seat privileges, a professional courtesy extended between flight crews to ride for free in the cockpit. In 1985, the new Continental pilot group, predominantly consisting of Lorenzo's replacement workers and picket line–crossing strikebreakers, voted to decertify the union. Lorenzo had achieved his goal.[86]

In 1986, Lorenzo set his sights on Eastern Airlines where he attempted to use many of the same union-busting strategies he developed at Continental. But Eastern was a different sort of airline, once the East Coast powerhouse led by World War I ace Eddie Rickenbacker. Unlike Continental, it had only recently fallen on hard times. Rickenbacker had been reluctant to expand the aging fleet, content to fly propeller-driven planes as other airlines bought jets. Eager to catch up, new CEO and former NASA astronaut Frank Borman adopted a "grow at all costs" approach, determined to integrate jetliners into the fleet. To achieve his goals, Borman overpurchased airplanes while demanding concessions from employees, creating a clash with union leaders and escalating company debt.[87] By the time Lorenzo arrived, Eastern was already in a tailspin, and most employees thought things couldn't get much worse.

However, Eastern became Lorenzo's Vietnam War: he couldn't win but he would never surrender. Mired in personality clashes with union leaders who were as stubborn as he was, Lorenzo continued selling off company assets just to keep fighting employees. Pilots, in particular, were a problem for Lorenzo because, unlike at Continental, Eastern aircrews refused to cross the picket lines. Lorenzo was convinced they would eventually break and became so obsessed with beating the unions that rational economic sense disappeared. What had started out as cutting costs, justified by deregulation economics, turned into a personal grudge match. If Lorenzo could not win, nobody would, he vowed.[88]

Meanwhile the Texas Air holding company, which already had New York Air, Continental, and Eastern Airlines in its stable, added People Express and Frontier Airlines: Lorenzo now personally controlled over 20 percent of the US airline industry and could rob assets from one airline, such as Eastern's valuable computerized reservation system, and sell it to another one of his airlines for whatever he wanted to charge. And his holding company, Texas Air, reaped all the profits. It was a masterful scheme, and Lorenzo became an instant favorite of Wall Street's moneymen. Lorenzo's aspirations to dominate the US airline industry were finally thwarted when a US bankruptcy court ruled that his shenanigans made him unfit to run Eastern Airlines. In 1991, under the operation of bankruptcy court trustees, the nation's oldest carrier vanished after sixty-three years in business, putting twenty thousand Eastern employees on the street.[89] Lorenzo, ever the moneymaker, had shielded himself from risk and left the debacle with a vast personal fortune. In 1993, he tried to found a new airline ironically called Friendship. However given his past record, the US Department of Transportation would not grant him permission.

What is important to note in this example is how the deregulated airline environment began to attract financiers like Lorenzo who could manipulate the fiscal aspects of managing an air carrier but had no ability to run the day-to-day operations of the airline itself. Rather than increase industry competition, as advocates of deregulation predicted, this environment actually offered new opportunities for airline executives to monopolize power and manipulate employees. Although Lorenzo may have been the worst example of this new breed, he was hardly alone.

Richard "Dick" Ferris became chairman of United Airlines in 1978 on the cusp of deregulation. He was one of the few major airline chief executives to advocate for deregulation, yet under his leadership United struggled more than most air carriers in adjusting to the new environment.[90] After serving in the army during the Vietnam War, Ferris majored in hotel management at Cornell University and then worked for Western (later Westin) Hotels in Chicago. In 1970, United bought Westin, and Ferris came over too as head of food services. Within a decade, he became CEO. Like Lorenzo, Ferris was a smooth-talking salesman, and like Lawrence he had a boom-or-bust vision: making United Airlines a one-stop travel empire.[91]

Ferris was young, handsome, articulate, and his "grow the airline" rhetoric was initially popular with United's workers. A pilot himself, he flew his Learjet around the United network, visiting airport outstations to share his vision for growth with employees. The plan was particularly popular with pilots, who were eager to move into the increasing number of captain seats as the airline expanded. In recognition of their support, United pilots made Ferris an honorary union member with a pilot seniority number. It seemed they may have finally found a CEO who could rival Pat Patterson.[92]

Under Ferris's leadership United quickly expanded, becoming the first airline to serve all fifty states. In 1985, it gobbled up industry mainstay Pan American Airlines, adding its equipment and vast array of international routes to United's network. Things were going well until, following Lorenzo's example, Ferris decided he needed wage-and-benefit concessions from employees to achieve his full vision. After American Airlines CEO Robert Crandall forced his pilots to adopt B-scale wages that put new employees on a lower salary schedule, Ferris saw his chance and argued that employee wage cuts were the only way for United to remain competitive.

However, at the same time that Ferris was demanding concessions from airline employees, he was mobilizing his plan to create a one-stop travel empire by bringing United Airlines, Hertz rental cars, and the Westin and Hilton international hotel chains under one company he called Allegis. It is easy to see why airline employees were disgruntled. To them it seemed that the sacrifices they made for the sake of their airline's survival were being squandered on rental car and hotel chains. United pilots resisted and claimed Ferris was trying to break the unions. They held a twenty-nine-day pilot strike in 1985, the longest in company history. Like Lawrence and Lorenzo, Ferris had gone too far.

Even the financial sector was skeptical about Ferris' strategies. Although some Wall Streeters liked the one-stop concept, ultimately Ferris's personality, like Lorenzo's, became the biggest detriment to the plan. One senior Wall Street analyst recalled how difficult it was working with Allegis executives: "They didn't want to tell you anything, share anything, do anything to make your life easier.'" But "the real killer" for Ferris wasn't his vision, the analyst emphasized, it was "that they were so goddamn arrogant it was not to be believed."[93]

Similarly, one senior United captain I interviewed described Ferris and the cultural discord he created this way:

> [Dick] was here when I arrived. He was a very, very charismatic fellow, very likeable. . . . He would come into our union meetings early on and take his jacket off, roll up his sleeves, and within five minutes—he was very perceptive—he'd catch names. . . . He'd be talking to you on a first-name basis, as if you were the best of friends. . . . Then it was like a light switch. He just became a different individual. He had a grand vision for the way he wanted to take the industry, and he fought for that and he lost. He became vindictive, and it was very ugly then. It was a fight to the death.

By 1987, United employees and the board of directors had had enough of Dick Ferris. After a special board meeting in New York, Ferris was forced to resign and the company announced plans to liquidate Allegis, selling both Hertz and the hotel chains and returning United Airlines to its original state. Ferris was, nevertheless, awarded a $3 million golden parachute.[94]

Although Lawrence, Lorenzo, and Ferris proved to be some of the worst airline executives in the period after deregulation—arrogant, insulated, and fixated on achieving their own personal ambitions at any cost—not all airline CEOs in this era were this destructive or unpopular. Herbert Kelleher, the charismatic cofounder of Southwest Airlines, served as CEO, president, and chairman for a total of thirty-seven years, retiring in 2008 at seventy-seven. Over the years, Herb, as he is fondly known to his employees, fostered a corporate culture that thrived on fun and rewarded individuality. And Kelleher led by example. With a glass of Wild Turkey in hand and a cigarette dangling from his lips, he dressed like Elvis, sang rap songs that poked fun at himself, joined employees in all-night parties, and settled disagreements with arm-wrestling competitions. In response, unlike other airline executives' good riddance goodbyes from their employees, when Kelleher retired Southwest pilots took out a full-page newspaper ad thanking him: "The pilots of Southwest Airlines want to express our sentiment to Herb that it has been an honor and a privilege to be a part of his aviation legacy."[95]

Like many other CEOs in the post-deregulation era, Kelleher came to the airline industry as an outsider with no aviation experience. A lawyer by training, he moved with his family to San Antonio in the mid-1960s with plans to practice law. However, as the now famous story goes, in 1966 Kelleher and a banker client, Rollin King, had the idea to mimic California short-haul operator Pacific Southwest Airlines in Texas and sketched out the basic plan for Southwest right then on the back of a cocktail napkin.[96] Kelleher provided some seed money, but by 1971 Southwest was profitable and has remained so ever since. Today, Herb's shares are worth about $86 million.[97] But he's not the only millionaire at Southwest Airlines. There are seventeen original Southwest employees still employed at the air carrier, and although most are quite wealthy as a result of the company's profit-sharing program, they continue to work anyway, just for the fun of it.[98]

As an industry outsider Kelleher was in some ways like other CEOs of the new era: highly educated but with no aviation industry experience. However, in character, motivation, and people skills he was more akin to airline pioneers like Patterson and Smith. A gruff, hard-drinking man of the people, Kelleher smoked five packs of cigarettes a day and often sprinkled his folksy reflections with expletives and off-color jokes. Although his airline is highly unionized like other air carriers, his leadership style included partying all night with employees to find out what they were thinking, rather than antagonizing them into strike actions like Ferris. His goal was not to run a megacarrier, like Lawrence, or personally dominate the industry through ruthless corporate takeovers, like Lorenzo. In fact, when asked by reporters what he thought his airline legacy should be, Herb responded, "I consumed more Wild Turkey and cigarettes than anybody in the industry."[99]

There are now at least nine books written about Southwest Airlines, and invariably the studies find the key to the airline's success in Kelleher's unorthodox personality and his engaging management style. Some predicted that with Herb's retirement in 2008, Southwest would suffer. However, some things have steadfastly remained unchanged. Today, Southwest is the largest air carrier in the United States in terms of domestic passengers carried. It has 37,000 employees, almost seven hundred jets, and operates over 3,300 flights per day to ninety-seven destinations in forty-two states.

Whenever asked about the secret to Southwest's success, executives past and present still echo Kelleher's statement to *Fortune* magazine in 2001: "You have to treat your employees like customers. When you treat them right, then they will treat your outside customers right. That has been a powerful competitive weapon for us."[100] He has also said, "We've never had layoffs. We could have made more money if we furloughed people. But we don't do that. And we honor them constantly. Our people know that if they are sick, we will take care of them. If there are occasions of grief or joy, we will be there with them. They know that we value them as people, not just cogs in a machine."[101]

To ensure this happens, Herb told *Fortune*: "People think of us as this flamboyant airline, but we're really very conservative from the fiscal standpoint. . . . We never overreached ourselves." His goal as CEO was simple, to "manage in good times so that [we're] ready for bad times."[102] And he offered an example. In contrast to the solution of other CEOs to lay off airline workers or slash wage and benefits in the post-9/11 period, Kelleher reached out to his employees in collaboration when costs escalated:

> We did two things. First, we asked our people to cut our nonfuel costs. I wrote a letter asking each of them to save $5 a day. It sounds like nothing, but, believe me, the little things can really add up. By each saving $5 a day, our people at Southwest helped cut our costs last year by 5.6%—which is extraordinary in one year. Then we also hedged 80% of our fuel costs—at $22 a barrel. Jet-fuel prices spiked precipitously shortly thereafter. When the [9/11] crisis hit, we were ready.[103]

The key to Southwest's success seems straightforward. The airline exploited a niche in the unglamorous short-haul aviation market, never abandoning this core in search of a more exciting vision. It simplified operations by using one type of aircraft, which reduced maintenance and training expenses. But, most important, the company has treated employees with respect and values their skills and commitment. It never furloughs, always pays a fair wage, and empowers people to do their job, allowing them to have fun at work.[104]

In contrast, other historical examples such as Lawrence, Lorenzo, and Ferris, among many others, depict airline CEOs chasing visions of grandeur, sacrificing their airlines and employees before moving on to other personal endeavors. Even Alfred Kahn observed that once airline deregulation occurred some airlines made "terrible mistakes." It became clear, he emphasized, "that deregulation calls for a different kind of management."[105] Herb Kelleher was able to be this sort of innovative airline executive, dedicated to one airline, passionate about aviation as a unique business enterprise, committed to employees, and holding a long-term vision of developing a safe, reliable airline industry. Unfortunately, as we will see in coming chapters, most executives in both aviation and finance in the post-9/11 period are more akin to Lawrence, Lorenzo, and Ferris than Kelleher.

5

ESCALATING RISKS

Although neither the airline industry nor the financial sector would welcome the characterization today, both industries were originally intended to operate as public utilities of a sort. By providing an intermediary function for Main Street America, both industries took people places they wanted to go: air carriers moved passengers and cargo around the world, and Wall Street matched investors seeking profits with companies needing capital. The purposes and goals of both industries initially seemed straightforward enough. So how then did managing and regulating aviation and finance become so complex?

What the parallel histories of these two boom-or-bust industries reveals is that changes in CEO personality types, industry ethos, and regulatory oversight strategies, combined with technological advancements in computers and mathematical modeling programs, brought the country to the risky precipice we face in 2014. The process expanded in the 1980s when influential politicians, enamored of deregulation theories, created laissez-faire government policies to empower big business while diminishing labor union influence. During this period, serving as a "public utility" was nei-ther as profitable nor as glamorous as either industry's new leaders desired. In aviation a new breed of CEO, such as Lawrence, Lorenzo, and Ferris, arrived on the scene with high ambitions but without the people skills or industry knowledge needed to successfully run an airline. Impatient to get rich fast rather than nurturing employee and customer relationships or long-term industry growth, this new breed of leader was interested in one thing: expanding his empire and making a quick profit for himself.

Similarly, a new kind of leader with a new way of thinking joined the financial industry as well during this time period: "quantitative analysts" or "quants" brought their new field "quantitative finance."[1] Like Kahn and Barnett applying their academic theories to aviation, this new breed, which included mathematicians, physicists, economists, and computer scientists, focused their academic skills on finance. More precisely, they focused on making money.[2] The result was the development of investment prod-ucts that took the art and science of risk management to new extremes.[3] Through the seductive influence of men like Ed Thorp, Jim Simons, Boaz Weinstein, and Ken Griffin, Wall Street fell for the apparent certainty and mathematical elegance underlying some of the riskiest investment vehicles in history. These products were called "derivatives."[4]

A derivative, in its most basic form, is simply a specialized contract that signifies an option to buy or sell the underlying asset at a prearranged price within an agreed on time period. Also called a hedge, it is similar to the in-surance policy on your house. However, in the hands of the creative quants, these exotic contracts quickly grew in size and complexity to become vast, intertwined, and inscrutable networks of finance. By programming com-puters to take on some-supervisory functions, Federal Reserve Chairman William McChesney Martin suggested, quants and their risk management systems would "pull back the punch bowl" when the party got too risky.

However, because many financial firms chose to program their risk management systems with overly optimistic assumptions and oversimpli-fied data, the alarm bells never sounded and the party roared on. Even after it became apparent that risk management systems were unable to accurately assess the risks, and a financial industry meltdown like the one that finally did occur in 2008 was looming, Wall Street partied on, continu-ing to trade complex securities concocted by their most creative bankers. Some financial analysts even believed "there was a willful designing of the systems to measure the risks in a certain way that would not necessarily pick up all the right risks."[5] The same could be said of mathematical models designed by aviation quants, which only include fatal jet crashes in their statistics, ignoring all other forms of aviation accidents and near misses.

Over time, risk taking became contagious on Wall Street, and the new breed of trader came to focus almost exclusively on mathematical models to justify investments. As was the case in aviation, these philosophical changes separated new managers from the ethos of their forebears. Unlike old guard leaders these new analysts ignored many market fundamentals and human factors that had been central in previous decision making.[6] Just like airline CEOs, Wall Street's new managers disregarded the social implications of their decisions, prioritizing the manipulation of numbers to achieve their goals. The result of this escalating risk taking and short-term profit seeking was the 2008 financial industry implosion. What happened to cause the Wall Street crash, and how might lessons learned in the finance industry be applied to aviation?

As Alexander S. Hoare, managing partner at London's oldest family bank C. Hoare & Company, founded in 1672, observed: "Greed took over." As bigger banks swallowed up smaller ones, just like airline mergers today, the financial industry became less of a gentlemen's club and more like a street brawl, impossible to police. Hoare observed in 2012 that, in response, "a highly alien culture [crept] into all these big banks," and "all this regulation has not solved the problem of excessive risk-taking."[7]

Wall Street executives gave up conservative traditions in favor of far riskier and less established business models, developing increasingly exotic securities that were difficult to understand, encouraging investors to sideline their concerns and to invest frivolously. Brokers would boast of "ripping the face off" their clients, meaning they had closed a deal so complicated the client could not understand it—and might not actually benefit from it in the long term—but one that nonetheless generated huge short-term profits for their bank and themselves.[8] Like the aviation industry changes discussed in chapter 4, this environment attracted corporate leaders who fostered a different organizational culture and ethos that shifted risk and safety to chase after big wins. Wall Street became a casino where it was possible to get rich quickly by speculating on the right stock, and technology companies in northern California's Silicon Valley intensified the excitement and risk through initial public offerings (IPOs).[9]

Before trading publically on the stock exchange, private companies hire an investment bank to establish an IPO share value and help market the initial sale. In exchange, bankers typically earn an 8 percent commission on the shares they sell. It is a lucrative business. In 2000 alone, Goldman Sachs pocketed over $24.5 billion for underwriting sixty-three IPOs. And, although two-thirds eventually traded below their issue price, losing money for investors, banks locked in their own handsome winnings at the day's closing bell. Across the board, Wall Street bonuses nearly doubled that year, topping $100,000 for the first time.[10] Compared to today's numbers this seems a pittance. For example, in 2006, Goldman CEO Lloyd C. Blankfein took home a $68 million bonus, and even in 2011, after so much effort to rein in Wall Street excesses in Washington, Goldman nonetheless set aside $12.22 billion for compensation and benefits.[11]

What cases like this exemplify is how industry leaders in both finance and aviation quietly sidestepped previous generations' risk-reducer role in favor of the entrepreneurial risk-maker role, leaving everyone else in the risk-taker seat. And bankers, like aviation managers, in the new era are unconcerned about the implications of their short-term strategies. After all, they say it's not their job to offer long-term value—the marketplace will regulate that.

Another cause of the crash and lesson to be learned is that both industries' escalating risk bred new forms of executive gamesmanship. For instance, however straightforward investment bankers would like underwriting IPOs to seem, there is a lot of gamesmanship involved in the managerial decision-making process. Consider Facebook's first day of trading in 2012. Although some investors questioned the company's long-term prospects, Morgan Stanley believed they could justify the offering price of $38 a share. When the market opened, the price stagnated and then flatlined.[12] Some claimed Facebook crashed, in part, because of electronic-trading problems when an automated program suddenly flooded the market. None of the technological circuit breakers worked to curtail trades, and turmoil spread across Wall Street.[13] Although one financial insider requested NASDAQ to stop trading "so we can all catch up and actually understand our exposure,"[14] the party just raged on. Two months later, Facebook traded at less than half its initial price. Yet, like airline CEOs exiting bankruptcy, Morgan Stanley and other underwriters still took home about $100 million.[15]

Finally, in lessons to be learned from the Wall Street disaster, in both aviation and finance decisions are often based on mathematical models that are vulnerable to manipulation. For example, in response to the Facebook debacle, NASDAQ was fined $10 million for poor systems design and ineffective managerial decision making, the largest fine ever levied against an exchange.[16] SEC spokesperson Daniel M. Hawke emphasized in 2013 that it has been too easy to shrug off incidents like this as "technical glitches" when "it's the design of the systems and the response of exchange officials that cause us the most concern."[17] As one finance industry analyst observed, "You think there is somebody watching the control panel somewhere," but there's not.[18] The same observation could be applied to decisions made at airlines today.

Facebook might have proven to be overpriced, but some IPOs are deliberately underpriced by bankers in another gamesmanship strategy to generate additional profit. In this scenario, investors quickly sell ("flip") their shares, focusing on short-term profits rather than engaging in a buy-and-hold position. One historic example of this strategy was the IPO for social networking provider theglobe.com in 1998. Underwriter Bear Stearns deliberately underpriced the stock at $9 per share, causing a bidding frenzy up to $97. Prices climbed 1,000 percent at the day's opening; theglobe.com was suddenly worth $1 billion, and Bear Stearns profited well.[19] Perhaps just as emblematic of problems in the system theglobe.com not only rose extremely rapidly but it had a drastic demise. The stock price collapsed the following year, and it ultimately traded at less than 10 cents a share. The company ceased operations in 2008. Airlines like Valujet used similar strategies to make millions for their executives before suddenly going under, leaving passengers at the gate still holding their boarding passes.

In 1999, theglobe.com founder Stephan Paternot was caught by a late-night news crew at a Manhattan nightclub, dancing on a cocktail table in shiny black pants with his model girlfriend, saying: "Got the girl. Got the money. Now I'm ready to live a disgusting, frivolous life." Instantly dubbed as "the CEO in the plastic pants," Paternot became a symbol of the poor leadership, inappropriate excesses, and financial delirium of the executive boardroom.[20] Businessmen like Paternot were not alone is seeking short-term gains with little sense of integrity or long-term responsibility. Government regulators, politicians, investment bankers, venture capitalists, research analysts, and investors big and small were all drawn into the dot.com mania as underwriters took countless companies public that had little chance of long-term profitability.

During the dot.com bubble "people were throwing money at businesses that wouldn't pass simple due-diligence screens five years ago," said one venture capitalist. "People overlooked almost all business fundamentals and drove valuations into the stratosphere."[21] For instance, previously, an IPO rule of thumb was that a company needed to generate at least $10 million in revenue in the twelve months before it went public. However, after theglobe.com, one venture capitalist recalled, "everyone realized the entire market was doing deals like this." People said, "Hey, if theglobe.com can go public, we can [too]."[22] In 1997, of the twenty-four domestic companies Goldman Sachs took public, a third were already losing money. Yet, underwriters knew if they did not jump on these opportunities, one of their competitors would.[23] A race to the edge of risk began as more risk-adverse practices of the past were ignored in pursuit of immediate profits, no matter how short lived.

The same is happening in aviation today. For example one pilot I interviewed, Charles, summed up the post-9/11 changes this way:

> [Airline executives] are only interested in making money—more, more, more money—for themselves, and that's all they care about. They really didn't care about the success or failure of the company, per se. They were just concerned about how much they could get out of it. And that was generally how much further can we cut, cut, cut. . . . Maybe those management people have figured out that they can afford to crash one airplane every two years, and they don't care because they're not riding on the airplane. Maybe that's what it comes down to; you have these new kinds of managers.

What is important to take away from this discussion are the ways in which both finance and aviation suffered from increased greed, which escalated risks, which bred new forms of gamesmanship as industry leaders justified decisions based on mathematical models that were vulnerable to manipulation. Most critical in this conversation is the fact that no formal decision was made to relax standards or modify decision-making policies. This change in industry ethos occurred organically, under the regulatory radar, as a result of an informal shift in attitudes toward risk and ethics within the competitive business environment.

In response to this shift, a new breed of executive entered both aviation and finance. Highly educated, confident in their theories, and aggressive in their tactics, these men—and they were predominantly male—had a high tolerance for risk and low concern for the implications of their actions, particularly for the wider repercussions of their decisions should they fail. These CEOs cultivated a new ethos within their organizations, an ethos not everyone was comfortable with.

Greg Smith worked at Goldman Sachs for twelve years, starting right out of college. He resigned in 2012 because the company had become too much about shortcuts and profit seeking and too little about risk management, long-term planning, and serving the client. He explained further, "I have worked here long enough to understand the trajectory of its culture" and "can honestly say that" Goldman Sachs is so "toxic and destructive [that] . . . I can no longer in good conscience say that I identify with what it stands for." He amplified, "It makes me ill how callously people talk about ripping their clients off [or refer] to their own clients as 'muppets,'"—Wall Street slang for a rube or easy mark. Over the years, Smith observed, "the firm changed the way it thought about leadership. Leadership used to be about ideas, setting an example and doing the right thing. Today, if you make enough money" for Goldman Sachs, you will be promoted. This fixation on quick profit influences junior people's values in disturbing ways, he noted, creating a self-fulfilling prophesy for future generations. What a surprise, Smith said, when a junior person, "sitting quietly in the corner of the room hearing about 'muppets,' 'ripping eyeballs out' and 'getting paid' doesn't exactly turn into a model citizen."[24]

Similarly, Frank Partnoy, a trader at Morgan Stanley, recalled how as his firm shifted from prestige to profits the company cultivated aggressive new tactics in its employees. "By the time I arrived" in 1994, Partnoy said, "any evidence of the old, stodgy Morgan Stanley had been washed away." "Half-geek, half-wolf" managers instructed their employees: "There's blood in the water. Let's go kill someone." As one boss instructed him, "We love desperate clients, we get excited about them. We've made a lot of money off desperate people." Like other Wall Street firms, Partnoy reflected, "Morgan Stanley carefully cultivated this urge to blast a client to smithereens." This cut-throat competition was not only rampant among derivative salesmen like Partnoy. Senior managing directors, who were already rich, collected seven-figure bonuses as trophies. "Each wanted to be paid more than his peers, not necessarily because the money was relevant to day-to-day life, but because it would signal that he had beaten the others," claimed Partnoy. As the market intensified, Wall Street "partners became greedier as they shifted to higher-risk, higher-profit activities," depending more and more on derivative salesmen like Partnoy. The goal, he was instructed, was to "lure people into that calm and then just totally fuck 'em." He elaborated, "No one seemed to care about how risky many of the hundreds of derivatives deals were. No one seemed to care about whether clients actually understood what they were buying, even when the trades had hidden risks. . . . Year by year, client by client, trade by trade, the venerable House of Morgan was building a precarious house of cards."[25] However precarious these transactions were in reality, the image of Wall Street was so Teflon that after twelve failed attempts over the years, executives and lobbyists finally convinced Congress to fully deregulate the financial industry.

In 1999, President Bill Clinton signed the Gramm-Leach-Bliley act repealing the Glass-Steagall act and removing government safeguards that separated commercial and investment banking that had been put in place after the 1929 stock market crash. Although this repeal is widely believed to have directly contributed to the 2008 financial industry implosion,[26] the act's coauthor, Senator Phil Gramm, celebrated it as "the wave of the future."[27] Similarly, Treasury Secretary Lawrence H. Summers noted, "This historic legislation will better enable American companies to compete in the new economy."[28] And Senator Bob Kerrey attacked critics by claiming, "The concerns that we will have a meltdown like 1929 are dramatically overblown."[29]

However, not everyone was a supporter. Senator Byron Dorgan prophetically warned, "We will look back in ten years' time and say we should not have [repealed this act]."[30] Similarly, President Obama echoed concerns about corporate behavior in deregulated environments during his election campaign. "Instead of establishing a 21st century regulatory framework, we simply dismantled the old one," he said, "[which encouraged] a winner take all, anything goes environment" with questionable benefits.[31] We know these changes directly contributed to the 2008 financial industry crisis, and, the same charge of a "winner take all" corporate culture in an "anything goes" regulatory environment can be leveled at the US airline industry today.

Was it possible to see the 2008 US financial industry crash coming? Several people both inside and outside Wall Street certainly had concerns. Billionaire financiers like Warren Buffett and George Soros shunned derivatives because the risks were complex and could not be properly understood.[32] Buffet called them "financial weapons of mass destruction."[33] Economist Nouriel Roubini warned in 2006 that a US financial implosion was imminent and would lead to a deep recession. Yet critics dismissed Roubini's predictions as pessimistic and unreliable because they were not supported by mathematical models, calling him a "permabear" and "Dr. Doom."[34] Economists Kenneth Rogoff, Robert Shiller, and William White, as well, repeatedly cautioned about inflated housing prices and escalating indebtedness. Raghuram Rajan warned about banking risk.[35] And financial historian Niall Ferguson drew parallels to past economic booms that also ended badly.[36]

In Washington, Brooksley E. Born lobbied hard for her organization, the Commodity Futures Trading Commission, to receive oversight authority over custom derivatives, which had grown into a $70 trillion market in just a decade. Yet Born's warnings were surprisingly opposed by other government regulators such as Robert E. Rubin, Lawrence H. Summers, and Alan Greenspan.[37] These influential policymakers believed that even discussing new regulatory rules would threaten the prolific derivatives market and prompt traders to take their business overseas. Even the near collapse of hedge fund Long Term Capital Management in 1998— a precise example of what Born was worried about—did not sway senior officials who continued to pressure Congress not to regulate. In fact, Federal Reserve Chairman Alan Greenspan was one of the most vocal fans of derivatives and never missed a chance to fiercely object whenever they came under scrutiny, saying that "it would be a mistake" to increase regulation.[38] And Congress listened.

Chair of the House Banking and Financial Services Committee Jim Leach recalled, "Alan was held in very high regard" on Capitol Hill, and derivatives were "an area of judgment in which members of Congress have nonexistent expertise." No one was going to argue with Alan Greenspan about derivatives. Senator Tom Harkin agreed, adding that Greenspan "was able to say things in a way that made people not want to question him." It was "like he knew it all." Greenspan was nicknamed "the Oracle." Senator Harkin emphasized, "Who were you to question him?"[39] Important to note is that, like the Boeing 787 battery fire debacle, it was easy for executives and lobbyists to find support for their cause in Washington, particularly among those tasked with oversight of their industry.

Ultimately, the problem in both aviation and finance is not that people do not see a crisis looming; it is that those who benefited from the existing system had too much inducement to continue their risky behavior and too little incentive to stop. In the end, greed, reckless competition, unchecked innovation, and extreme willingness to embrace risk, along with minimal regulatory supervision, put Wall Street, and the entire country, in peril. As Morgan Stanley chairman John Mack described it, "We did our own cooking and we choked on it."[40]

CEO of Goldman Sachs Lloyd Blankfein claimed that the underlying cause was that "we talked ourselves into complacency."[41] A Silicon Valley lawyer summed it up differently: "As it turns out, they screwed up; Wall Street didn't understand what they were doing well enough to manage the risk associated [with its practices]."[42] And *Rolling Stone*'s Matt Taibbi offered an even more graphic depiction of powerful investment banks' motivations. He wrote that they are like "a great vampire squid wrapped around the face of humanity, relentlessly jamming its blood funnel into anything that smells like money."[43] Whether the cause is complacency, greed, or just plain bad management, similar managerial risk taking is occurring in the US airline industry today, with just as far-reaching and dangerous consequences.

I have highlighted the ways the deregulated environments in both aviation and finance attracted a new breed of leader with a different skill set, an increasing appetite for risk, and an eagerness to reap short-term profits for themselves with a corresponding disregard for the long-term implications of their actions. In sum, for these managers it was all about "the now." In the finance industry, there is ample evidence that these attitudes and behaviors ultimately contributed to the 2008 Wall Street crash and the Great Recession that followed and that government leaders had a hunch things were going awry but did little to intervene. For example, the Federal Reserve Bank of New York learned as early as April 2008, when the financial crisis began to escalate, that at least one bank was reporting false interest rates. A Barclays Bank employee told a New York Fed official that "we know that we're not posting um, an honest" rate but that there was pressure to "fit in with the rest of the crowd."[44] Even today, pressures to conform continue to escalate risks at airlines and on Wall Street.

In finance, traders at American International Group (AIG), J. P. Morgan Chase, and the Swiss global financial services company UBS accumulated

billions of dollars of losses.[45] Although financial industry regulators recommended reforms, they failed to stop the escalation because they did not
have "explicit proof" of intentional wrongdoing.[46] These revelations once
again fuel the argument that regulators in both finance and aviation are
ill-equipped to police big companies that have become adept at gaming the
system for their own purposes. "Too big to fail" has morphed into "too big
to jail." Frank Partnoy, the Wall Street derivatives salesman, now turned
law professor, has a response. "I wish I could say I'm shocked, because it is
shocking," he said. "But regulators have not been particularly effective or
aggressive in the past two decades of finance."[47] And this pattern continues
to the present day, even after 2008 and the supposed increase in regulatory
supervision called for in the 2010 Dodd-Frank Wall Street Reform and
Consumer Protection Act. Questions remain about these patterns of escalating risks, weak regulatory oversight, and poor accountability at organizations that are too big to fail—whether in finance or aviation.

To understand how similar factors to those in Wall Street are affecting
aviation safety in equally risky ways, I turn the analysis back to the airline
industry and evaluate the commonalities of several aviation accidents that
occurred in the post-deregulation period, the same period in which risks
began to escalate exponentially in the finance industry. Like Wall Street,
these risky aviation practices have not been checked by introducing adequate safeguards either.

Although Alfred Kahn conceded that his deregulation experiment
turned out to be hard on airlines, they were even tougher on employees
who rode the roller coaster ride of airline expansion and contraction over
the past three decades. In fact, many airlines' struggles to stay solvent in the
post-9/11 period originated with flawed managerial decisions made during the 1980s and 1990s. During this period intense competition brought
on by executives' pursuit of bigger is better, often in service to their own
personal ambitions, led to extensive purchases of new airplanes and record
hiring of employees. Between 1985 and 1988 alone, nearly thirty thousand
commercial pilots were hired in the United States. As a result, in 1987, the
head of the FAA, Trusten Allan McArtor, called for a review of the FAA's
pilot-certification process—the first such examination since 1952. Mc-
Artor noted that "the overall experience of pilots is of some concern [and]
the overall flight hours of pilots is of some concern. But we don't know
whether that means a safety problem."[48] Yet, little substantive change occurred as a result of this study.

To contextualize this rapid expansion period, consider that there are only about 70,000 commercial pilots currently employed in the entire US aviation industry (fig. 5). In 1989, Future Aviation Professionals of America estimated that US airlines would hire another 32,000 pilots by the year 2000, and the FAA estimated airline fleets would increase by 25 percent or nearly 4,200 additional commercial aircraft.[49] This rapid aviation industry expansion exhausted the available labor supply and put younger, less experienced pilots in the cockpit of nearly every US air carrier. As Captain Vern Laursen, vice president of flight training at TWA, cautioned, by 1999, "every airline in the country will have 30-year-old captains."[50] This prediction, made in 1989, became a reality within the decade.

Contributing to the pilot shortage was the mandatory retirement of large numbers of experienced Vietnam-era pilots at age sixty, competitive bonuses paid to keep military pilots in the service, and the high cost of civilian flight training. To overcome this pilot paucity, airport flight schools sprang up, and commercial pilot-training programs thrived, changing the background and demographics of the professional pilot. It was now possible for someone with little experience, or proven aptitude, to buy accelerated flight training leading to employment as a regional airline copilot.

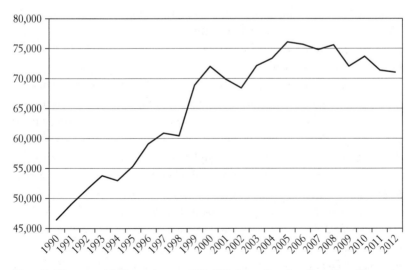

Figure 5. US commercial pilot employment, 1990–2012. *Source*: Data from Research and Innovative Technology Administration (RITA), US Bureau of Transportation Statistics, http://www.bts.gov/programs/airline_information/.

In addition, airline executives negotiated with universities offering aviation degrees to promote professional pilot educational programs while simultaneously reducing previous standards for age, vision, height/weight, and experience. For example, in 1986 most major airlines only hired college graduates. By 1989, one new hire pilot in ten had no college diploma. The impact of this demographic change had an immediate effect on air safety. Consider the following five examples.

Continental Airlines in 1987   On November 15, 1987, Continental Airlines Flight 1713 was delayed leaving Denver's Stapleton Airport by almost two hours due to snow, fog, freezing temperatures, and reduced visibility. Once cleared, the airplane deiced and awaited takeoff clearance for another twenty-seven minutes as snow continued to fall. The takeoff roll was initially uneventful until the first officer, flying the aircraft, over-rotated on liftoff, stalling the jet, which impacted the runway and rolled inverted, killing twenty-eight of the eighty-two occupants on board.[51]

Both pilots were inexperienced in their crew positions and unaccustomed to their required duties during cold-weather operations prompting questions, in hindsight, about why they were paired: The forty-three-year-old captain had just 166 total hours in the DC-9, of which only 33 were as captain. The twenty-six-year-old first officer was hired by Continental just four months before the accident and had only 36 flight hours in the DC-9. He was assigned to the accident flight, only his second assignment as a Continental first officer, because he had not flown in twenty-four days and needed to gain proficiency.

Yet, unknown to the captain, the first officer had a documented history of poor performance and problems during training. A previous employer's chief pilot described him as "tense and unable to cope with deviations from the routine." At Continental, his DC-9 instructor also voiced concerns during training, commenting: "Completely lost control of the airplane"; "Pitch control jerky"; "Altitude control when pressure is on is somewhat sloppy"; and "Airspeed control generally way out of limits".[52] These piloting deficiencies all were factors on the day of the accident.

The NTSB determined the probable cause of this accident was "pilot error." Yet, in their final report, the NTSB included an unusual systemic indictment: "The rapid growth of the aviation industry at a time when fewer experienced pilots are in the workforce has reduced the opportunity for a pilot to accumulate experience before progressing to a position of greater responsibility. This loss of 'seasoning' has led to the assignment of pilots who may not be operationally mature to positions previously occupied by highly experienced pilots." Although specific ways to address these deficiencies were not offered, the NTSB urged regulators to become more proactive: "The time has come for the FAA to establish and the industry to accept" operational safeguards and increased regulations to compensate for this "loss of seasoning."[53] This observation was made twenty-five years ago, and little substantive change in this area was ever forthcoming. Airline executives' interest in expanding quickly trumped air safety resulting in twenty-eight deaths.

GP Express Airlines in 1992   In 1992, there was another fatal aviation accident involving unseasoned airline pilots, new to their roles in the flight deck and in over their heads when a challenging situation occurred. GP Express Airlines Flight 861, a Beech C-99, impacted terrain killing three people when the inexperienced crew lost situational awareness while maneuvering in clouds to land in Anniston, Alabama. It was the twenty-nine-year-old captain's *first day* as an airline pilot and his twenty-four-year-old copilot's second month as a first officer. Both pilots had logged a large percentage of their flight experience in small single-engine airplanes and had minimal actual instrument flight experience flying in clouds.[54]

One unusual company cost-saving strategy central in this accident was GP Express's policy of providing only one aeronautical approach chart to each crew, which, during this accident, was held by the first officer. As pressure built, the new captain became disoriented, overwhelmed, and increasingly reliant on the first officer's erroneous flight guidance. Yet, without his own aeronautical chart for verification, the captain had no way to identify the copilot's mistakes or reorient himself.

Approximately three minutes prior to impact, the first officer joked sarcastically about the captain's obvious task saturation, seeming to enjoy his discomfort: "Didn't realize that you're going to get this much on your first day, did ya?"

"Well, it's all kind of ganged up here on me a little fast," the captain confessed.[55]

Two minutes later, the captain discussed executing a missed approach—akin to going around for another try—but the first officer convinced him to continue the landing. They crashed one minute later.

The NTSB determined that both "pilot error" and "organizational failures" contributed to this accident. The pilots failed to use approved instrument-approach procedures, and GP Express senior management failed to provide adequate training and operational support when they paired an inadequately trained captain with an inexperienced first officer and without sufficient aeronautical charts. For want of a few dollars' worth of navigation materials, three people died. In addition, neither pilot completed a formal crew resource management program, a team-building and resource-management training program standard at most airlines, which would have enhanced their workload management skills, and perhaps even prevented this accident.

Scenic Air Tours in 1992   A third example of a fatal aviation accident caused by oversight failures, cost cutting, and a young pilot who lacked "seasoning" involved a commercial sightseeing company on the island of Maui in Hawaii. The twenty-six-year-old captain had been employed by Scenic Air Tours for about eight months prior to the accident. He took off on April 22, 1992, in a 1957 Beech-18 on the Volcano Special sightseeing tour. Although the flight was single-pilot visual operations, not certified for instrument conditions, the pilot entered the clouds over Mount Haleakala and became disoriented; he collided with the rising terrain and killed all nine people on board.[56]

Particularly disturbing was the postaccident discovery that the young captain, eager to advance his commercial aviation career, falsified his employment application by stating that he had accumulated 3,200 flight hours when in fact he only had about 1,600—well below Scenic Air Tours 2,500 minimum. Over the previous four years he had worked for at least nine different aviation employers, five of whom dismissed him for cause such as "below standard work," "failure to report for duty," "poor training performance," and "misrepresentation of qualifications,"[57] Yet, this information was not made available to Scenic Air Tours.

In the ten years prior to this disaster, the NTSB investigated twelve sightseeing company accidents resulting in ninety-six fatalities; six crashes were caused when, similar to Scenic Air, a fully functioning aircraft was mistakenly flown into the ground. These commonalities prompted more questions about safety, training, and oversight in the aviation industry, in particular, the FAA's failure to require that commercial operators conduct a substantive background screening of pilots before employing them.

In at least three accident investigations between 1987 and 1992, the NTSB urged the FAA to require aviation employers to screen pilots more thoroughly. However, using their cost-benefit analysis, the FAA dismissed these recommendations in the belief that the benefits of these require-ments would not outweigh the cost of promulgating and enforcing the new regulations.[58]

GP Express Proficiency Check in 1993   Another fatal airplane crash in-volving immature pilots who had quickly worked their way up the com-mercial aviation ladder during the rapid expansion in the period after deregulation occurred at 11:50 p.m. on April 28, 1993, in Shelton, Ne-braska. The official purpose of this flight was for a company check airman, age twenty-eight, to administer a required proficiency check to another check airman, age twenty-nine, both commuter airline captains at GP Ex-press Airlines. Yet the actual goal of the flight later emerged to be a late-night opportunity for the two young pilots, known to be good friends who liked to joke around, to conduct unauthorized aerobatic maneuvers in the company's Beech C-99, a fifteen-seat turboprop airplane.[59]

The flight started with the accident pilot asking the check airman if he was "up for a 'vertical thing'" on takeoff as he radioed company ground personnel at the airport to "look out the window" and watch.[60] Once airborne, the two continued with other stunts, including a lethal "aile-ron roll" that, moments prior to ground impact, both pilots confessed to never having attempted before. Postcrash investigation revealed that an Airmen Competency/Proficiency Check Grade Sheet, the FAA paper-work required to document completion of the required flight maneuvers, was found in the check airman's company mailbox—already completed and signed. Clearly, the pilots never intended to conduct a proper FAA check ride.

Based on this evidence, the NTSB determined that both pilots were willing participants in unauthorized, hazardous aerobatic maneuvers that violated company policies, FAA regulations, and prudent airmanship. Yet, in a shift toward a more systemic analysis of team breakdown, the NTSB also cited GP Express management for failing to establish and main-tain a corporate culture committed to pilot professionalism and safety, noting once again the lack of crew resource management training as a delinquency.

GP Express emerged in the 1980s and expanded quickly to provide Essential Air Service to midwestern and southern US states, a by-product of the Airline Deregulation Act of 1978 discussed previously. By 1992, it served eleven states and, like Colgan Air today, was doing business as Continental Connection. However, GP Express also had an alarming number of accidents, with crashes in 1987, as well as the ones in 1992 and 1993 discussed here. In 1996, its pilots decided to fight back and voted to accept pilot labor union representation. That same year, the airline declared bankruptcy and ceased operations, leaving behind a trail of fatalities.

ValuJet Airlines in 1996   Like examples from the history of US finance, the history of ValuJet Airlines includes evidence of how greed and cost cutting generated an alien company culture, escalating risk while reaping huge profits for executives unconcerned about the implications of their short-term profit-seeking strategies as they "ripped the face off" customers and employees. The case of ValuJet, like the others discussed here, includes exploiting regulatory loopholes to save money and hiring inexperienced employees who disregarded standard procedures and skirted regulations. However, it also exemplifies the need to regulate in new ways the new elements in the world of aviation that lead to crashes, similar to the concerns Brooksley Born and Nouriel Roubini raised before the 2008 Wall Street crash. At ValuJet there was a complex array of business management practices that intertwined with operational errors, resulting in the crash of Flight 592. The business factors were all perfectly legal and even encouraged by industry regulators, and thus the case can be used to sum up what went wrong with all the accidents discussed here.[61]

On May 11, 1996, ValuJet Flight 592 departed from Miami International Airport on a clear afternoon and then mysteriously disappeared. Ten minutes later it crashed into the Everglades, killing all 110 people on board. Ground scars, wreckage scatter, and witness statements indicated that the jet impacted in a near vertical nose-down attitude, which means that both pilots were either completely incapacitated or somehow unable to control the aircraft. The probable cause of the crash, an in-flight fire in the airplane cargo compartment, eventually seemed clear enough.[62] However, nothing was straightforward about this accident. A subsequent investigation by the inspector general of the US Department of Transportation, Mary Schiavo, found that "ValuJet was primed for a major crash."[63] Yet, no one seemed interested in hearing about it.

The story of Flight 592 begins in early 1996 when ValuJet purchased several used MD-80 aircraft and sent them to a contract maintenance facility in Miami called SabreTech for various mechanical modifications and inspections. One item to check was to make sure that the oxygen canisters—steel devices the size and shape of large beer cans, kept in the overhead cabin, that provide oxygen to passengers through dangling yellow masks—were within their service life. During inspection, SabreTech discovered 144 were out of date and removed and replaced them. Because oxygen canisters can explode and generate temperatures up to five hundred degrees, there are specific shipping and handling warnings in the MD-80 maintenance manual with a direct call to "obey the precautions." When shipped, unexpended canisters should have a safety cap on the detonator and be in special shipping containers that are clearly labeled "hazardous waste."[64]

At SabreTech there was a great deal of managerial pressure on employees to complete the contracted work on Valujet planes; mechanics were working twelve-hour shifts, seven days a week.[65] Some reported knowing about the shipping hazards and safety requirements of unexpended canisters, others did not, but all were focused on getting the airplanes airworthy. As a result, most of the removed canisters were thrown, without safety caps, into unmarked boxes and left on a parts rack in the hangar. Several weeks later, mechanics gathered the unexpended canisters into five unmarked boxes and delivered them to the shipping area where a clerk closed and labeled the boxes as "aircraft parts" for shipment to ValuJet's Atlanta headquarters. Unknown to the aircrew, these five potentially explosive boxes were loaded into the forward cargo hold of Flight 592. Shortly after takeoff the canisters detonated, igniting other flammable materials in the cargo area and filling the plane with smoke and noxious fumes. The plane impacted the ground shortly thereafter.[66] The NTSB postcrash investigation blamed the crash on SabreTech for improperly packaging and illegally transporting dangerous materials, ValuJet for not properly supervising SabreTech, and the FAA for not properly supervising ValuJet.

However dismal this story is, we can learn a lot about changing airline industry ethos and the influence of inexperienced CEOs fixated on short-term profits from the ValuJet example. Although today ValuJet is more likely to be associated with the Ford Pinto as a managerial case study in what *not* to do, the airline started out as a phenomenal success story. Founded in 1993 with three airplanes flying eight routes in the competitive southeastern corridor, going head-to-head with major carriers and winning, ValuJet expanded to fifty-one jets within two and a half years.[67] Based on Southwest's model of fun, low-frills service and cheap fares, ValuJet's DC-9s were painted with a cartoon "critter" and filled with bargain hunters. It seemed the perfect formula.

After just one year ValuJet went public, earning $21 million in 1994 alone and creating a windfall for its founders and investors. Wall Street fell in love, smitten in ways ironically similar to its initial response to Frank Lorenzo. Even the FAA touted ValuJet as an innovative new business model, perfect for the competitive deregulated environment.[68] As part of the new breed of airline executives, ValuJet's chairman Lawrence Priddy was unabashed about his aspirations: "Every other start-up wants to be another United or Delta or American. We just want to get rich."[69]

The secret to ValuJet's success was to buy older used aircraft and parts from foreign countries and then outsource airplane maintenance to the lowest bidder; these were highly suspicious shortcuts, yet all were perfectly legal by FAA standards. As a result, many aircraft had questionable mechanical histories and averaged about twenty-six years in age, significantly older than airplanes at other US air carriers.[70] Emulating long-distance bus travel, ValuJet provided no tickets, refunds, seat assignments, onboard refreshments, airline clubs, or frequent-flyer programs. Employees were paid below-average wages but were encouraged to perform by the possibility of receiving year-end bonuses if the airline profited that year.[71] Cutting costs in this fashion allowed ValuJet to offer cheap tickets and turn a big profit. A Miami to Atlanta ticket that cost about $200 on a major carrier was just $59 on ValuJet.[72]

However, the airline's safety record deteriorated almost in direct proportion to its rate of phenomenal growth and profitability. Like Colgan Air (discussed in chapter 6), there were many signs of impending doom. ValuJet pilots made fifteen emergency landings in 1994, fifty-seven in 1995, and fifty-nine in the months preceding the crash of Flight 592 in 1996.[73] In the airline's three years of flight operations, the FAA had scrutinized it 4,858 times and issued 34 violations, a serious list of discrepancies in a short period of time, yet curiously the FAA never grounded the airline.[74] It is important to note, once again, that near-misses like these that do not result in a fatal jet crash are not included in aviation quants' statistical modeling data.

Even after the crash of Flight 592, instead of heightening its scrutiny of ValuJet, the FAA circled its wagons to protect the airline. In a strange role reversal for an industry regulator, Secretary of Transportation Federico Peña, whose task it was to monitor ValuJet's operations through the FAA, instead made a statement on national television endorsing the airline's safety, stating, "I have flown on ValuJet. ValuJet is a safe airline, as is our entire aviation system." In a surprising public relations move for a government regulator, Peña insisted, "If ValuJet was unsafe, we would have grounded it."[75] It was as if the chairman of the US Securities and Exchange Commission claimed Bernie Madoff, the infamous Ponzi schemer, could never have defrauded thousands of investors of billions of dollars over several decades because, if he had, the SEC would have known about it and stopped him.

Weeks later, after increasing social and political pressures, including a Congressional inquiry and demands by crash victims' families, the FAA finally grounded ValuJet.[76] During the hearing on Capitol Hill, Rep. William O. Lipinski voiced a common concern: "I still don't understand," he said after more than five hours of FAA testimony. "It is my humble opinion that the evidence you had prior to the crash would have been sufficient to shut them down."[77] FAA administrator David R. Hinson responded enigmatically, "It is a logic problem."[78] By this he apparently meant that the FAA found no evidence of any deliberate intention by ValuJet executives to violate aviation regulations, and since the FAA is charged to both "promote" and "regulate" the airline industry, the FAA stuck with promote mode by default. Eerily similar to the Gulfstream Airlines inquiry that took place over fifteen years later (examined in chapter 6), the FAA gave ValuJet executives the benefit of the doubt, stating: "ValuJet itself acknowledges in hindsight that there were things it could have done to insure that its infrastructure was better equipped to handle its growth. However, there is no evidence [that ValuJet] intentionally disregarded safety."[79]

This is another curious distinction, commonly emphasized by regulators within both finance and aviation. Regulators operate under the notion that explicit proof of specific intentional violations is required to pursue disciplinary action, and therefore they can ignore the ample evidence provided by whistleblowers and industry insiders of patterns of reckless and unethical actions that increase risk and often result in catastrophe. It seems an odd distinction when so much is at stake.

Just three months after the crash of Flight 592, the FAA recertified ValuJet to fly again. Although the FAA may have been satisfied that there was "no intentional disregard" for safety at ValuJet, employees and passengers were not. ValuJet's flight attendants union said that the airline was still unsafe. Just because managers claimed to have addressed the issues, they argued, it should not overshadow the severity of the problems or the fact that the issues occurred in the first place.[80] While the FAA may not have listened to employee complaints, the public did, and passengers stopped flying the airline. In response, ValuJet changed its name to AirTran in a futile effort to escape the long dark shadow of Flight 592. In 2011, AirTran merged with Southwest Airlines, creating the largest low-cost carrier network in America.[81]

Unfortunately, little substantively changed in the airline industry as a result of the ValuJet accident. As demonstrated in the coming chapters, instead of its being a system-wide warning, it did nothing to stop the cost-cutting models of airlines like ValuJet from continuing to be championed as examples of innovative management. Airlines continue to outsource maintenance to the lowest bidder, pressure fatigued employees, and cut corners on training to save money. Even today, another airline like ValuJet could emerge, make millions for executives and a handful of investors through aggressive cost cutting and then disappear a few years later after a major crash and the death of hundreds of people.

Shortly after the crash of Flight 592, ValuJet's president, Lewis H. Jordan, was asked at a news conference whether he exercised responsible leadership growing ValuJet at such a remarkable rate. He replied, "We never grew the airline faster than we could be sure that we were operating safely and reliably."[82] However, even the FAA, once staunch advocates of ValuJet as a model airline, finally conceded mistakes had been made. FAA administrator David R. Hinson confessed, "We did learn some lessons [from ValuJet]. It is apparent now that the extraordinarily rapid growth of this airline created problems that should have been more clearly recognized and dealt with sooner and more aggressively."[83] Yet, the question remains: How do regulators and airline executives know whether air carriers are operating safely and reliability or if they have grown too aggressively before a crash occurs? One would think, like spies, they would gather "humint" by listening to employees, the frontline operators who are most at risk and can best see when things don't seem right before a major problem occurs. Unfortunately, as we will see, that is not occurring either.

6

Strapped In for the Ride

What are some of the implications of the post-9/11 airline industry changes? A 2009 white paper by the Air Line Pilots Association (ALPA), the world's largest pilots' union, noted how industry decisions made after 9/11 significantly altered the business models of major air carriers, encouraging them to cut costs by parking larger airplanes and furloughing their more experienced—and therefore more expensive—pilots, shifting flying to commuter affiliates and their regional jets (RJs) to save money.[1] Since their introduction in the early 1990s, RJs have grown in size, complexity, and performance capability, from about 40 seats to upward of 110 today, while increasing their flight range to 2,000 nautical miles. At this size and power, RJs now blur the boundaries between the narrow-body jets nearly all major airlines once flew like DC-9s with about a 100-seat capacity and 1,000 mile range and early 737 models with about 100 seats and a 1,800 mile range.

For years, strong labor unions like ALPA controlled this form of outsourcing through labor contract negotiations and side letters of agreement at the major air carriers. But after 9/11, with contracts voided by bank-ruptcy judges, airline management was empowered to negotiate freely, unions were rendered powerless to intervene, and regional airlines jumped at the chance to expand their service. This strategy proved to be especially profitable, increasing major airlines' virtual network while reducing their overhead costs. But what this means operationally, says ALPA vice president Paul Rice, was that major airline management could go out and solicit new regional partners and "start siphoning off the business to whoever will fly for cheaper." Unfortunately, he noted, "the American public is only just starting to wake up" to the fact that "what they are buying is the lowest-cost operation that's available," not the best or the safest.[2]

In 2010 Delta Air Lines, for instance, had nine commuter airline affiliates—Atlantic Southeast Airlines, Chautauqua, Comair, Compass Airlines, Freedom Airlines, Mesaba, Pinnacle, Shuttle America, and SkyWest—flying a variety of RJs under the Delta Connection name.[3] A Delta 737-300 requires 81 passengers to break even, but their commuter partner Comair only requires 21 on a regional jet on a similar route.[4] An average Delta pilot earns about $100,000 per year while a Comair pilot averages $36,000.[5] It's easy to see the economic advantages.

Passengers have also demonstrated a clear preference for jets rather than the noisy, vibrating turboprops the regional airlines once flew. And the European Aviation Safety Agency found good reason to avoid them. Their study of global aviation accidents between 1997 and 2006 determined that "on average, the fatal accident rate for turboprops was three times that for jets, based on flights flown, and nearly seven times greater when using hours flown as the rate measure."[6] The *Wall Street Journal* reported that one commuter carrier developed a passenger "turbo-prop avoidance factor," calculating ticket sales would increase by as much as 20 percent just by switching from turboprops to RJs on some routes.[7] One 2006 industry study estimated that RJs can accommodate "80–85% of passenger demand in the top US domestic markets," making it the air-plane of choice well into the future.[8] Why should we be concerned about such trends if they afford the flying public what it wants?

As exemplified by the crashes discussed in chapter 5, the furloughing of ex-perienced airline pilots by major airlines and outsourcing of flying to their regional partners, which employ cheaper, low-experience pilots, raises safety concerns in the present as well as for the future of air travel. Today, uncertain career prospects, the high cost of initial pilot training (about $60,000), low starting pay for their commercial pilots (about $20,000), and diminishing chances of these pilots ever flying one of the dwindling numbers of larger jets at a major carrier, make it increasingly difficult to attract top-notch civilian applicants to entry-level jobs. "The best and brightest" are not interested, as Captain Sullenberger forewarned.

Experienced military pilots are in short supply as well. Wars in Iraq and Afghanistan have shifted the battlefield, and military pilots are now as likely to fly an unmanned aerial vehicle (UAV), which is a remotely controlled aircraft, as a real airplane. The Air Force, for example, now has more than 1,300 UAV pilots stationed at thirteen bases across the United States, and by 2015 the Pentagon estimates it will need 2,000 more.[9] The Air Force already trains more UAV pilots—350 in 2011—than it does fighter and bomber pilots combined, and it is likely that within the next thirty years nearly all military flying will be done via remotely piloted aircraft. Initially, UAV pilots went through traditional flight training just like real pilots. However, now pilots are fast-tracked after only about forty hours of basic flight training in a small Cessna-type plane.[10] As a result, their military flying skills will likely not be as transferrable to commercial airline jobs as they were for previous generations of military pilots.

The military pilots who do have actual aircraft flight experience, formerly the backbone of commercial aviation, are increasingly staying in the armed forces as well. Attracted by big signing bonuses—for instance, I received a $72,000 bonus when I re-upped for eight years as a Naval Aviator after my initial commitment ended—and new generations of sophisticated aircraft, military pilots are at the same time put off by the airline industry's low entry salaries, uncertain career advancement, and the likely prospect of being furloughed. Because there are fewer experienced military pilots available to hire, ALPA emphasized, regional airlines lower their minimum employment criteria even further, often hiring pilots with minimal operational knowledge, skills, professionalism, and proficiency and only a few hundred flight hours that are accumulated in small, slow single-engine aircraft.[11]

ALPA noted with concern, "Today's archaic regulations allow airlines to hire low-experience pilots into the right seat of high-speed, complex, swept-wing jet aircraft in what amounts to on-the-job training with paying passengers on board." Unless significant changes are made in FAA regulations, ALPA concluded, "this trend of hiring pilots with less and less experience is expected to continue well into the future."[12] Such low-time copilots with experience accumulated in small aircraft via flight instruction, sightseeing tours, or banner tows not only represent a safety risk, they place an inordinate amount of pressure on the captain—who may not have a lot of experience either—to instruct and mentor while continuing to perform his or her own duties. Ironically, it's all perfectly legal by current FAA standards. This is yet another industry secret that airlines hope no one will alarm the passengers about.

To understand the depth of the problem, let's put these concerns about employee competency within the context of Boeing's prediction that the aviation industry will need to hire more than one million aviation workers worldwide over the next twenty years to cope with a wave of thirty thousand new aircraft deliveries. In particular, Boeing estimated, airlines will need to hire 466,650 pilots and 596,500 mechanics between 2010 and 2029—an average of 23,300 new pilots and 30,000 maintenance workers annually from now on.[13] The skill shortage is predicted to increase in the United States after 2012 when airline pilots allowed to delay mandatory retirement from age sixty to sixty-five in 2007 will once again hit the age limit and be forced to resign, opening about another 2,000 positions annually.[14] These data make it clear that airlines' fixation on short-term profits at the expense of safety will likely have dire consequences. Let me be even more specific.

In the decade following 9/11, there were fifteen fatal aviation accidents resulting in 430 deaths involving FAA Part 121 scheduled air carriers, the technical term for commercial airlines.[15] Not an extraordinary number. Yet after analyzing each accident, the NTSB, which is the independent federal agency charged by Congress to investigate accidents, identified an unusual pattern—a pattern that would not have emerged through applied probabilistic and statistical fatality modeling. In nearly every crash, the NTSB cited aspects of pilots' and/or mechanics' lack of professionalism and a failure to adhere to established procedures as factors. It criticized the FAA for lax oversight and inadequate regulations.

To consider the commonalities between these crashes and their implications for customer air safety, let us first eliminate cargo operations and ground-personnel mishaps that do not involve passengers. This leaves the seven fatal passenger airline accidents for consideration. Five of these

TABLE 2. Fatal commercial air carrier accidents in the United States, September 11, 2001, to September 11, 2013 (FAA Part 121 Commercial Air Carriers)

DateYear	Airline	Aircraft Type	Deaths	Description	Probable Cause	Other Contributing Causes
2001	American Airlines	Airbus A300-600 (jet)	265	Crashed after encountering wake turbulence on takeoff from JFK Airport, NY.	In-flight separation of vertical stabilizer as a result of first officer's unnecessary and excessive rudder pedal inputs	Characteristics of Airbus rudder system design and elements of American Airlines training
2003	Air Midwest (DBA US Airways Express)	Beech-craft 1900D (turboprop)	21	Crashed on takeoff at Charlotte-Douglas International Airport, NC.	Loss of pitch control during takeoff resulting from incorrect rigging of elevator control system compounded by center of gravity substantially aft of certified limits	Maintenance oversight, procedures and documentation FAA lack of oversight
2004	Pinnacle Airlines (DBA Northwest Airlink)	Bombardier CL-600-2B19 (RJ)	2	Crashed on ferry flight after both engines flamed out due to pilot-induced aerodynamic stall near Jefferson City, MO.	Pilots' unprofessional behavior, deviation from standard operating procedures, poor airmanship, and inadequate training	Engine design and aircraft flight manuals
2004	Corporate Airlines (DBA American Connection)	British Aerospace BAE-J3201 Jetstream (turboprop)	13	Crashed on approach to Kirksville Regional Airport, MO.	Pilots' failure to follow established procedures and protocols in the conduct of instrument approach	Pilots' unprofessional behavior and fatigue; FAA inadequate regulations
2005	Flying Boat, Inc., (DBA Chalk's Ocean Airways)	Grumman Turbo Mallard G-73T (turboprop)	20	Crashed following separation of right wing shortly after takeoff from Miami Seaplane Base, FL.	In-flight separation of right wing resulting from maintenance failure and FAA lack of oversight	None noted
2006	Comair	Bombardier CL-600-2B19 (RJ)	49	Crashed during takeoff from closed runway, Blue Grass Airport, KY.	Pilots' failure to follow established procedures and verify position on correct runway before takeoff	Pilots' nonpertinent conversation and loss of position awareness; FAA inadequate regulations
2009	Colgan Air, Inc., (DBA Continental Connection)	Bombardier DHC-8-400 (turboprop)	50	Crashed during instrument approach to landing at Buffalo–Niagara International Airport, NY.	Captain's inappropriate response to stick shaker leading to an aerodynamic stall and loss of control	Pilots' failure to monitor instruments and adhere to sterile cockpit procedures; captain's failure to effectively manage flight; Colgan Air's inadequate procedures

Source: Compiled by the author using NTSB accident reports.

accidents involved regional airlines doing business as another entity, an airline outsourcing strategy with new and as yet unidentified air safety risks that were nearly unheard of in aviation before 2001.

Colgan Air in 2009   Let us begin the analysis with the most recent fatal accident, Colgan Air Flight 3407 doing business as Continental Connection. This twin-engine turboprop airplane was on approach at night for landing at Buffalo-Niagara International Airport in icy weather when the captain allowed the plane's airspeed to become dangerously slow. This caused a warning device called a "stick shaker" to turn off the autopilot and vibrate the control yoke, indicating impending stall, as designed. Although the aircraft was in no imminent danger, the captain panicked. Distracted by the icing, startled by the warning, and confused by the autopilot, he lost control of the aircraft and crashed five miles from the destination, killing all forty-nine aboard and one person on the ground.[16]

The cockpit voice recorder revealed that both pilots were not properly monitoring the aircraft instruments but were instead distracted by nonessential communications on such subjects as commuting, applying to major airlines, and changing aircraft. Particularly distracting was a discussion about the implications of the copilot's annual gross salary of $15,800—several thousand dollars below industry standards and well below the US poverty line— and her eagerness to upgrade to captain to improve her quality of life.[17] This lack of situational awareness was compounded by fatigue: both pilots could be heard yawning repeatedly throughout the flight. To save money, they had both slept in the flight-crew lounge the night before the accident.

Although the forty-seven-year-old captain had two years of captain experience and over 3,000 logged flight hours, he only had 109 hours in the accident aircraft. He was hired in 2005 with only 618 hours, 250 of which were accumulated in a pay-for-training program at Gulfstream Training Academy in Florida. Aspiring pilots could enter Gulfstream's program with as little as 200 flight hours and no college degree and, for $32,699, would receive accelerated training as a regional airline copilot and then build flight time with the academy's affiliate airline, Gulfstream International. After completing the program, most pilots, like the accident captain, have accumulated enough flight time to land an entry-level job at one of the many US commuter carriers. These are airlines that, due to major air carrier outsourcing in the post-9/11 period, now fly over 50 percent of America's passengers.[18]

However, there are serious questions about the quality of this pilot preparation for the fast-paced, challenging environment that lies ahead for them. For instance, the accident captain's training records showed that although he successfully completed the Gulfstream program, he had several documented areas of difficulty with aircraft control. Prior to attending Gulfstream, he failed three FAA check rides, and then later, at Colgan, he failed to earn his Airline Transport Pilot Certificate—all of which required remedial training before he finally qualified.[19] Other pilots claim there is an unhealthy relationship between Gulfstream's training academy and its airline. Since it guarantees students first officer training for a hefty fee, there is a strong incentive for Gulfstream to just pass students along in order to collect their money. As one pilot explained, "Gulfstream is selling the [regional pilot] job. When you've got a guy fronting the cash, there's a lot of pressure on the company to keep him onboard no matter how bad [a pilot] he is."[20]

The twenty-four-year-old Colgan copilot had gone through a similar civilian training track. She'd been hired a year before the accident with about 1,600 flight hours accrued through two years of part-time flight training in Arizona. This may have been an adequate amount of flight time, but it was questionable preparation for airline operations during the winter months in the northeastern United States. By her own admission, "all of that [flight time] in Phoenix" was of little help in preparing her for a challenging airline career. "I had more actual [instrument flight] time on my first day" flying at Colgan Air "than I did in the sixteen hundred hours I had" logged before I was hired, she joked on the cockpit voice recorder just minutes before her death. Eager to make more money but clearly uneasy about the depth of her training and lack of operational experience, she shared, "I really wouldn't mind going through a winter in the Northeast before I have to upgrade to captain." And, in an eerie case of foreshadowing, minutes before the crash, she confessed, "Back in Phoenix, if I'd seen this much ice [I'd have] thought, 'Oh my gosh, we were going to crash.' . . . [I'd have] freaked out. . . . I've never seen icing conditions. I've never de-iced. . . . I've never experienced any of that."[21]

One has to wonder if any other post-9/11 aviation accidents had similar characteristics, namely, inexperienced pilots, new to their crew position, over their heads in a challenging environment made worse by weak basic skills provided through civilian pilot-training programs. Table 3 can help us analyze this question. But first we must eliminate Air Midwest Flight

TABLE 3. Pilot training and background in fatal US airline accidents due to pilot error, September 11, 2001, to September 11, 2013 (FAA Part 121 Commercial Air Carriers)

Accident Date	Flight Information	Personnel	Training Highlights	Date Hired	Approximate Time in Current Position	Total Flight Time	Time in Model
Nov. 12, 2001	American Airlines Flight 587	Captain, 42	Air Force	Jul. 1985	3 years, 3 months	8,050	1,723
		*First Officer, 34	Bolivar Flight Academy	Mar. 1991	3 years	7,623	1,835
Oct. 14, 2004	Pinnacle Airlines Flight 3701	Captain, 31	Embry-Riddle Aeronautical University, Gulfstream International Airlines	Feb. 2003	1 year, 7 months	6,900	973
		*First Officer, 23	Broward Community College, Gulfstream Training Academy, Gulfstream International Airlines	Apr. 2004	6 months	761	222
Oct. 19, 2004	Corporate Airlines Flight 5966	*Captain, 48	Unknown	Mar. 2001	1 year, 1 month	4,234	2,510
		First Officer, 29	Embry-Riddle Aeronautical University, Eastern Cincinnati Aviation	Jul. 2004	4 months	2,856	107
Aug. 27, 2006	Comair Flight 5191	Captain, 35	Comair Aviation Academy	Nov. 1999	2 years, 8 months	4,710	3,082
		*First Officer, 44	American Flyers, Gulfstream International Airlines	Mar. 2002	4 years, 6 months	6,564	3,564
Feb. 12, 2009	Colgan Air Flight 3407	*Captain, 47	Gulfstream Training Academy, Gulfstream International Airlines	Sep. 2005	2 months	3,997	111
		First Officer, 24	Sabena Airline Training Center	Jan. 2008	1 year, 1 month	3,714	774

Source: Compiled by the author using NTSB accident reports.

* Pilot flying at the time of the accident, if known.

5481 and Flying Boat Flight 101 from consideration. Both of these crashes involved mechanical failures that no pilot could have recovered from. Air Midwest suffered a loss of pitch control on takeoff due to incorrect installation by mechanics, and Flying Boat's right wing separated in flight due to faulty maintenance. Problems with aircraft maintenance have also become a major concern, a result of the same drastic cost-cutting and poor oversight practices. However, for now, I will focus on fatal post-9/11 accidents found to involve pilot error.

Table 3 shows the flight experience, training, and background information for the ten pilots involved in the five fatal passenger airline accidents involving pilot error in US commercial airlines in the decade following 9/11. The findings are revealing. All but one crash involved a regional air carrier, the area of the US airline industry that had expanded so quickly in the post-9/11 period due to major airline outsourcing. Fifty percent of these accident pilots had fewer than 1,000 hours of flight experience in the accident aircraft. Sixty percent had been in their flight-crew position for less than two years. And almost a third crashed within their first year on the job. Nearly all had been trained in civilian flight programs. Perhaps most alarming is that 50 percent of the accidents involved pilots who had received their basic training in accelerated professional pilot-training programs—an astonishing 40 percent of the accident pilots had a direct connection to Gulfstream—and all crashes had elements of lack of professionalism and/or lack of adherence to standard procedures as factors, just like the Colgan Air accident.

Comair in 2006 To break this down further, I will start with Comair Flight 5191, a regional jet that crashed on a dark early morning takeoff from Blue Grass Airport in Lexington, Kentucky, in 2006.[22] After lining up on the wrong runway, which the pilots noted was curiously unlit, the crew nonetheless attempted to take off, ran out of runway, and crashed. The aircraft was destroyed by impact forces and fire, killing forty-nine people on board. The first officer, the pilot flying at the time of the accident, was the sole survivor.

The captain graduated from a professional pilot-training program at Comair Aviation Academy in 1998 and then flight instructed at the academy until he was hired by Comair about a year later. The first officer initially trained at American Flyers flight school and then in 1997 was hired by Gulfstream International Airlines where he worked until he was hired by Comair in 2002. Both pilots had a significant amount of flight experience in their aircraft, had been employed at their company for several years, and had flown around the Lexington airport many times before. How is it they could have made such a basic—yet fatal—mistake?

Like the Colgan crash, it's hard to discern exactly what went wrong within the team dynamics of this crew on the day of the accident. The morning seemed to have gotten off to a bad start. The crew awoke at 4:15 a.m., checked in at the airport at 5:15 a.m., and proceeded to board the wrong airplane and begin their preflight. It wasn't until a ramp agent notified them that they were in the wrong jet that the pilots corrected themselves. Later, sometimes yawning as they ran through checklists, the crew made more mistakes, but they seemed to catch each other and rectify the problems. Unfortunately, when it came time to taxi they had run out of backup.

Throughout the morning the first officer seemed distracted and distracting, generating a stream of non–work related chatter. Like the Colgan copilot, he was concerned about making captain and discussed transferring domiciles in order to upgrade faster. He strategized about flying overseas as a way to log flight time as captain, called pilot-in-command or PIC time, so he could apply to a major air carrier. He debated the pros and cons of borrowing money from his father to pay for a 737-type rating, a requirement for employment at Southwest Airlines. Although the captain did not initiate these non–work related conversations, he did participate in the dialogue.

The NTSB found that as the crew taxied for takeoff this nonpertinent conversation was distracting them from their duties, which contributed to their loss of situational awareness and caused them to fail to cross-check their position to make sure they were on the correct runway before takeoff. Unlike the crew's previous mistakes, no one was there to correct them, and the sole air traffic controller on duty allowed them to take off from the shorter, closed runway without challenge. This error ultimately led to the crash and the death of forty-seven passengers. Like the Colgan Air accident, fatigue, finances, and substandard working conditions directly contributed to these deaths—distractions that are reported by pilots at most all airlines post-9/11.

Corporate Airlines in 2004   Another fatal accident occurred in 2004, this one involving Corporate Airlines Flight 5966 doing business as American

Connection.[23] This twin-engine turboprop descended below approach minimums on a cloudy, foggy evening, striking trees and then crash-landing short of the runway at Kirksville Regional Airport in Missouri. The captain, first officer, and eleven of the thirteen passengers were fatally injured; two passengers received serious injuries; and the plane was destroyed by postimpact fire.

Similar to the previous accidents discussed, Corporate Air pilots continuously produced a stream of distracting, non–work related white noise that made it difficult for them to concentrate on the deteriorating weather and challenging flight conditions. As they approached the airport in the clouds, task assignments broke down as both pilots searched for visual contact with the runway, violating standard operating procedures and federal aviation regulations that require the pilot at the controls to level off at a prescribed altitude and fly by reference to instruments until a safe landing is assured.

As with the Comair accident, the Corporate Air pilots' duty day began early, about 5 a.m. They were completing their sixth flight within almost fifteen hours of duty time when the accident occurred about 7:35 p.m.[24] The NTSB found the probable cause of the crash was the pilots' failure to follow established procedures and comply with regulations in the execution of their instrument approach. And, as with both the Colgan and Comair accidents, the NTSB also concluded that the pilots' unprofessional behavior and fatigue likely contributed to their degraded performance.

Pinnacle in 2004   Days before this Corporate Airlines accident, a third post-9/11 crash involving Gulfstream-trained pilots occurred, this time near Jefferson City, Missouri, when Pinnacle Airlines Flight 3701 crashed into a residential area.[25] In what seems to have become a not-so-surprising post-9/11 accident trend, Pinnacle Airlines was doing business as another airline, Northwest Airlink, and had ties to Colgan Air through their parent company. The crash occurred about 10 p.m. while the captain and first officer were repositioning their RJ from Arkansas to Minneapolis–St. Paul for the next day's flight schedule. Although they planned the flight for a lower altitude, the pilots intentionally climbed their jet to its maximum operating altitude of 41,000 feet, ostensibly to see how the aircraft would handle. Their bizarre decision did not go unnoticed by air traffic control, who radioed, "I've never seen you guys up at forty-one [thousand feet]."

The captain laughed, "We don't have any passengers on board so we decided to have a little fun."[26]

As the jet struggled to maintain its maximum certificated altitude, the aircraft repeatedly stalled, causing the pilots to laugh. One joked, "Dude, it's losing it," while the other went in back to retrieve sodas to drink from the galley. Although they recognized the deteriorating aircraft performance, neither pilot responded with urgency until airflow became so disrupted that both engines failed and the jet began a glider-like descent toward the ground. Both men died on impact, and the aircraft was destroyed. Similar to the previously discussed accidents, the NTSB found the probable cause of this crash was the "pilots' unprofessional behavior, deviation from standard operating procedures, and poor airmanship."[27]

These Pinnacle pilots' lack of professionalism, unabashed thrill seeking, juvenile effort to impress each other, and blatant disregard for safety prompted regulators to evaluate other aviation crashes. They found five troubling examples involving a similar "lack of cockpit discipline and adherence to standard operating procedures."[28] Yet, curiously, both the NTSB and FAA blamed the individual pilots for this immature behavior and made no recommendation to examine the aviation industry system, the recently introduced practice of outsourcing by major airlines, regulations governing training, company hiring practices, or organizational culture at airlines for clues to this unusual pattern. It would not be until four years later—prompted by pressure from irate family members after the Colgan Air crash in 2009—that government regulators finally began examining the wider industry.

American Airlines in 2001   The final airline crash under consideration here occurred just weeks after 9/11 in Queens, New York. American Airlines Flight 587 departed John F. Kennedy International Airport at 9:14 a.m. en route to the Dominican Republic.[29] The beautiful, clear fall morning was jarringly transformed when, less than two minutes after takeoff, the Airbus A300 encountered wake turbulence from a previously departing Boeing 747 and broke apart in flight. All two hundred and sixty people on board as well as five people on the ground were killed, making this accident the second-deadliest single aircraft crash on US soil to date.

Problems began a few minutes after liftoff. "Little wake turbulence, huh?"[30] the captain inquired nonchalantly to his copilot who was flying the airplane. However, moments later, the tone changed as the jet encountered a second pocket of disturbed air. Already in a moderately banked turn, the airliner rolled steeper causing the first officer to panic and overreact with increasingly aggressive flight control inputs, slamming the yoke from left to right while simultaneously jamming both rudder pedals to their limits. Unable to tolerate the resultant aerodynamic loads, the aircraft's tail snapped, causing the vertical stabilizer to detach from the airplane fuselage making the jet uncontrollable.

The NTSB determined that the probable cause of this accident was the first officer's unnecessary and excessive rudder pedal inputs, which produced aerodynamic loads beyond the aircraft's design.[31] Contributing to this crash were aspects of the American Airlines training program and characteristics of the Airbus rudder-control-system design. Unlike the four previously discussed crashes, this crash was more of an anomaly. These two pilots had thousands of hours of flight experience and years of employment history with their airline. Yet, similarly, the first officer had been trained through an accelerated civilian pilot program and failed to follow the airlines' established procedures for wake-turbulence recovery.[32]

Although each of these five cases—Colgan in 2009, Comair in 2006, Corporate and Pinnacle in 2004, and American in 2001—involved crews trained through civilian pilot-training programs, at first glance the details of their occurrence makes them seem distinctly different. One involved takeoff, two involved landing, and two involved en route operations. Two were regional jets, two were turboprops, and one was an Airbus jetliner. It is only after I evaluated the crashes together that a behavioral pattern emerged, a problem that would not have been identified using mathematical formulas or applied probabilistic and statistical modeling.

I found seven common elements. The first four involve intracrew or individual pilot characteristics: (1) lack of cockpit discipline, (2) poor understanding of aircraft systems and operating characteristics, (3) disregard for standard procedures, and (4) general devaluing of the seriousness and responsibilities of the piloting profession. In addition, there are three organizational factors: (5) questionable basic training, (6) airline crew scheduling leading to fatigue, and (7) an organizational culture devaluing air safety.

How could an organizational culture like this emerge, escalating risks and decreasing safety? One pilot I interviewed, Captain Jimmy, shared his regional airline experiences. Jimmy trained at Gulfstream Academy and returned to fly as captain for its commercial air carrier side after building experience at other commuter airlines. He recalled:

> I kept in touch with several of my friends at Gulfstream, and they were having a massive expansion up north back in early 2007. . . . I put my application in, and I got a call from the director of operations to come out and interview [at Gulfstream International Airlines]. I was offered a job after about a two-minute interview, and they hired me as an "off the street captain." . . . Gulfstream was just a different company when I went back. They'd changed ownership. . . . These guys who bought the company—I think they were a holding company out of New Jersey and they had never run an airline before. Of course, it was "Let's cut costs any possible way." . . . [But it was too much.] Guys were leaving left and right, saying they'd just sold their soul. . . . I found out real quickly what they were talking about. If you didn't violate an FAR [i.e., a federal aviation regulation] for them it was like you became a pariah immediately. And it wasn't just little things. I'd experienced that at the other carriers I'd flown with. . . . But with Gulfstream it was every day, all the time. . . . With my level of experience, I knew that if something didn't look good I'd just get the hell out of there. But I knew that they had a bunch of twenty-three-year-old hotshot captains that had never had any real-world experience. . . . It was an accident waiting to happen. I'd never seen anything like it before.

As one might hope, the pattern of commercial airline crashes that occurred in the post-9/11 period and the troubling trend of data previously discussed did finally raise warning flags with the FAA. In 2009, they launched an investigation into Gulfstream's operations.[33] FAA spokeswoman Laura Brown said the inquiry uncovered hundreds of instances in 2007 and 2008 in which Gulfstream violated federal aviation regulations. As a result, the FAA slapped Gulfstream with a $1.3 million fine—one of the largest ever levied against a regional airline.[34]

Yet Gulfstream, encouraged by the FAA's laissez-faire approach to regulation, was not going to give in easily. They claimed the alleged violations were simply paperwork errors and, while not conceding any guilt, eventually agreed to pay just $550,000—less than half the initial fine. The FAA accepted this concession calling it "fair and reasonable" because they said they found no evidence that Gulfstream's violations, although plentiful, were deliberate.[35] This has become a point of contention for regulators in both aviation and finance—must violations be deliberate and intentional in order to merit prosecution?

In addition to fighting the FAA, Gulfstream confronted its other critics as well. They argued that it was just coincidence that so many accidents involved graduates of their pilot-training academy. Captain James Bystrom, director of Gulfstream training, claimed it was unfair to blame accidents that occurred at other airlines on Gulfstream's training program. After all, he argued, Gulfstream graduates had successfully passed tests administered by FAA representatives and had subsequently completed training at their respective airlines.[36] Gulfstream's CEO David Hackett explained, "The analogy we like to use is: You're 25 years old; you had a car accident; who taught you to drive at 16?"[37]

Yet, this is precisely one of the glaring shortcomings of our current aviation system: airlines like Colgan, Comair, Corporate, Pinnacle, and American blame trainers like Gulfstream for providing pilots with poor basic skills; trainers like Gulfstream blame airlines, claiming they cannot be responsible for an individual pilot's professionalism or what their academy graduates might *eventually* do; and everyone hides behind FAA regulations, which are routinely criticized as being archaic and irrelevant in today's technologically advanced, high-tempo operational environment. This is another part of the secret the aviation industry would rather not alarm the passengers about.

Airline passengers should be concerned about this shifting-the-blame game by trainers, airlines, and regulators, and their corresponding lack of responsibility for pilots' skill deficiencies. As vice president of training at Airbus, Captain Larry Rockliff, observed, these examples of skill deficiency found in every post-9/11 US airline accident are particularly disconcerting at the commercial-pilot level because "once you're already in the profession and simply transferring or transitioning from one aircraft type to the next, it's very, very late to be teaching basic skills that were missed."[38] It is also extremely difficult to teach professionalism, critical thinking, and sound decision making in an organizational culture that does not value it. Where then are young pilots supposed to learn this type of basic skill?

The Colgan Air crash in 2009 so shocked the American public that Congress convened a hearing, and the FAA hosted regional meetings to investigate commuter airlines' safety standards. They subsequently issued a *Call to Action* report that identified ten FAA milestones.[39] Encouragingly, the FAA noted, the single defining theme that emerged after the Colgan Air accident was that "quality of training and quality of experience are far more important" than quantity of flight time "in determining an individual's readiness to operate in the air carrier environment." What seemed to be universally recognized was that "a generational 'paradigm shift' in the pilot population" at regional airlines had occurred involving "a fundamental shift in experience, expectations, and work practices," which required corresponding organizational changes in training, supervision, and managerial practices.[40]

Yet, there was no exploration into the root causes of this pilot population shift or the repercussions of this experience gap for air safety. Nor was there any consensus about what changes in training and work practices should take place at regional airlines. Concerned by this lack of critical evaluation, and the fact that the FAA met only one of its self-assigned Call to Action milestones, in 2010 the Department of Transportation's own inspector general, Calvin L. Scovel III, reported to Congress that "critical issues" that emerged as a result of the Colgan accident "remain unaddressed, such as potential correlations between aviation accidents and pilot experience and compensation."[41] He also observed that the FAA's "progress has been limited in implementing initiatives with the greatest potential to improve safety" because of a lack of understanding about air carrier programs, which leaves the FAA ill prepared to evaluate their effectiveness. In addition, Scovel noted, a lack of standardization, oversight, and guidance by FAA leaders has resulted in "remarkably varied regulatory approaches among [frontline] inspection staff, which could drastically affect the consistency of decision making processes" and enforcement actions at airlines.[42]

In closing, Scovel cautioned, the "FAA maintains that it ensures one level of safety for all air carriers—both regional and mainline. However, recent fatal accidents and the resulting scrutiny raise questions as to disparities in regional and mainline operations that could impact safety, particularly in terms of pilot training, fatigue, and professionalism."[43] These were interesting safety criticisms by a spokesperson from the very federal department tasked to provide a "safe" and "efficient" transportation system for the nation. And they weren't the last. In 2013, another DOT administrator, the assistant inspector general for aviation and special programs,

Jeffrey B. Guzzetti, voiced similar concerns to the US Senate about the FAA's lack of progress in addressing these important safety issues.[44] Meanwhile, FAA administrator Michael P. Huerta repeatedly told Congress, "Safety is FAA's number one mission. Nothing is more important. Our system has never been safer."[45] Once again, the American public is left wondering who to believe.

In 2013, the FAA finally instituted the regulatory changes that it had been considering since the Colgan crash four years earlier, that is, increasing the experience requirements of airline pilots. First officers, or copilots, are now required to hold an Airline Transport Pilot (ATP) certificate and aircraft-type rating, which means being at least twenty-three-years-old with 1,500 flight hours. Copilots with fewer than 1,500 flight hours may qualify for a new "restricted" (R-ATP) category if they are at least twenty-one and a military-trained pilot or have an aviation degree. Airline captains must also possess an ATP and type rating, as previously required, but must now have at least 1,000 flight hours in air carrier operations before taking command.[46]

This is all good news. However, during the course of its study, the FAA identified fifty-eight accidents resulting in ninety-nine fatalities and twenty-eight serious injuries between 2001 and 2010 that could have been prevented if these new standards had been in place earlier.[47] Is this a surprising number of accidents and fatalities? It shouldn't be. These crashes involved small air carriers and propeller airplanes, not jets, and therefore they do not figure in the statistical modeling programs of aviation quants.

One might wonder, if there are so many experienced airline pilots on furlough from the major air carriers, why is there a dearth of flight experience and professionalism at the regional pilot level? The answer to this question is covered in more detail in chapter 7. For now, let me simply say that the prospect of low pay, grueling flight schedules, and starting over at the bottom of a regional airline pilot seniority list, often flying as copilot for a young low-experience captain, makes most laid-off major airline pilots prefer unemployment. Randy, a furloughed copilot from a major airline, explained:

> The regionals were expanding and getting more and more RJs. So they were in need of a bigger hiring boom [in the post-9/11 period], whereas the majors were furloughing people. But not every guy working at the majors

would want to go back [to the farm leagues]. . . . Most of us that got furloughed just didn't want to start over [as copilots] in the right seat, commuting to another regional airline with no seniority, no pay, that kind of stuff.
Most of us have found either different careers or different options. . . . For
me, it didn't make any sense to go back to the regionals when I can take my
skills overseas and work as captain in different companies and command
better work rules and better pay than to sit in the right seat of a Brasilia [i.e.,
a small turboprop airplane] for twenty bucks an hour.

For other furloughed pilots, like Doug, it wasn't just poor pay, bad schedules, and low seniority; it was the lack of a "safety-first" culture that de-
terred them from working at a regional carrier:

> I flew at [regional airlines], and there's a different level of professionalism
> there. You're flying with a bunch of young kids. . . . There's just a differ-
> ence; there's more goofing off that goes on. . . . [For example,] I was based
> in Salt Lake City and the runways out there are super long, and while we're
> still rolling out after landing [the captain] would scoot up and grab his cell
> phone out of his pants pocket or out of his flight bag and turn it on and
> check messages as we were taxiing in. Now, he's taxiing, and he's got his
> phone next to his ear. I mean just crazy stuff.

In sum, the lack of professionalism and safety at the regional airlines
drives the more experienced commercial pilots away from flying for them.
Yet, even in 2014, there is little incentive for aviation industry change, in
part, because no regulatory agency is specifically tasked with monitoring
airline business practices. As long as air carriers seem to comply with federal aviation regulations, some of which are decades old, airlines are free to
operate as they like. Meanwhile, nearly all major airlines continue to shift
flying to their regional affiliates, which outsource to smaller subsidiaries
such as Colgan, Pinnacle, Corporate, and Comair, often unknown to their
passengers, who believe they purchased a ticket on a major air carrier.

In fact, the situation is even more insidious. In 2010, Colgan Air's parent
company, Pinnacle Airlines Corporation, provided regional airline service
to nearly all major US airlines doing business as Continental Connection,
Delta Connection, United Express, Northwest Airlink, and US Airways
Express, flying nearly 10 million passengers annually on 1,650 daily flights
to 182 destinations.[48] With only four hundred pilots, forty-eight turboprops, and a low cost overhead, airlines like Colgan can operate much

more cheaply than major air carriers—albeit with questionable safety, as Flight 3407 proved.

Was the crash of Colgan Air Flight 3407 an anomaly? The facts suggest otherwise. Colgan Air had been in trouble before. Inspired by the Southwest Airlines whistleblowers testimony to Congress, Colgan Air's FAA inspector also came forward, filing for whistleblower protection with the Office of Special Counsel. He described numerous safety violations at Colgan dating back to 2005—four years before the fatal crash—such as inadequate operational manuals, poor internal-evaluation programs, and insufficient managerial oversight of safety operations. Some of these safety concerns were also identified in Department of Defense audits of Colgan in 2005 and 2007. Particularly alarming, in light of these ongoing managerial problems and safety concerns, was that Colgan Air had doubled in size in just four years. Nonetheless, similar to what happened after other FAA employees made complaints, any effort to bring enforcement action against the growing airline met with resistance. When safety inspectors tried to intervene, they were told by FAA management that "[Colgan Air president] Mike Colgan is a friend of this office."[49] The obvious inference was to leave Colgan, and his airline, alone. Today, however, there is no need to worry about inadvertently winding up on a Colgan Air flight when buying a ticket on Delta, United, or US Airways. Just like accident-prone air carriers ValuJet and GP Express, both Colgan Air and Comair ceased operations after their fatal accidents.

Safety concerns about major airlines' outsourcing their mainline flying to low-cost regional partners in the post-9/11 period are still common within the aviation community. Pilots I interviewed overwhelmingly answered the survey question, "What is your biggest safety concern about airlines today?" with worries about outsourcing of major airline flying to regional operators and the inexperience of their crews (table 4).

What are the repercussions of all this? Will the United States soon see a major airline disaster? Nearly every pilot I interviewed agreed that it's likely. Ninety-six percent reported witnessing increased stress on the pilot workforce due to post-9/11 cost-cutting measures with 71 percent reporting this as a daily occurrence (fig. 6). Ninety-eight percent of pilots I interviewed witnessed mistakes or distractions on the flight deck as a result of airline cost cutting and work-rule changes, and 60 percent saw this on a daily or weekly basis (fig. 7).

TABLE 4. Typical pilot responses to interview question "What is your biggest safety concern about airlines today?"

- "Outsourcing to the lowest bidder that has the lowest wages and the least experienced pilots."

- "Young, inexperienced, poorly trained, low-paid pilots flying small jets under the mainline carrier's name, while mainline outsources the experienced pilots to the lowest bidder."

- "Inexperienced pilots at regional carriers."

- "Outsourcing to regional airlines with less-experienced pilots."

- "Professional attitude due to a lack of respect."

- "Matriculation of inexperienced pilots into Part 121 operations."

- "Inexperienced express pilots."

- "Outsourcing flying to other carriers with less-experienced pilots."

Source: Data compiled by author during study of US airline pilots.

Figure 6. US airline pilots' observation of increased stress. *Source*: "While flying at your airline, how often did you witness increased stress on the pilot workforce due to post-9/11 company cost cutting measures?" Author's survey data, no. 11.

Examples of repercussions from this post-9/11 stress and distraction are readily available throughout the aviation industry today. Take for instance the United and Delta jets, transporting a combined 300 passengers, that came within one hundred feet of colliding in Fort Lauderdale in 2007, or the Northwest Airline pilots who, out of radio contact for an hour, overflew their Minneapolis destination by 150 miles in 2009 with 147 passengers on board. After investigating the incident, the NTSB reported, "The

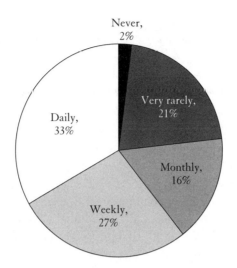

Figure 7. US airline pilots' observation of increased mistakes and/or distraction. *Source*: "How often did you witness mistakes and/or distractions on the flight deck because of post-9/11 cost cutting and work-rule changes?" Author's survey data, no. 13.

crew stated they were in a heated discussion over airline policy and they lost situational awareness."[50] That same week, a Delta Air Lines crew also lost situational awareness when they landed their 767 with 194 passengers on a taxiway at their hub airport, Atlanta-Hartsfield International, instead of their assigned runway.[51] Just months before these two incidents, Delta had acquired Northwest through merger. The deal nearly fell through when a standoff emerged between the two pilots' unions, each wanting greater seniority for their labor group.

In 2008, two fatigued GO! Airline pilots (a subsidiary of regional carrier Mesa Airlines) fell asleep during their fifty-minute midmorning flight from Honolulu to Hilo, Hawaii.[52] Out of radio contact for eighteen minutes, they flew twenty-six miles past their destination before they woke and returned to land uneventfully at Hilo. On the ground, the captain phoned FAA personnel and told them they must have lost communications by selecting the wrong radio frequency. Perhaps even more disconcerting than this blatant lie was that the pilots elected to fly back to Honolulu because they were now "feeling very alert as a result of the incident." After landing in Honolulu, they eventually confessed the truth and removed themselves from the flight schedule.[53]

That same year, United Airlines was forced to cancel a flight when the captain announced to passengers that he was "too upset to fly" after a dispute with another employee about wearing his hat. The pilots' union had urged pilots to remove their hats to protest a managerial decision to set aside $130 million in stock for an executive incentive plan while cutting routes, parking planes, and laying-off employees. The hat protest was a sign to show management that pilots were "serious about regaining what was stripped" from employees "during bankruptcy."[54]

In 2012, another flight was cancelled because of a stressed-out pilot. A JetBlue captain apparently suffered a mental breakdown in flight. Captain Clayton Osbon, a twelve-year veteran, was locked out of his cockpit and restrained by passengers while aloft between New York and Las Vegas after shouting about bombs, terrorists, September 11th, Al Qaeda, Iraq, and Iran. Several security officials on board, en route to a professional conference, helped restrain the captain. As one put it, "Clearly he had an emotional or mental type of breakdown."[55]

The FAA, JetBlue, and ALPA, the pilots' union, quickly moved to diminish the significance of the event, blaming the captain and calling it an extremely rare and unfortunate medical situation.[56] Friends of the pilot described him as friendly and even-keeled, and said they were shocked at how unusual this behavior was for this experienced aviator; one friend described it as "100 percent out of character."[57] Even JetBlue CEO David Barger defended Osbon as a "consummate professional," someone he has "personally known for a long period of time."[58] Yet, Captain Osbon was brought up on federal charges of interfering with a flight crew. In July 2012, a Texas judge found Captain Osbon not guilty by reason of insanity.[59] One has to wonder if this experienced pilot and consummate professional could snap in flight, who might be next?

Even seasoned pilots like Chesley Sullenberger and his crew were not immune to post-9/11 industry turmoil. In fact, they had discussed the implications of airline mergers and work-rule changes just minutes before their Hudson River landing. Noticing a Northwest jet taxiing behind them during engine start, First Officer Jeff Skiles commented, "[I] wonder how the Northwest and Delta pilots are getting on."

"I wonder about that too," Captain Sullenberger responded, "I have no idea—hopefully better than we and [America] West do."

"Be hard to do worse," Skiles quipped.

"Yeah. I can't imagine it'd be any better," Sullenberger replied.[60]

Although technically a violation of the FAA's sterile cockpit rules, these types of distractions are common on the flight deck of nearly every airline today as pilots struggle to cope with the drastic changes that have befallen their profession.

In addition to pilots, other less-visible sectors of the aviation industry have also been reporting problems. In 2012, an American Airlines flight attendant launched into a rant on the airplane's public-address system about 9/11 and airplane safety until she was wrestled into a seat and then later taken to the hospital. In 2010, an upset JetBlue flight attendant swore at a rude passenger, grabbed a beer, and slid down the emergency chute to the tarmac at JFK. And flight crews are not the only people tired and stressed; maintenance and ground crews experienced problems as well. In 2011, fatigue cracks were found in the fuselage of at least five 737s that had reportedly passed the required maintenance inspections. Some cracks emerged while airplanes were airborne. For example, a five-foot hole ripped open midflight on a Southwest jet revealing daylight and forcing an emergency landing in Yuma. This was not an anomaly; Southwest had a history of similar maintenance problems. In 2008, the FAA slapped them with a $10.2 million fine for failing to conduct the mandatory fuselage inspections.[61]

What is happening in the US airline industry? Are these just individual mistakes made by rogue employees who don't follow procedures and whose lives are filled with self-inflicted personal problems, as airlines and regulators would like us to believe—inconsequential events that we should forget about because we are, after all, statistically safe when on board airliners—or are these more signs of the fracturing of the US aviation safety system?

7

Airlines Today

In September 2010 I contacted people at my former employer, United Airlines, and inquired about posting a note on the labor union forum inviting pilots to complete an internet survey investigating aviation safety and airline working conditions in the post-9/11 period. One hundred twenty-seven captains and first officers from nearly every major US airline responded to my questionnaire. (See appendix B for survey questions.) Some were actively employed at their airline, while some had transferred to a new airline, many of them overseas. Others had taken voluntary leave or were on military duty. A large majority of the pilots were on furlough, airline parlance for laid off, awaiting recall to work. The last survey question asked if the respondent would be interested in participating in a follow-on telephone interview. Seventy-two pilots volunteered, and I completed forty-three interviews between September 2010 and July 2011. (See appendix C for interview questions.) Their observations and interpretations are provided in this book under first name pseudonyms.

Although pilots were candid in their answers and forthcoming with their responses, they uniformly reported that their profession was widely misunderstood by the general public and acknowledged that they rarely, if ever, spoke to outsiders. As Anthony, a furloughed first officer, put it:

> [I] only [talk] with fellow pilots who have been furloughed. You can't talk to anyone else unless it's another furloughed pilot. . . . No one else understands. They don't. They say things that are so stupid. . . . They don't have a clue. I don't ever discuss it with anybody other than a pilot or somebody who's in the know.

Greg, another furloughed first officer, voiced similar frustration about the general public's lack of awareness of their plight:

> With family, I can share stuff because they obviously have a little bit more understanding than most people. But if I'm in a social situation, I don't even tell people what I do. All it does is get you worked up when they make the comments that they do—"Oh, you were overpaid," "Oh, you get free travel," or "Oh, you get to stay at wonderful places"—and it's very tough to deal with. . . . Very few people out there have any clue what has gone on [in the airline industry since 9/11].

So what is it that the general public does not understand? Before I share more of my pilot interview responses, it is worth separating fact from fiction about an airline pilot's life. Hollywood typically portrays airline pilots in one of three stereotypes: the nomadic playboy like Leonardo DiCaprio in *Catch Me if You Can*, the weathered stalwart like Sam Elliott in *Up in the Air*, or the selfless hero like John Wayne in *The High and the Mighty*. Airline uniforms have helped perpetuate this image with pilots in crisply pressed military-style jackets and hats surrounded by sexy young flight attendants wearing fashion-forward outfits by modern designers, particularly at style-conscious airlines like Braniff and Southwest in the 1970s. Airlines actively tried to promote this image with advertising slogans like Braniff's "When you've got it, flaunt it," Southwest's "Long legs and short nights," or National Airlines' "Fly me!" Although less prevalent in airline advertisements today, these images have nonetheless endured over time creating a romantic mystique around airline employment that, in most cases, is not grounded in reality.

To understand the real life of an airline employee, especially a pilot, one must first understand the airline seniority system. When a worker is hired by an air carrier, he or she is assigned a seniority number on the first day of work. In short, this seniority number becomes the most important indicator of quality of life for the rest of that employee's career, particularly for pilots. It is both a gift and a curse. For instance, it is in order of seniority that schedules are assigned, vacations awarded, and equipment bid. If furloughs are required, layoffs and recalls are done in seniority order as well. Because of the seniority system, if an employee is furloughed, there is a big incentive to wait for recall, even if it takes years, rather than start over at the bottom of another airline's seniority list.

In addition, the more years of service, the higher the employees' pay level. Unlike airline managers who may job hop every few years, when frontline employees join an airline they are expected to stay there for their entire thirty-or-forty-year career. Although flight attendants and mechanics may work on a variety of aircraft, pilots typically fly just one type at a time, such as a Boeing 737 or Airbus A320; the larger the airplane, the higher the pilot pay rate usually is.

In sum, being a junior employee on an airline seniority list is not a very good place to be in terms of quality of life. However, new employees recognize that everyone must pay their dues and that they will become more senior over time with quality of life improving accordingly. How quickly these changes occur has to do with two simple factors: the rate at which an airline hires new people and the number of senior employees retiring. This fact of life has been particularly frustrating for airline employees in the post-9/11 period as few new workers have been hired while airlines downsized. At most major airlines, the most junior employees have eight to ten years of tenure with their company—a significant amount. Yet, they are still working the most basic of entry-level schedules. In addition, post-9/11 airline restructuring has forced many senior employees to delay retirement plans because of financial shortcomings.

Jasper, a senior captain, talked about how his airline's bankruptcy and subsequent pension plan default affected his retirement plans:

> I'm one of those [pilots] that was definitely affected by [my airline's pension plan default]. I was counting on a halfway decent retirement had not [my airline] gone through bankruptcy and gutted our retirement. My retirement pay went from—I would have gotten—$6,000 a month, and now I'll get $2,200. One a livable pension, the other not so much. . . . I've changed all my retirement plans.

To help offset this disparity and catch up with international regulations, the FAA changed the mandatory retirement age for airline pilots from sixty to sixty-five in 2007.[1] Those who do risky work such as police officers, firefighters, air traffic controllers, and pilots continue to have enforced mandatory retirement ages that may seem premature compared with other professions. For those who work in jobs such as these, employers can adopt lower retirement age requirements if they can show it supports legitimate aims like public safety.

When the FAA instituted the new regulations, senior captains like Jasper benefited. However, for most airline employees, it was bittersweet. Many senior pilots would have preferred to retire at sixty but now felt driven to continue working by an uncertain future and the loss of their pension plan funds. Jasper explained:

> I'm very grateful to have the opportunity to work for an extra few years, I'm grateful to be able to supplement my retirement so I can at least have some sort of dignified retirement. . . . There's a lot of resentment—I see it around me—a lot of people talking about the "over-age-sixty guys" who are still flying. But people don't realize sometimes what forced them to do that. Nobody wanted it; nobody planned on it or wanted to work after age sixty.

Although Captain Jasper's plight warrants sympathy given the risks of today's new economy, he is right to sense resentment. For junior pilots, the age change was particularly problematic because it either slowed their career progression into the better-paid captain seat or prolonged their furlough. They argued that the retirement of just one senior captain, like Jasper, creates over a dozen job opportunities for other pilots. For example, if a 747 captain retires, that opening allows a 777 captain to move up to take his seat, a 767 captain to move to the 777, a 737 captain to move to the 767, a 777 first officer to now bid 737 captain, and so on down the seniority list until a furloughed pilot is recalled to work.

Captain Henry is a former US military pilot and major airline captain. After 9/11 and his airline's drastic downsizing, he wound up back in the copilot seat. Frustrated by this experience, Henry left the United States to work for an Asian airline and now flies as captain again. Henry is not alone in making this choice; several pilots I interviewed sold their airline skills overseas, often making more money with better benefits working for healthier companies. Just as Silicon Valley imports Indian computer engineers, so has the United States been exporting some of its most valuable aviation professionals over the last decade, particularly to Asian and Middle Eastern air carriers. For instance, Captain Murray flew for twice-bankrupt US Airways and chose to retire early because he was apprehensive, like Captain Henry, about his air carrier's uncertain future. Today Murray and his family live in Dubai, and he flies around the world for Emirates. He says safety standards are high at Emirates and pilots are "treated with respect in this part of the world." "Captains are treated as vice presidents of the organization," Murray said.[2] Few US-based pilots I interviewed reported this experience in the post-9/11 period.

Similarly, Captain William doubled his pay by moving to Taiwan to fly for EVA Air and then transferred to a Korean air carrier. "It was the smartest thing I've ever done," he said. And it's not just US captains who are emigrating; US copilots are in international demand as well. After Andrew was furloughed from Northwest Airlines he moved to Hawaii and now flies as a first officer for a Japanese airline. "A lot of my [laid-off] friends are sitting at home or working for Home Depot," waiting to be recalled by their US airline, he said. "I'm glad to have this job." ALPA president Duane Woerth is apparently optimistic about the long-term international opportunities for US pilots: "This one looks like a permanent structural shift," he observed. Some industry analysts claim this is only the beginning of the diaspora, estimating China alone will need more than 35,000 new pilots over the next twenty years.[3]

Captain Henry explained his decision-making process to leave the United States:

> One of the reasons that I decided to [go to Asia] was because I didn't like the way things were going. I didn't have confidence that the airline was going to survive. Based on the things they were doing and the people who were running the place, it looked to me like [my US airline] was in a death spiral.

Henry also said that increasing the retirement age to sixty-five directly contributed to his demotion and the plight of so many other pilots:

> I was very strongly against [the age change]. I think there are a lot of pilots furloughed right now who wouldn't be furloughed except for the fact that

there are guys who are sticking around longer. The guys that are over sixty now, flying until sixty-five, are guys that for their entire career had been able to take advantage of . . . retiring at sixty for their job security and their advancement. And then all of a sudden there's a five-year delay for everybody else to advance.

This five-year delay, combined with the years that thousands of furloughed pilots have spent "on the street" awaiting recall, puts them way behind in their career advancement.

Greg, another very experienced yet furloughed pilot, was upset about the age change as well. Although the change was prompted by regulatory changes outside employees' sphere of control, he felt it nonetheless divided the pilot group into subfactions:

> I'm not happy with [the age change]. I wouldn't be furloughed right now, so no I think it was a bad decision. I think it was a greed issue. These guys were pissed off that they lost their retirement and they wanted the age changed to sixty-five so they can continue to work. . . . It definitely pitted one group against another. . . . It's painful for everybody. It's painful for us because we got laid off again. But it's just as painful for those that are still there that didn't get their upgrade. So now they have to sit in the left seat of an Airbus instead of going to the 757. So it's painful for a lot of people to advantage just a small group.

Although both sides articulated their concerns clearly—senior captains like Jasper want the chance for a dignified retirement, and junior pilots like Henry and Greg resent becoming the victims of regulatory gamesmanship— what often gets missed is how this situation was exacerbated by airline executives' fiscal mismanagement and air carrier bankruptcy. Instead, younger pilots are pitted against older pilots in an unwinnable war over resources made scarce by short-term managerial thinking and ineffective leadership.

In addition to policy changes such as the retirement age change, which led pilots to fight among themselves, many pilots mentioned how airline management seemed to strategize ways to keep labor groups fighting one another other, increasing employee discord in ways that were not present prior to 2001. For example, Greg, noted:

> The company did their best to make sure all employee groups were pitted against each other. That was a noticeable change [after 9/11]. They always

blamed one group or another, always trying to get one group pitted against the other, and it was noticeable when I returned [from my first furlough] in 2003.

Captain Gilles, another senior pilot, agreed:

> One thing that's constant at [my airline] is they've tried to divide the employee groups and always keep one group against the other. Whether it was the mechanics and pilots, or flight attendants, they'd always stir up animosity among them so that they couldn't coalesce and form coalitions and be supportive. So [managers] always tried to sow dissent and just breed mistrust and bad blood between the groups as a tool.

Although it would seem logical for workers to band together, Henry recalled how difficult it was to accomplish this as the mood of employees declined in response to management's divide-and-conquer strategy:

> All the employee groups—flight attendants got a little more surly over time, gate agents.... [Airlines] encouraged the groups to go against each other.... Everyone has similar problems. Everyone was working with less: people doing the same job, working harder for less money, and nobody was happy.

As Henry points out, money is often the source of friction between airline employee groups, and each union often believes that it has given up more than the others during difficult times like the post-9/11 period.

To more fully understand how creating organizational discord can be helpful as a management tool for airline executives, yet disastrous for employees and air safety, it is important to understand airline labor unions. Most airline employees, but not all, belong to a labor union that represents their particular professional group. Pilots, flight attendants, and mechanics, for example, typically have different union representation. This differentiation can be a double-edged sword. It can be good because each union understands the needs, desires, and demographics of its particular professional group and can better negotiate compensation and work rules on their behalf. However, as noted, many airline executives have become adept at playing one group against the other. Unions can band together, like employees at Eastern Airlines did when they resisted Lorenzo's tactics in 1989, or unions can undermine others' power and job action strategies by not supporting them.

One post-9/11 example of the success of airline management's divide-and-conquer strategy is the mechanics strike at Northwest Airlines in 2005. Almost 4,500 members of the Aircraft Mechanics Fraternal Association, which represents mechanics, cleaners, and other employees, walked off the job to protest the company's request for $176 million in wage-and-benefit cuts, their share of the $1.1 billion in concessions Northwest management demanded from employees.[4] Although strikes like this are not unusual at airlines—in fact, prior to deregulation, only 1968 went without a strike—what happened next was surprising.

Like President Reagan's tactics with striking air traffic controllers in 1981, airline managers immediately threatened striking workers with replacement, a threat they were prepared to back up. Over the previous year, Northwest had spent more than $100 million to hire and train 1,500 substitute mechanics, as well as 1,100 flight attendants, just in case there was a sympathy strike.[5] But something didn't add up: the $100 million that airline managers spent preparing for the strike was nearly as much as the $176 million they were demanding in concessions from employees. Similar to Frank Lorenzo at Eastern, it seems something more personal than money was at stake, and like Continental's strike in 1983, many Northwest employees crossed the picket line and went to work.

Why didn't a sympathy strike among other employees emerge at Northwest to support the mechanics? First Officer Hal Myers, a committee chairman for the Northwest pilots' union, explained that, ironically, it was for "strength in unity" reasons.

> Crossing another union's picket line is obviously distasteful to us. But we've been trying for two years to get the other Northwest unions to join with us in creating a solution to Northwest's cost problems. If we had joined in a sympathy strike, Northwest management very likely would have grounded operations and filed for Chapter 11 immediately. And we still think that, if we can get through these tough times, Northwest can avoid Chapter 11.[6]

Even though pilots and flight attendants did not strike because they wanted to prevent the airline from going bankrupt, Northwest executives filed Chapter 11 bankruptcy proceedings within weeks anyway. Other employee behaviors also undermined the mechanics' job action, such as when baggage handlers and customer service agents pitched in to cover some strikers' duties including cleaning aircraft between flights. And in Detroit, a 757 captain even hopped into a pickup truck and went to the hangar himself to fetch his plane rather than waiting for mechanics to bring it up to the gate.[7] Although these may seem like small, inconsequential gestures, in the broader scheme, these picket line crossings by fellow employees undermined other employees' unions, which reduced their collective industry influence. And this is exactly what airline managers hope for. A lack of solidarity across labor groups is not unprecedented, but the extent to which it occurred at Northwest in 2005 was an extreme example of the shift in ethos in the post-9/11 airline industry.

Several other factors contributed to weaken Northwest strikers' bargaining position as well. For example, due to post-9/11 layoffs at other airlines, there was a ready supply of experienced aircraft mechanics who were desperate for aviation jobs and willing to cross the picket line. This made it easy for Northwest executives to find replacement workers. In addition, the federal government was behind Northwest management from the start. President George W. Bush was prepared to step in, like President Reagan had done, and order striking employees back to work as permitted in the Railway Labor Act. In addition, although striking mechanics complained about safety and shoddy workmanship, the FAA saw no problem in authorizing aircraft maintenance by replacement workers.[8]

Critics at the time claimed these were signs that, like Lorenzo at Continental, executives at Northwest intended to provoke a strike all along so they could file for bankruptcy, outsource maintenance, and restructure the company with lower-paid replacement workers. And, it turns out, they were right. Just like United and US Airways before them, Northwest executives were "right sizing" the airline for merger. Following this now-common managerial script, executives used the bankruptcy process to reorganize the airline, slash costs, dump unwanted routes, and retire planes, while paying themselves handsomely. And then the company rose from the ashes two years later.

It's clear that there are big financial incentives for airline executives during both bankruptcy and merger, and these same CEOs often leave the airline business shortly after these occur. Northwest executives were no different. Doug Steenland, a lawyer by training, became Northwest's CEO in 2004, just in time for the strike and bankruptcy; he then departed in 2008 with over $18 million in compensation after Northwest merged with Delta. Now he works as an executive in the food-service industry.[9]

Richard Anderson, another lawyer by training, became CEO of the resultant Delta-Northwest combined airline and made about $17.4 million in compensation that year for landing the deal.[10] Although the airline's stock price has since declined by more than a third, Anderson nevertheless gave himself a pay raise in 2011 and took home $8.9 million.[11] Anderson has more aviation industry experience than most airline CEOs today, having cut his teeth at Continental as part of the legal staff that investigated the wintery crash of Continental Flight 1713 in Denver discussed in chapter 5. He joined Northwest shortly thereafter at the invitation of then-CEO John Dasburg. When Dasburg left the airline business in 2001 to run Burger King, Anderson stepped in to replace him.

Like Steenland, Dasburg, and many other airline CEOs, just three years later Anderson moved on to his next career opportunity and a correspondingly huge compensation package. He joined Minneapolis-based health insurer United Health Group for a few years until he was wooed away to lead the Delta-Northwest merger. Although some of Anderson's past employees, like Dave Stevens, head of the Northwest pilots' union, concede that Anderson has some "excellent operating experience" on his résumé, most remain wary because Anderson "doesn't always show his true agenda." And perhaps most important for this discussion, Stevens warned, "If the Delta employees think that they will be his first priority, they are mistaken."[12]

Like most executives in the era following deregulation of the airlines, United Airlines' CEO Glenn Tilton was not an aviation industry insider. He was an oil industry executive at Texaco with no prior airline experience before he took United's helm in 2002. Only three months later, United declared bankruptcy and remained in Chapter 11 for a record 1,150 days. It was a lucrative strategy for Tilton and his management team.[13] When United emerged from bankruptcy, executives had agreed to deal four hundred managers in for 8 percent of the total company, worth an estimated $115 million on top of their annual salaries. Tilton received a total compensation package of $23.8 million for 2006 alone.[14]

Although United employees were understandably irate about these managerial payouts, given the extent of their own personal sacrifices during bankruptcy, Tilton's tenure did not begin antagonistically. On the contrary, pilots I interviewed, like Captain Jasper, recalled a general feeling of optimism among employees when Tilton arrived. After the challenges of 9/11, Jasper thought that United employees were hopeful that a positive change might be forthcoming at their airline:

> I met Glenn Tilton on his first day. . . . He waded right though all the reporters, answered a bunch of questions, and really came across that first day pretty well. [We thought] here was a guy that "god, maybe we finally got a leader again." And as it turned out he was more of the same—just there to line his own pockets—very disappointing.

United spokesperson Jean Medina defended the airline's postbankruptcy managerial compensation scheme as "appropriate to enable United to attract and retain top performers. It's in everyone's interest for management to have this component of management compensation tied to future performance of United's stock price."[15] However, ironically, United's stock has declined steadily, down almost 60 percent in 2012 from its peak. Other industry analysts were not convinced by United's retention-of-top-performers argument either. Executive pay expert Brain Foley noted that "the basic concern here is that the players don't seem to discipline themselves as much as they should," "external forces aren't executing any braking power," and bankruptcy "courts don't seem to hold people as accountable as they should."[16]

When questioned about airline executives' frequent recourse to the bankruptcy courts, Tilton defended this strategy: "So long as we have to fall under the scope of the Railway Labor Act of 1926," he said, "Chapter 11 is the only way to gain leverage with the unions."[17] By this statement, he presumably means CEOs are bound by the federal government to recognize employees' collective bargaining rights and negotiate fairly with labor unions, which is the stated purpose of the act. However unsettling negotiating with employees might have been for Tilton, he did not apparently mind authorizing over $200 million for legal advice and consulting fees while in bankruptcy and $20 million developing an employee-training program called Business Education Training (BET).[18]

Several United pilots I interviewed said that it was actually not airline bankruptcy, pay cuts, or employee furloughs that was most unsettling to them. It was managerial strategies like BET, which was undertaken after downsizing to indoctrinate the surviving employees into the new post-9/11 organizational culture, that troubled them the most. As one pilot described

BET, about a hundred employees assembled to play a board game designed to expose workers to various business scenarios. Another called it a "Business 101 briefing for kindergartners." A third described the goal as convincing workers how hard managerial decisions had been during bankruptcy:

> You rolled the dice and moved forward and you'd land on a space, like a Monopoly game, and it would say "Fuel prices have spiked up $5 a barrel. Do you want to: (a) park some of your airplanes; (b)"—and then you'd have to make choices. Based on the choice, you'd lose money or make money.

Besides being offended that they were required to attend this training unpaid on their day off and "embarrassed" to be playing "a stupid board game," many employees resented feeling forced to drink the company "Kool-Aid." Several were appalled that United spent millions of dollars developing the training while simultaneously furloughing employees and cutting workers' wages and benefits.

Many people reported "riots breaking out" and "security" being called because employees became so enraged. One pilot observed that managers had "grossly miscalculated the depth of pilot anger and hostility." Another reported that all the experience accomplished "was to highlight just how out of touch our management team was. If they couldn't gauge morale within their own employee group, how could we then have any confidence in their decision making as it related to a complex business?" A third recalled people crying, they were so humiliated: "Here was a company who had clearly broken employee spirit and morale" and "now they had the audacity to talk about things like quality and working together as a team. What a two-faced joke!" It seems everyone from high-priced consultants and trainers to airline managers and lawyers made out during United's three years in bankruptcy—everyone except for United employees that is. This trend has continued ever since. Tilton earned $10.3 million in 2007, $3.9 million in 2008, and $3.9 million in 2009.[19] During the same period, United began to recall its nearly two thousand furloughed pilots, some of whom had not worked in years. However, by 2009, most of these same pilots were back on the street again, laid off for a second time as United parked one hundred of its 737s.

Continuing to tick the boxes on his post-9/11 to-do list, Tilton now set his sights on merger. He entered discussions with Delta, Northwest, and US Airways, all of which cost millions in associated fees, before settling with Continental in 2010, allowing him to safely exit with his golden parachute. Where is Tilton employed now? You guessed it: just four years after his hefty "retention pay bonus," he left the airline industry and headed for Wall Street. He is now working for JP Morgan Chase.[20]

Most pilots were not surprised by Tilton's departure from aviation. Many, like José, a furloughed United first officer, thought that Tilton lacked any sense of commitment to aviation as a unique service industry and was just there for the money:

> I don't think Tilton was ever motivated to run an airline. I think he was brought on to either merge or split the company up. And he was never really interested in running an airline company.

Similarly, Captain Gilles emphasized the disjoint between airline executives, like Tilton, with their quick payout decision-making orientation and employees' long-term commitment to one airline. It is a relationship fraught with tension:

> I'm disgusted by Tilton. He's what you'd expect; he's a self-serving businessman. . . . He has no leadership skills whatsoever—one hundred percent self-serving. Most of us believe honestly that if he could make an extra nickel through liquidation, he would just pull the trigger and liquidate: "It's just business, don't blame me. Thanks for your thirty or forty years. You'll probably find another job, but if you don't, too bad."

Gilles comments about Tilton's self-serving nature and insulated attitude exemplifies the anger and disappointment so many airline employees feel about managerial downsizing and cost cutting in the post-9/11 period. Although most pilots concede that cutbacks were required after 2001, it was the manner in which they were accomplished that has been so disturbing to them. The ramifications continue to be felt throughout the US airline industry. But the most important consequence to emphasize is how this widespread employee dissatisfaction is creating a toxic culture that increases risk and negatively affects air safety.

Although Tilton may have left United Airlines, his legacy and the impact of his managerial strategies will remain embedded within United's culture and its employees' memories for a long time. Unfortunately, Tilton's legacy will be more akin to Frank Lorenzo's than Pat Patterson's. His employees uniformly reported increased stress, distraction, and suspicion with a corresponding reduction in trust, morale, and organizational commitment under his tenure.[21] These findings should raise concerns about air safety at United as well as other US air carriers, since they are dealing with the same self-inflicted wounds brought on by bankruptcy, downsizing, and merger. Although executives have departed unscathed, employees have not.

Pilots described feeling "constant turmoil" at work, observing that employees were "unhappy," "beat down," and pushed to the "breaking point." As a result, there was a "mood change" between employees and airline managers after 9/11 with management becoming "more of a big brother" looking over workers' shoulders. Respondents felt this surveillance was "almost punitive and pervaded the whole environment," which "made people even more angry," "stressed," and "distracted."

When asked about the roots of this organizational discord, Anthony provided a common pilot response:

> I blame management, bad management, greedy management. . . . Rather than looking at what's going to make this a great company in the long run, they say what's going to make us a buck today? . . . [We] get one CEO after another. . . . They want to outsource everything. They want to outsource the flying. They want to outsource the maintenance. . . . All they would like to do is to sell a ticket and make a dollar. If they had no pilots, no flight attendants, no airplanes, they would be happy [because] they don't really want to be an airline.

It was not always like this at US air carriers. Kevin, a military reserve pilot and airline first officer, grew up in an aviation family. Like me, he was airborne on 9/11 and diverted to a small Midwest city when the air traffic control system shut down. After over a decade in commercial aviation, he had some insightful comparisons to make about the post-9/11 culture:

> When I was first [hired in 1997] I didn't feel like I was at odds with management. I knew there was a labor-versus-management perspective, but there

always appeared to be an ability to work that out. In the last decade, that doesn't seem to be the case. . . . [Airline executives] are just ruthless. They don't care about their employees. They are sold out to a buck. It has become a me-versus-you industry.

Other pilots voiced a similar sense of disillusionment about the weak leadership skills and pervasive greed of airline managers who have no regard for the long-term ramifications of their decisions for employees or air safety. For example, Greg observed:

I blame corporate greed, and I blame people that run [my airline]. They don't care about the employees; they don't care about people. When I got hired at [my airline in 2000] we had over one hundred thousand employees, and I think today there are around sixty thousand. . . . Meanwhile, the executives that run this company were paid lavishly for doing that, for when they took the company to bankruptcy, and it's just ridiculous. It's very upsetting.

Tom, a furloughed first officer, believed it was not just executives and managers who are self-indulgent. He blames labor union leadership for selling out the junior employees or "eating their young" for money, a common perspective among the younger generation:

I don't have faith in anybody. Nobody's looking out for my interests . . . it is all about collective greed and selfishness. . . . The one word I would use is "cannibalistic"—those in charge really want to hold on to what they have, so they can get what they can for themselves and their contemporaries, at the expense of the junior members. . . . A lot of guys rail on the company about everything, but that's what they're there to do—make money. I have a bigger problem with the way the union has handled things because they are the ones that are supposed to be on our side.

In addition, several pilots voiced concern that pilot unions such as ALPA often represented both major airline and regional airline pilots in negotiations, resulting in a troubling conflict of interest that leaves both pilot groups vulnerable.

As a result of this sense that both managers and union leaders do not care about the long-term health and success of employees or the airline, only 3 percent of pilots surveyed thought that decision makers at their

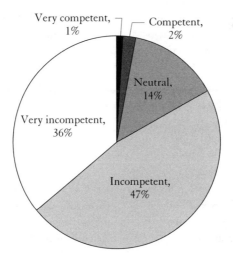

Figure 8. US airline pilots' rating of airline leaders. *Source*: "How competent are decision makers at leading your airline?" Author's survey data, no. 14.

airlines were competent (fig. 8). Aaron, a furloughed pilot, articulated the diminished trust that many pilots felt: "The company's burned us twice, and I think collectively that the union has burned us to a point too. We just don't want to subject ourselves to that again." Doug, another furloughed pilot, was even more blunt: "I just don't trust those executives."

The same could be said for industry regulators. Only 5 percent of pilots surveyed thought that regulators are competent at supervising safety in the US commercial airline industry. Similarly, nearly every pilot interviewed described how out of touch the FAA is in dealing with real industry operations. For example, Doug emphasized the FAA's dual mandate as a fundamental flaw:

> It's that classic "the mission of the FAA is to both promote and enforce." The same organizations can't do it. It's too intertwined. You can't have the same agency promoting and policing. It just doesn't work.

José supported Doug's observation and emphasized that what the US airline industry needs is an agency whose sole mandate is regulating flight safety:

> I don't think the FAA can handle it. They want to promote the industry, to make sure the industry grows, but if they shut down every airline for things

that they see going wrong they're not really promoting that industry. . . . You need to separate the two—someone that regulates the industry and someone that regulates just safety. It's a conflict of interest from the get-go.

In addition, Jason observed how political the aviation safety issue has become in Washington, where lobbying and a cost-benefit approach continues to dominate:

[Regulators] are so beholden to the political machine that they will do whatever it takes to either be reelected themselves or to maintain their good standing with whatever political action group is funding them. There's too many outside influences, especially in Washington, DC, that they're unable to effectively perform their jobs with an eye towards safety like they should. It becomes more about the almighty dollar than it does about the safety bottom line.

And Henry similarly emphasized how regulators are reluctant to be proactive about investigating safety concerns:

The only time that [regulators] really get involved is (a) there's an accident that crashes a plane, injures or kills a lot of people, or (b) a whistleblower comes out and says this has been going on and nobody's doing anything about it. Those are the only two times that the safety people, the regulators, get involved. So, no, I don't have a whole lot of faith in them.

The combination of ineffective government regulators, self-serving airline executives, and weak union leadership led several pilots to identity the post-9/11 culture as a "toxic" environment that made it a very difficult place in which to work.[22] As Henry described it:

Before 9/11 . . . quality of life was very good. I enjoyed the people I was working with. Going flying was a good thing. . . . Immediately after 9/11, things were dramatically different. . . . Going to work was becoming a drag. It was [caused by] really, really bad management and really poor decisions by senior management. . . . Everybody from gate agents, flight attendants, mechanics, ramp guys, and the other pilots, of course. Nobody was happy. . . . It became a really unpleasant environment to be in.

Jason, who flew as a regional airline captain for ten years, resigned to accept employment at a major airline and was furloughed shortly thereafter.

Unable to fly in the majors or go back to his previous employer, he was stuck in limbo. Although upset about this experience, Jason confessed, after being in the majors for six months, "it was almost a relief to find out I was getting furloughed because then I wouldn't have to deal with that poisonous atmosphere anymore." Similarly, Greg noted how a toxic culture was driving good airline employees to other job opportunities: "I think the realization is—at least for those of us still at [my airline]— if we get hired [somewhere else] we're probably not going to leave that company to go back. . . . I've never worked in such a toxic environment."

This is a radical change in employee opinions in the decade since 9/11. Prior to 9/11, many pilots dreamed of working for a major airline. Karen explained, "I knew this was what I wanted to do from the time I was five years old." Christopher, a double-furloughee, said, "I was going to be [an airline] pilot. It's as simple as that. And I've had that dream probably for thirty years. . . . [It] is who I am; this is who I've always wanted to be." Similarly, Captain Andrew reflected on his excitement about joining United during the Employee Stock Option Plan (ESOP) period (1995–2000):

> The whole idea that this was an employee-owned airline—this is our airline. Isn't it great to work here? And then everybody wanted to work at United! I had friends, students actually from the military, jump seat on my airplanes. I remember one lady specifically. She was a Fed-Ex pilot, which in retrospect would be a great place to work now. She got on the airplane saying, "Oh, you guys are so lucky. It must be nice to work here at United." And I was sitting in the right seat of the Airbus at the time, and I thought, "Yeah, this is pretty great."

Charles agreed, explaining how happy he felt when he was first hired at [his major airline]. He was the envy of others:

> Once I joined [my airline] I thought that I was going to be set for life. Good retirement, good benefits, good opportunities to fly nice equipment. Everything just seemed like I'd won the lottery . . . I couldn't have been more happy. I think everybody wanted to be a [major airline] pilot before 9/11.

This was an image the airline sought to actively produce. For example, Anthony described his first days at work during which flight managers indoctrinated new pilots into the organization culture, helping them celebrate their career success:

> [Flight managers said,] "You won the lottery. Burn your old uniforms, you'll never need another one"—ker-ching, ker-ching [sound of cash register ringing] all the way home. . . . They had a party for us, and that was nice at the time. I really was on cloud nine for that week. . . . That was just a magical moment for me. That was the pinnacle!

Bill, another a furloughed pilot, recalled managers instructing pilots the first day, "Look around, you are in a room full of future millionaires." Christopher added:

> When I got hired, they had just been awarded the world's richest pilot contract. So, you know, pinch me! I was like, "Oh it's sweet. I'm done [job hopping]. I won't have to interview again. I can burn my interview suit. I can burn all my résumés."

Through these managerial strategies pilots were made to feel privileged that they were hired by their company and indebted to the airline itself, because it was only through employment there that they had achieved professional success and could now enjoy the stability their steady climb up the commercial pilot career ladder had earned them: a stable career path, a strong labor union, clear work rules, established seniority numbers, and orderly bidding processes for everything from vacation time to aircraft assignments. Yet, embedded in this dialogue is an inference that in exchange for career stability and an identity as a major airline employee, pilots should willingly make sacrifices—any sacrifices, no matter how painful—for the company's survival. Awareness of just how much sacrifice was expected of airline employees in the post-9/11 period came to people in different ways with varying intensities.

Charles explained how the cumulative impact of these post-9/11 managerial strategies created a battlefield, pitting employees in a war against their own airline:

> I don't know what business [airline] executives have been in the last five years, but I don't think it was the airline business. They talk a good talk,

but when you are constantly at war with your employees, nothing good can come of that. . . . It really is destructive to people's lives. I don't think these people care.

After taking an average 56 percent pay cut, the sense of being antagonized by managerial policies and "at war" with the company in a toxic environment further exacerbated the mistrust for airline decision makers, causing many pilots to withdraw their organizational commitment.[23] For example, Aaron said:

Before 9/11, I was always willing to help out the company if they called me and needed a favor. Post-9/11, when I went back [to work from furlough], I was never willing to help out. I felt like I'd been burned by the company, burned by the union. I just wanted to do my job and go home.

Another pilot explained, "Before 9/11 being an airline pilot was a career. After 9/11, it was just a job. There's a big difference in your frame of mind going to your job verses going to your lifelong career. . . . I don't have that pride anymore." Similarly, Jason observed that he thought airlines were less safe "because of the bitter atmosphere and people not caring. I never saw anybody say, 'I don't care about safety.' They never had that attitude. It was just, 'I don't care about the company.'"

Within this toxic environment, air safety hangs in the balance. Captain Gilles noted how managers' attitudes about these escalating risks have changed during his tenure:

I'm afraid for some [managers air safety] is just a distant connection, and if we should have an accident it's just, "Oh my goodness, that's why we have insurance. That's really unfortunate. Don't take it personally. Let's put a flower on their grave and move on."

In addition to seniority, unions, and managerial influences, another frequently misunderstood factor is pilot pay. A 2007 industry study, for instance, blamed airlines' "unionized labor force" for driving costs skyward because "pilots of some of the larger airlines work only seven days per month and senior pilots earn between $250,000 and $300,000 per year."[24] In other words, not much work for lots of pay while taking exotic trips to destinations most people can only dream about. Nothing could be further from the truth. What gets missed in these assumptions is the manner in which pilots' pay is calculated and the reality of the airline-scheduling process.

A pilot's time clock for pay purposes does not start until the airplane's brakes are released and the aircraft is pushed back from the gate, and the time clock stops when brakes are set again at the destination airport. Although pilots are required to be at the airport to brief at least one hour prior to every flight, they are only paid for the time they are actually strapped into the seat. Using this criterion, it is as if a surgeon only earns when he is actually operating on a patient, a lawyer can only bill for the time spent arguing in the courtroom, or an athlete for time on the playing field.

While, according to 2012 salary schedules, US major-airline captains can make between about $124 and $189 per hour, or up to about $189,000 a year (the FAA limits annual flight time to one thousand flight hours), the starting pay for most first officers at a major airline is about $32 per hour, less than $35,000 a year.[25] Although this copilot pay may be two or three times what regional airlines pay their pilots—I took home about $800 per month when I flew for Continental Express—it is nonetheless alarmingly low for a midcareer professional who may have served as a military pilot or spent $60,000 or more on civilian training to acquire FAA certification.[26]

For pilots, it is like a professional football player's challenge to stay healthy long enough to make a lifetime's worth of money for retirement in the decade or so of their prime-earning years. By the time most NFL players are thirty-five, their careers are over. Conversely, the peak decade for pilots is when they are senior wide-body captains—around fifty-five to sixty-five. As a result, health is as important for a pilot as it is to an athlete. Pilots must pass a full physical every six months to maintain the required FAA first-class medical status for an airline transport pilot certificate. In addition, pilots must pass performance checks that require both written and flight-simulator evaluations. A failure of either could result in a loss of license and therefore a loss of job. Like professional athletes, an airline pilot's career may be temporarily lucrative but only for a finite period of time, and the risks and personal investment are high.

In addition to the complexity of pilot pay schedules, the way that pilots accumulate their monthly flight hours is not straightforward either.

Another post-9/11 change that raises safety questions, and was mentioned by nearly every pilot interviewed, is the inefficient ways airlines now schedule flight crews. Rather than flying their flights and then going home, or to their overnight hotel, pilots are forced to hang around for hours at airports waiting for their next flight. In the same way that airlines offload passengers and park planes at their hubs, so too do they park their employees there as well.

For a pilot to earn just five hours of flight pay, or "hard time," it might take fourteen hours on duty, with long, fatiguing periods of downtime, called "sits," in between flights. What this means for passengers and air safety is that the flight crew that flew into an airline's hub in Atlanta, Dallas, Denver, or Chicago at 6 a.m. might be eventually flying your family home at 8 p.m. that night—perhaps sixteen hours since they last rested. Karen, a furloughed first officer who gave up waiting for recall and joined the bottom of the seniority list at another major US airline, described post-9/11 crew scheduling this way:

> [The problem is] incredibly inefficient schedules from a pilot perspective. So you might only fly five hours of hard time, but your duty day would be right up at thirteen to fourteen hours of maximum duty, which the contract permitted with multiple, long sits. For example, a 3 hour and 59 minute sit in Chicago, which is one minute less than the contract would stipulate to give you a day room [at a hotel to rest]. You would do that, and then you would go fly to an out station and have a 1 hour and 47 minute sit, thirteen minutes under what it would take to get a day room at that location. And you'd do that all day. It was surprisingly fatiguing!

Once pilots finally made it to their overnight hotel, post-9/11 scheduling also made getting a good night's sleep difficult as well. Karen explained:

> Between the transportation to and from the hotel and your one-hour report the next day, it wasn't even possible to get eight hours of sleep then. To get back to the hotel, get into your pajamas, brush your teeth, and then get up the next morning and take a shower. You were lucky if you could get six hours of sleep. And if you did that three or four nights in a row on a four-day trip—or even just one night on a four-day trip—you just felt like garbage.

Although there are FAA regulations as well as union work rules that dictate how long a pilot's duty day can legally be, airlines offered incentives for pilots to waive their required rest and fly fatigued. Karen said:

> There was a financial incentive to wave that rest period. You would get five hours of "incentive pay" if you waved that rest. So they were putting a financial incentive—the company—on basically you offering, in my opinion, to fly fatigued. It is literally called "incentive pay." It's incentive to waive your rest. . . . [The company built inefficient schedules knowing people would waive their rest] because those pilots are going to want to get home, start their days off, or get heading home on their commute.

As Karen described, airlines' efforts to increase productivity in the post-9/11 period has resulted in employees working longer hours for less money over more days per month with less time for recuperation. In addition, more pilots were forced into commuting to work, often because of employment uncertainty, changes in their scheduling, or the now-unaffordable cost of living in their assigned cities such as San Francisco or New York. Many pilots described ways that commuting became a big factor for them in the post-9/11 period. Like the scheduling challenges described here, the commuting problem begins with the new ways flights are planned. To put in the required eighty to ninety flight hours per month typically requires about eighteen days away from home. For example, a five-day trip will start at a pilot's domicile, which is the airport at which he or she has been assigned as their home base. I was domiciled in San Francisco, and so I would commute from my home in San Diego either the morning of, or the evening before, my assigned trip, depending on when my first flight took off. Commuting is not unusual for airline employees. I knew a captain who lived in San Diego and was domiciled in New York. The longest commute I ever heard about was a flight attendant who was based in Paris but lived in Christchurch, New Zealand.

In these cases, airline employees either stay with a friend or relative, find a hotel, or invest in a crash pad, a small communal apartment filled with minimal household goods and several beds and storage areas for transient airline workers. Some commuters even use RVs parked in the airport employee parking lot as their overnight accommodations. It can be a very restless existence, increasing stress and distraction for employees at work. Greg noted:

> At the pilot level, with the stress of not only having to go through bankruptcy but through the merger, people are worried about losing seniority, what's going to happen with their bases, are they going to close their base, are they going to have to commute.

Similarly, Dan, a National Guard pilot and airline furloughee, observed how outside stressors like commuting affect a pilot's personal life, adding to the distractions:

> I noticed that there were a lot more people than before making these horrible commutes, and they'd been divorced, their families had issues, they'd taken pay cuts. Everyone is flying more in order to make up for all the pay cuts.

Even under the best circumstance commuting is often unpleasant, but for many pilots, like Karen who felt forced into it by post-9/11 industry changes, it was even more disturbing:

> I never wanted to be a commuter, so I moved out to Chicago [when I was first hired], and then when I got furloughed I had to move back into my parents' basement back in Minnesota until I could get a job. . . . The bottom line is sometimes decisions that the company makes about furloughing and things like that have other implications I don't think people realize.

The worst implication is obviously a crash. Many pilots, like Kevin, observed how stress and fatigue associated with commuting directly contributed to the Colgan Air crash, an accident that should never have happened:

> There's so much dialogue going on in the cockpit about what's going to happen to your seniority, what can you bid [if you have to commute]. It's a huge distraction. . . . It's sad because those [Colgan] pilots were set up by management. They were inadequately trained, and then they are so poorly paid that they are having to commute in. . . . To save a dollar, they sleep on a cot in the crew restroom. That's what these companies are getting away with. Then they want to blame it on the pilots.

Randy, another furloughed first officer, offered a similar story. He worked for several regional airlines before 9/11 and described his experience of post-9/11 industry restructuring and the impact it had on employees' finances, families, and quality of life:

> [Airline management] would say, "Yeah, we don't need you for a few months," lay a bunch of people off, and then later start bringing people back. In the process they closed almost every single one of the domiciles. . . . This might help people relate to incidents that have happened like the Buffalo crash. . . . We started at around $24 an hour, and then second-year pay was up around $35 to $36. . . . [Captains' pay] was mid-$60s. . . . The majority of people were forced to commute—our company even opened a base in Atlanta and then closed it within a year. The entire time they said, "Everything is going fine, don't worry, the base is going to be good." Some people moved there permanently, bought houses, and then the company just closed it. So when they started opening new bases, everybody was pretty leery about moving. . . . Most of us chose to commute. . . . It put a lot of pressure on getting to and from work, took up time from your days off traveling back and forth in the back of an airplane. People were a little more fatigued and a little more frustrated by the situation, and it always puts a thought in the back of your mind—just worrying about your job. What are you going to do? So you weren't completely rested and happy and excited to be at work.

Commuting is so stressful, time consuming, and fatiguing, many pilots will go to great lengths to avoid doing it. Christopher is a first officer living in the Chicago area who was furloughed in 2002. Unlike many of his peers, he was able to stay in the cockpit, landing a job flying for JetBlue out of New York's John F. Kennedy International Airport. He liked the company. However, once recalled by his airline, he left JetBlue anyway. Christopher described his decision-making process this way:

> It was a tough decision, I made it based on the auspices that I did not want to commute to New York City for the rest of my flying career. . . . On the best of days, the commute took four to five hours. On the worst of days, it took all day. And that was time away from my family. I did the math, and I knew I was taking a pay cut to go back to [my airline], but in the long term I felt that I would be money ahead eventually. But it wasn't because of the money. It was because I didn't want to commute.

José was also forced to make difficult employment decisions and even risked giving up his airline career in order to avoid commuting:

> [Since I was laid off] I've been applying to—you name it, Target, Wal-Mart, any place, I could not get a job! Nobody would call me back. . . . I didn't try other airlines; I thought I was completely out of the airline industry. I didn't want to start over [at the bottom of the seniority list] anywhere else at $30,000 a year and have to commute and not have a good quality of life.

In addition to commuting, every pilot interviewed named fatigue as one of their biggest safety concerns in the airline industry today. Although fatigue has been on the NTSB's "Most Wanted" list of transportation safety risks since they began the list over twenty years ago, fatigue-related issues have become more acute for pilots in recent years because of the post-9/11 airline-scheduling practices discussed here. With drastic reductions in pay and an increased need to commute, the problem will only escalate, and the impact could be disastrous. As NTSB chairwoman Deborah Hersman explained, "While alcohol is often associated with impairment, operating a vehicle while fatigued can be just as deadly."[27]

Karen provided some specifics about the detrimental impact the grueling post-9/11 work schedules have had on pilot health. It was a common complaint:

> When I came back [from furlough] I was, to be quite honest, *shocked* at how different the [working] conditions were. . . . I had never been so tired in my life. . . . I had flown for a commuter airline, and a kind of crummy commuter airline to boot. . . . We'd fly seven legs a day, really long days; we could fly up to eighteen hours of duty in a day. So it wasn't that I wasn't used to long days, but it was kind of a whole different mentality in terms of how fatiguing it was . . . I was shocked. It was the most tired I had been in my professional life. . . . I was sick a lot; I'd have bronchitis. I was just kind of always under the weather.

Similarly, Captain Gilles described how the combined influence of increased flying and outside stressors made it difficult for pilots to function at optimal levels:

> Fatigue has been a huge issue. Pilots are working many, many more hours than they ever used to. Fatigue is just as debilitating as any substance abuse.

Your brain can't function well. So that's a big concern. . . . Many people were completely behind the power curve in terms of rest. . . . It just added layer upon layer of stress.

Examples of the repercussions of the fatigue and stress Gilles mentions are readily available. Ninety-eight percent of pilots interviewed witnessed mistakes or distractions on the flight deck because of post-9/11 changes; 60 percent saw this on a weekly basis.

The pilots I interviewed provided many examples. Like Gilles, Henry observed how fatigue and stress had become linked in pilots' day-to-day experience affecting both work and home life:

Fatigue became a big issue; stress was certainly an issue. Between people getting furloughed, people having trouble paying their bills, there's financial stress. It put a lot of stress on pilots from a lot of different angles. . . . I went through a divorce. I knew other people who did as well. Personal lives took a real beating. . . . Financial stress, stress on the home front, being away much more, it kind of snowballed.

The manner in which airlines chose to downsize exacerbated the stressors as a pilot could continue for months with unresolved questions about an impending layoff hanging over his or her head. Aaron reported how frightened he felt when he finally found out he would be furloughed:

There was a letter that went out, and then there was a phone call. I knew [the layoff] was happening, but that phone call felt like the guillotine blade was coming down. . . . There were others relying on me, and so I pictured the worst: bankruptcy, losing a home, losing my family. . . . All the worst scenarios went around in my head. . . . I was very scared.

Christopher related similar feelings of fear and uncertainty about his impending layoff:

I knew that the furlough was coming. And it is a stressful event. And you have to try to keep it out of your mind. . . . When they announced they were parking one hundred airplanes in June 2008 at United Airlines, all I had to do was the math. That's a good 1,500 pilots right there, and that's essentially what they furloughed. . . . The second time, it was about a year that I spent with that hanging over my head. It was at least a year. I had a gut feeling even before that.

Stress was not just a factor for the furloughed employees. For both down-sized pilots and the remaining survivors, financial unpredictability and working with soon-to-be-laid-off employees were frequently mentioned as causes of stress and distraction.

Captain Jasper recalled that nearly every flight "I was flying with a co-pilot that was being furloughed either that month or the next month. The stress [was] unbelievable." And "when there's stress on one pilot, there's definitely stress on both." Prompted in part by his experience of being air-borne on 9/11 and suffering from post-traumatic stress syndrome, Jasper took time off, went into therapy, and completed a master's degree in coun-seling. He noted, "I have quite a bit of background in the effects of depres-sion and stress [now]. It was really obvious to me that at least half of the guys I was flying with were clinically depressed." They "were probably at the level where they really shouldn't have been flying."

Similarly, Gilles reported how desperate some pilots' lives had become:

> The whole financial stress. It's not just a minor budget adjustment—marriages have been destroyed; houses have been lost. We've had suicides. It was unheard of here decades ago. We've had a number of pilot suicides. That's just a symp-tom of how difficult things have gotten for many, many individuals.

As fatigue, stress, downsizing, financial uncertainty, and family concerns combined, distraction became a huge issue for pilots. The safety implica-tions of these distractions are obvious, as Doug succinctly observed:

> I think it's almost a miracle that there wasn't bent metal and dead people at [my airline], in particular, post-9/11 because you talk about the distraction. Everybody was distracted for all kinds of reasons—change in fleets and seats, change in domiciles, major pay cuts, losing jobs, unemployment—all these kinds of things.

Gilles was even more specific:

> You'd see pilots that were so distracted by trying to make ends meet finan-cially, they'd be in operations getting ready to launch off into a blizzard and

they'd be on the cell phone trying to close a mortgage deal. They're trying to make a few dollars for themselves, not paying attention fully to the mission, trying to pay full attention to life and trying to survive financially while being distracted by all this other junk.

Another distraction that became common in the post-9/11 period was second jobs. Sixty-nine percent of surveyed pilots reported that they had pursued supplemental sources of income while employed at their airline because of pay cuts and their need for additional funding streams. To offset their loss of income, alleviate financial concerns, and better support their families, many pilots started outside businesses in addition to flying at their airline. For example, Karen recalled:

> When I came back from furlough, I'd say at least 50 percent plus of the captains I flew with had at some point gone into some type of side business to supplement their income. . . . A lot of guys started businesses with their spouses as another way to access health insurance, thinking, "Gosh, if [the airline] goes under we're going to lose our health insurance." . . . That just provided a tremendous amount of distraction.

As a result, the pursuit of supplemental income to offset pilot pay reductions after 9/11 took a physical and emotional toll on both crew members. Karen explained:

> Having these businesses on the side was a tremendous amount of outside pressures and distractions. . . . It was like everybody was burning the candle at both ends. . . . Everyone had this kind of feeling that the rug can get pulled out from under you at any time. . . . There was just a level of "rush, rush, rush. I need to hurry up." . . . For example, everyone needed to hurry up and get to their commute home because their businesses were waiting for them if they didn't live locally. Or they wanted to get to the gate as quickly as possible because their cell phone would be ringing.

Dan also witnessed several forms of new distractions on the flight deck, not present before 9/11:

> I flew with one guy who had four or five sandwich franchises in Chicago. The whole trip he was on the cell phone, every little opportunity . . . I flew

with another guy who had the nearmiss in Fort Lauderdale [in 2009]. I wasn't in Fort Lauderdale, but I flew with him after. I can see how he wouldn't have his head in the game. He had a lot of things happening in his life.

Another very common safety concern for pilots was cost cutting during training. This was a particular concern for furloughed pilots returning to the flight deck after years spent not flying. They found that training had been shortened and the evaluation processes streamlined in order to get pilots through as fast—and therefore as cheaply—as possible. Several furloughed pilots, like Aaron, had not flown an airliner in years, and they were uncomfortable with the shortened training:

> When we returned [from furlough] post-9/11, training was very compressed. Before I had done the 737 course and it was six weeks; when I went back it was four weeks. It was very compressed. You really didn't feel that you were getting a deep knowledge. They just wanted to give you enough to pass the test and get out and go fly.

Kevin even asked for more training time when he returned from furlough, but it was not provided:

> The training that I received when I went back [from furlough] was woefully inadequate. I passed the training. I was a safe pilot, but I was by no means well prepared for my job. The union has made a point of it, but the company doesn't care because they are trying to save every dime they can. . . . When I took my 767 training, that course was two to three weeks longer pre-9/11 then when I took it [after 9/11]. I told them after my first week that this is inadequate training. . . . Then at the very end, the way they play the game is they say, "Well, you've been certified" [by the FAA]. . . . It's stunning to me we don't have more safety incidents.

Similarly, Karen explained that even though she had not flown at her airline for three and a half years, she received the abbreviated training too:

> Everything in training just has been done on the cheap. . . . If I was brand-new to this airplane I would have really, really been upset at how poor the training was. For me, it ended up being a review because it was an airplane

I already had three thousand hours in. . . . Not only was the training bad, but I thought the testing was a joke, which I just found shocking that the FAA would buy off on.

Captain Ralph, a former military pilot and twenty-five-year airline veteran, had similar observations about training shortcuts and ineffective testing. He shared a conversation he had after his latest proficiency check ride:

We were sitting there filling out the paperwork, and I said to the standards captain, "So how long do you think it will be before I won't even have to bother coming out for the check ride? We can just do the paperwork. . . . Every time I come out here you ask less and less of me. I figure eventually we'll get to the point where I don't even have to come."

Why have things become so lax? Ralph provided a clue: "Failing is expensive and costs money, so they're not going to fail you."

Besides cutting back on training expenses and demanding employees work more hours for less pay, airlines pursued other cost-cutting strategies that pressured employees, further increasing stress, distraction, and risk. One new policy instructed pilots to taxi the airplane on one engine in order to save fuel. Dan explained how much of a potential safety problem this post-9/11 change was:

They wanted you to taxi out on one engine as long as possible, so that would leave the whole rest of the checklist open, and that just added to the workload [before takeoff]. . . . So you have a distracted captain, and the first officer was starting the other engine, looking inside, and the next thing you know it, you are on an active runway. I remember that's happened a couple of times. . . . All to save twenty ounces of gas. The company was constantly—not forcing people— but trying to get guys to squeeze more margin out of your day. I was always concerned that sooner or later there was going to be an accident.

In addition to new policies like single-engine taxiing increasing stress and distraction, cutbacks in other areas also increased the pilot workload, as Christopher explained:

[To save money] mechanics no longer parked the aircraft. They just had regular ramp people parking the aircraft. That put the onus on the pilots [to provide safety] because people parking the aircraft didn't really know what the heck they were doing. So that was another increased workload on the pilots.

These types of short-term cost savings, perhaps just a few dollars per hour in wages or gallons of fuel, create potentially dangerous situations that could result in millions of dollars in human injury or equipment damage. Yet, airlines continue to increase the risks. Karen described a situation that happened on one of her flights:

Mechanics don't push back the airplanes [any longer]. . . . It was amazing the inability and sloppiness of a lot of the push-back crews by switching it to just regular rampers. You could get all ends of the spectrum. So if you were in Chicago you could get somebody doing a great job, who follows the procedures to the letter. . . . But then the next time you showed up in Chicago to push back you'd have the tug come unhooked. That's actually something that happened to me on the Airbus in LA—they somehow hooked the tug up incorrectly, and midway through the push, the tug separated from the aircraft. Then they used all kinds of nonstandard phraseology to try to communicate with the captain to set the brake immediately, which created a whole scene. The airplane came to a flying stop. It was bad. It could have really done some serious damage to the airplane and the flight attendants who were up doing a safety demo.

Problems like Dan, Christopher, and Karen described were due to maintenance cutbacks, the furloughing of certified mechanics, and outsourcing of maintenance work to inexperienced subcontractors. Almost every pilot interviewed had a disturbing story to tell, often of pressures applied to captains by management to accept aircraft with mechanical problems called "deferrals" for deferred or postponed airplane maintenance. Henry explained the safety issue:

Over 50 percent of the mechanics—it maybe even closer to 60 percent of the mechanics—that had been working here, don't work here anymore. So we saw maintenance levels drop significantly. . . . When I was a captain on the Airbus, we were getting a noticeable amount of airplanes with deferrals. And not just a simple deferral but more significant [safety related] ones. At the end, I had mechanics tell me, the new policy is if it can be "deferred" [they] were going to "defer" it unless the captain refuses the airplane. So

things they would normally fix in a few minutes, they were not fixing. . . .
The company was certainly trying to pressure us to take it. . . . That to me is
a potential safety problem.

Greg similarly observed the maintenance cutbacks and managerial pressures that became commonplace:

The only way we could get aircraft fixed was for the pilots to turn the airplane down. Other than that, they'd defer it and send them on their way.
That's how bad it had become. Part of the reason was before I got furloughed they started parking the 737s so they stopped maintaining them. It
took pilots walking off the aircraft to get things fixed. Then you had to deal
with management asking why did you do that. "Well, we didn't feel it was
safe." And then they'd press and press and press. They would basically challenge the captain asking, "Why did you make that decision?"

Christopher explained the grey area between "legal" and "safe" in aviation. He said:

[After 9/11 there was] greater pressure on pilots to accept aircraft that were
not in a good condition to fly. Legal to fly—yes. But safe to fly—no. That
was something due to cost cutting. They wanted to have less overhead inventory of parts; they wanted to do less in-house maintenance, and that all
manifested itself in pilots having to accept aircraft that were not as ready for
flight as they were prior to 9/11.

Aaron had similar experiences and used the term "pilot pushing" to describe airline management's pressure to fly broken airplanes:

Before 9/11, I was on the 727, an old fleet at the time. But even with the
fleet's age we hardly ever carried forward deferred items. Post-9/11, on the
737 it was not uncommon to carry forward deferred items almost on a daily
basis. On any given flight you might have one to two deferred items. If
you wanted to get something done, you had to actually refuse to fly the airplane. . . . It felt like pilot pushing.

"Pilot pushing" was a term used by several pilots to describe a list of safety-
related post-9/11 cost-cutting measures that managers tried to enforce. For
example, José explained:

I was called by a flight manager because I had called in sick four, maybe five times in a year. . . . The company started pushing pilots to fly sick, to question pilots for turning down an airplane for mechanical reasons—a lot of things that weren't there before 9/11. It just made it a hassle to go to work, to actually do your job. People were getting in the way of you doing your job.

Greg explained some of the ramifications of these cost-cutting pressures on employees and their decision making:

Part of it was management had started scaring people, and people were afraid for their jobs so they weren't making the best decisions, the decisions they should have made. You just can't have that, especially in such a dangerous environment. When people start questioning what their decision is going to be based on [management's] repercussions and putting money savings over safety, that's not the way we should be doing things in aviation.

Greg also emphasized how pervasive this pressure became throughout the airline, as cost cutting trumped safety in all facets of organizational life:

It's not only the pilots, it was everybody—customer service, ramp agents, almost bordering on unsafe business practices. Pushing people to load the aircraft quickly to the point where people were running on the ramp, really hustling, trying to get stuff done. And it's not the type of environment to rush anything in.

Several pilots observed that not only is the airline industry in danger of not attracting the "best and brightest" as Captain Sully noted, but if things do not improve soon the current employment group will "vote with their feet" and find work in other countries or other professions. Kevin explained how pilots had learned a lot of about their marketability in the last decade, and many now know they can land jobs elsewhere:

Underlying it all is the experience in the cockpit. You have a bunch of experienced professionals who have the ability to rise above this stuff. I certainly won't stay in this industry if it doesn't get better. I'm a smart guy; I can find other ways to make a living. I've already proven that for the last decade [while on furlough]. Guys are going to find other places to go.

Jasper voiced a similar concern about airlines no longer attracting quality employees:

> I don't know who would go into this business. . . . Who's going to fly all these airplanes twenty years from now? I think that's really something the industry's going to have to face. I don't think there's an easy answer unless they make this industry more attractive through better pay, better work rules, and more sensible allocation of people's time. . . . Where do you get people? Do you start training people out of the Middle East or out of China or whatever? It's scary.

Aaron similarly noted the long-term impact of this skill shortage on air safety:

> I don't know what caliber of people the airlines are going to attract any more. It's more public knowledge now about what the lifestyle is and what the pay really is. . . . Therefore they are going to have to make it more attractive by loosening the schedules, increasing the pay, or you are going to attract a lower caliber of people, and it's going to make the aviation industry that much more less safe.

As a result, Kevin emphasized the biggest challenge facing the future of commercial aviation is

> a competent pilot in the cockpit. And you're not going to have it if you're not going to pay for it. And that's it. If that decision maker up there is not adequately compensated in the next decade, he won't be there. . . . It's a capitalist society; guys will go and find another way to make a living.

Movies, clothes, seniority lists, pay schemes, and time clocks aside, the next time you see an entourage of airline employees walking through the airport or hotel lobby, take a closer look. You will find underneath the pilot hat or flight attendant makeup, there is a tired person. A person tired of safety shortcuts, providing substandard service to irate customers, making excuses for their airline's poor performance, bilking passengers for amenities that should be free, and tired of working more hours for less money. In sum, all the things that you are tired of as a flying customer, airline employees are twice as frustrated by.

To find out for yourself, I suggest you consider asking them some questions, if they are willing to talk. Find out what their work schedule was like the past few days, how their day is going, or how they are feeling. Ask how their retirement plan looks, how their finances have changed, or how their family has coped in the post-9/11 period. You might be surprised by their candor and the breadth of their insights.

Airline employees today understand the complexity of the financial issues that have plagued their industry since deregulation. They know that without a healthy airline to work at, they would not be flying or working around airplanes doing the job they love. Yet, they also know firsthand the potential impact of the escalating risks that have become commonplace in aviation in the post-9/11 period. They do not want to be responsible for the next crash brought on by myopic cost cutting by inexperienced aviation managers who are eager to lock in their personal payday before jumping to another industry such as food service, health care, or finance. But do not take my word for it, ask them yourself. That is, if you are willing to risk finding out what is really going on in the airline industry today.

EPILOGUE

Although US air carriers took in over $2 *trillion* in revenue between 2000 and 2012, much of it untaxed, entire books have been written about the airline industry's inability to make a profit. The topic never seems to lose its appeal for economists, consultants, academics, and journalists—each trying to crack the code on the cryptic industry.[1] The findings are typically the same: employees are overpaid, labor unions obstinate, airplanes expensive, fuel costs volatile, economies unpredictable, and regulations restrictive; weather, recession, travel scares, and war hurt business; and competition is high because internet websites allow passengers to lock in the cheapest possible airfares. However interesting this perennial debate is, it misses a key point: some people *are* making big money working for US airlines, just not employees.

The evidence indicates that while US air carriers may have floundered in the immediate post-9/11 period, airline executives managed to maximize their own profits without much trouble. As it turns out, putting in a few years as an airline CEO is an excellent ticket punch on the way up the corporate ladder. And, just like Wall Street bankers, airline executives seem to believe that as long as they lock in their own take, the market will sort out the rest. Meanwhile, at the same time that airline executives furloughed employees, eliminated pensions, and cut workers' wages and benefits, they authorized costly expenditures such as $200 million for legal advice and consulting fees during bankruptcy and merger, and $20 million for Business Education Training to acculturate employees. Even post-merger paint schemes came with a high price tag. At about $30,000 an airplane, most major airlines spent around $200 million stripping and repainting their fleet in the post-9/11 period.

Although awareness of the details of these fiscal magic tricks may still be emerging for the general public, the high costs were not overlooked by airline employees. Ralph, a senior captain and former military pilot hired in the mid-1980s, noted how much has changed in the airline business during his tenure:

> The business model was so badly broken after 1978, it probably took twenty years just to rationalize what kind of business this business wanted to be, and I think they're still doing it. But it has certainly become all about the MBAs and their management techniques. . . . We used to have people in this industry who loved this industry, who loved aviation, who wanted to build great companies. . . . And they have been supplanted by MBAs and professional managers—we've had seven CEOs at [my airline] since I've been here. . . . We've become just like every other business in America where the management teams and the board of directors float in and out and try to maximize "shareholder value"—although it seems they shrink shareholder value as much as they maximize it. They certainly maximize their own value. That seems to be the only common theme.

Captain Jasper has thirty-five years of aviation experience and a valuable insider's perspective on industry developments and their cause, and he spoke similarly:

> Deregulation was a horrible mistake. . . . If you value commercial aviation as something that deserves the public trust, you've got to regulate it. The only way to make it stable and sustainable is to regulate it. To make sure that greed doesn't drive where the industry's going. Unfortunately, for the last twenty years, that's all it's been: greed has driven where the industry has gone.

Could things get even worse in the US airline industry if we don't change course soon? A look across the Atlantic at the Irish low-frills airline Ryanair gives us a glimpse into the possible future for US airlines.

In 2013, Ryanair Pilot Group, the pilots' union, developed a safety petition expressing concern about airline working conditions and air safety to be submitted to the Irish Aviation Authority. Rather than proactively addressing these deficiencies, Ryanair management instead warned pilots if they signed the document they risked dismissal. At most airlines this warning might have been discounted, however Ryanair pilots were fearful because they had recently been recategorized as "self-employed" subcontractors—not airline employees. Thus, pilots were not provided a guaranteed salary, pension, or medical insurance and were required to pay for all their own business expenses from uniforms and ID cards to ground transport and hotel accommodations—costs typically covered by airlines directly.[2] Could employee subcontracting be the next cost-cutting strategy for US airlines too? Many US air carriers already employ the tactic for mechanics, caterers, and aircraft cleaners. Why not pilots?

As long as airlines appear safe on paper and airfares remain cheap online, no one seems to care much about employees' concerns. Seventy percent of pilots interviewed believe it is likely that a major airline accident will occur in the coming years due to post-9/11 airline cost cutting, and *24% think an airline crash is very likely*. One captain I interviewed summed up the situation:

> [Airlines today aren't] doing things the right way. They are doing things that are economically expedient for them because they are foolish about safety. . . . We haven't had any [major airline] accidents. . . . But, I still say I think it's going to happen sometime. . . . Nobody would be surprised. We would all go back and look at the data and say, "Yeah, of course."

Just like Wall Street before the 2008 financial industry implosion, risks have been escalating in the US aviation industry, and airline employees today are primed for the next crash. However, general awareness of this growing problem has been spreading only gradually. Most of us now recognize that 9/11 did not create this airline industry instability—weak regulatory oversight, ineffective managerial strategies, and self-serving executives did. It is time to stop allowing profit seeking to trump safety concerns and to reconceptualize the idea of air safety before it is too late. So what should be done to address this problem now?

Major US airlines need a new business paradigm. In the current environment, any air carrier that does not follow the crowd into downsizing, cost cutting, and merger will be annihilated by the others, particularly air carriers allowed to operate for years under bankruptcy protection. What seemed to be economies of scale provided by these large airlines and their vast networks have become burdens of size in the new flexible economy.

Although not a new theoretical construct, per se, *conscious capitalism* has made a resurgence in the literature over the past decade, with American business scholars calling for improved ethics, sustainability, servant leadership, and value-driven decision making.[3] The underlying argument is that companies can do well financially while also behaving ethically, creating sustainability in their market. By subscribing to five characteristics, companies can be purpose driven and create benefit not only for shareholders but for employees, customers, the community, and the environment.[4]

First, companies need a higher purpose. Company profitability needs to be directed toward a greater end than making CEOs wealthy, as was the case with early airline pioneers who tried to create a safe and reliable aviation industry for America. Second, airlines must commit to meeting the needs of all stakeholders, including employees and customers, not just investors. Any passenger who has flown commercially over the last decade knows what a frustrating and dismal experience air travel has become. Third, executives must integrate ethics, social responsibility, and sustainability into their core business strategies. Fourth, airlines must foster a healthy organizational culture through a strong sense of community. And fifth, CEOs and senior managers must become "servant-leaders," committed to the long-term health of the company,[5] not celebrity names passing through on the way to their next impressive title and seven figure paycheck.

Southwest Airlines has been touted as a good example of *conscious capitalism*, and it is a great airline. However, for several reasons, Southwest's low-frills model will never work for major US air carriers and, after chasing after this image since airline deregulation in 1978, it is time for government policymakers to face this fact. For example, Southwest keeps training, maintenance, and other overhead costs down by flying one type of aircraft on largely short-haul point-to-point routes to airports in cheaper cities on the outskirts of major metropolitan areas. In contrast, major airlines fly a variety of domestic and international routes, which requires a range of airplane sizes to meet different operational needs. It cannot be done with just one type of airplane.

Larger aircraft require a different infrastructure than Southwest's planes do, such as longer runways capable of supporting more weight, ground obstacles to clear wider wingspans, terminal jetways to meet higher airplane doors, and refueling capabilities to meet high international fuel loads. Many smaller airports cannot accommodate this, so major airlines must land at bigger airports with higher landing fees. In addition, flying a variety of aircraft requires different training protocols and larger stockpiles of spare parts. The list of expensive challenges goes on. However, these are unavoidable costs for major air carriers. Southwest's 737s are never going to fly from the United States to Europe, Asia, or the many other international destinations passengers demand.

Yet, that does not mean that major airlines cannot follow Southwest Airline's example of *conscious capitalism*. It would be to their benefit. A 2009 book about US air carriers after 9/11 found that the managers who paid attention to the connection between relational reserves and financial reserves before and during the crisis best contributed to organizational resilience after the crisis. More specifically, this book explained why Southwest—an air carrier that has never furloughed employees—recovered the fastest of all US airlines after 9/11, while United and US Airways—air carriers that laid off the most employees—recovered the slowest. By 2005, Southwest's stock traded at 92 percent of its pre-9/11 level, while United and US Airways stock remained at 12 percent and 23 percent, respectively.[6]

A key difference during the post-9/11 period was Southwest's "employees first" philosophy. As CEO Jim Parker observed, "We are willing to suffer some damage, even to our stock price, to protect the jobs of our people."[7] This prioritization of employees' rights over shareholder interests is obviously in opposition to many managerial strategies and economists' opinions. However, Southwest's founder Herb Kelleher explained it this way: "Nothing kills your company's culture like layoffs. [It is] shortsighted." In contrast, refraining from furloughing, particularly when times are tough, "breeds loyalty," "a sense of security," and "trust." As a manager, he said, "you want to show your people that you value them and you're not going to hurt them just to get a little more money in the short term."[8]

In order for major airlines to accomplish this shift to conscious capitalism, there are three major areas warranting immediate attention: government, regulators, and the flying public.

Government   The US government has had a love-hate relationship with aviation from the beginning. While foreign countries were eager to invest in and develop their commercial airlines, the United States was dragged reluctantly into supporting the fledgling industry through airmail and other subsidies. This ambiguous beginning in some ways colors government's engagement even today. Nevertheless, a country of the size and wealth of the United States needs a strong and vibrant commercial air transportation infrastructure to support interstate commerce and the travel needs of its citizens, as well as for national defense in wartime. To support this safe and vibrant industry, America needs a national aviation policy that addresses all its needs—not a one-size-fits-all business model. It's time to recognize that Alfred Kahn's deregulation experiment has run its course and that the federal government should at least partially re-regulate the airline industry. It is in every American's best interest to increase safety and decrease risk, and government action is required because, just like Wall Street, airline executives have shown they can't—or won't—control themselves. As outspoken aviation leader Robert Crandall, retired CEO of American Airlines, noted:

> [The airline industry] is simply not an industry where the market will produce a solution. Leadership needs to come from the government. We need a coherent national transportation policy, new labor law, new bankruptcy law . . . [with] the objectives of preserving reasonable competition and an acceptable standard of service and taking the needed steps to ensure US airlines are competitive on the world stage. If the Germans and French can do it, we can do it. There is a national interest involved here.[9]

The reason why this has not happened is a lack of leadership at the federal level. Just like in the days of Alfred Kahn, Crandall observed, the United States is "in the grips of ideologues" who are "convinced the market will solve the problem." That will never happen, therefore the solution is "sensible government regulation," he said.[10] But how should we get started?

First, government should make bankruptcy a less convenient path for airline executives by restricting their ability to declare Chapter 11, pay lavish fees to consultants, and reap millions in bonuses for themselves while employees' wages and benefits are slashed. Aviation deserves leaders committed to safety, stability, and the long-term health of the industry like the airline pioneers, not short-sighted opportunists eager to game the system. Second, Congress should display the same interest in airline safety as they have shown in airport security in the post-9/11 period. They should commission a study by the Government Accounting Office of airline employees' opinions and experiences. The research questions could be simple: Have post-9/11 airline industry cost-cutting strategies—such as bankruptcy, outsourcing, downsizing, merging, and restructuring—affected employees' health and work performance? What are the long-term implications for risk and air safety? Then develop a plan to address the study's findings.

Regulators   One of the most glaring similarities between the Wall Street crash of 2008 and the evolving crisis in aviation is the mismatch of intentions and differing views of regulator's roles and responsibilities within the wider system. Financial industry regulators erroneously assumed that investment banks would police themselves, insurers would provide protection, credit-rating agencies would be objective, and market forces would keep increasingly risky deals in check. Similarly, transportation industry regulators like the DOT and FAA have assumed that airline managers will monitor safety, labor unions will police management's risk taking, and market forces such as passenger demand will keep things in check. After all, they assumed, airline employees would not fly for unsafe airlines and passengers would not buy tickets solely based on the lowest price. We know from the 2008 financial industry implosion and Great Recession that followed that this system of balancing forces did not work effectively on Wall Street. And we now know it is not keeping commercial airline safety in balance either. This is not the first time the FAA has been criticized.

The airline regulatory structure has been under attack for decades for its inability to accomplish its wide variety of missions. Like the CAB in the 1970s, the time has come to update aviation's regulatory system. Developed over fifty years ago, the FAA was simply never intended to provide all of the services it is burdened with today. It is time for the pilot training and airline policing functions to be separated from the FAA and assigned to new government agencies that can provide the leadership and attention these important functions rightly deserve. To echo Captain Sullenberger's comments, it is time for government, regulators, and airlines to refocus their attention and resources on the recruitment and retention of highly experienced, well-trained pilots with safety a priority at least equal to the financial bottom line. The only way this can be accomplished is through government intervention.

Military-trained pilots, previously the backbone of the commercial airline industry, will no longer be available either because they are increasingly staying in the service or because they are now trained in remotely piloted aircraft. This means the future of airline safety lies in civilian training programs, and if the crashes discussed in this book are any indication, this is an area that warrants intense restructuring. Although the FAA has increased airline pilot flight-time minimums, it remains unclear how other identified problems, such as a lack of professionalism, poor cockpit discipline, or a general devaluing of the seriousness and responsibilities of the piloting profession will be addressed. During World War II, President Roosevelt instituted the Civilian Pilot Training Program to provide a pool of well-trained civilian pilots from all walks of life—across gender, ethnicity, and class lines—to support America's aviation needs. It is time to reconsider this approach and take control of airline pilot training away from airport flight schools and companies like Gulfstream academy so as to provide well-trained pilots for our commercial infrastructure. Without an industry-wide commitment to attracting—and retaining—the best and brightest for our airlines, Asian and Middle Eastern air carriers will likely benefit while US air safety suffers.

The Flying Public The changes I propose will not happen unless the flying public embraces its collective power. We need to pressure airlines to prioritize safety and the federal government to increase accountability, just like during the New Deal in the 1930s. As consumers, we must be willing to pay more, if need be, to ensure that pilots are well trained, rested, and safe.

Although my arguments may be persuasive, I know the next question will be: How can Americans pay for these regulatory changes? It is not as difficult as one may think. Here are five steps I suggest to get started:

1. After 9/11, every roundtrip airfare in the United States incurred a $5 surcharge to pay for the establishment of the TSA.[11] With over 800 million passengers embarking in 2012,[12] and an anticipated 1.2 billion flying by 2032,[13] a small surcharge could help subsidize the changes I have recommended here.

2. In 2011 alone, the flying public paid over $12 billion in untaxed airline ancillary fees—fees like checked baggage, seat assignments, and rebooking—pure profit for airlines. Tax this profit, just like the government taxes airfare revenue.

3. Stop subsidizing flights through Essential Air Service, a program developed in the 1970s and never intended to still be in place thirty years later. Instead, urge airlines to make these routes profitable by meeting customer demand. This would have saved taxpayers $143 million for fiscal year 2012 alone.

4. Separate the FAA's dual mandate to both supervise and promote aviation into separate government agencies. This will allow regulators to develop a successful pilot-training pipeline and to properly police airlines. Enforcement actions will increase revenue.

5. Aviation industry fines must be paid in full, not negotiated down like Gulfstream's reduction from $1.3 million to $550,000.

The airline industry once shone like a beacon on the horizon, solid and steady. Airlines were a place where generations of employees dedicated their lives and worked with pride, happy to provide a service and enjoy a shared identity. For many airline employees, it's now a nightmare from which no awakening is in sight. The economic tsunami, as Captain Sully described it, hit the aviation industry in the post-9/11 period and has left employees reeling. Although airlines have returned to profitability and executives earn handsomely, airline employees continue to give up more than $12 billion a year in wages, benefits, pensions, and various work rules. As of 2010, nearly 200,000 airline employees remain out of work and over 10,000 pilot jobs at major air carriers have disappeared, many outsourced to questionably safe air carriers like Colgan Air.[14] Airlines have become the discount stores of the travel industry—"Expect More. Pay Less," as the Target slogan goes. Employees and passengers may expect more, but airlines will provide less. Meanwhile, industry leaders continue to hope no one will "alarm the passengers" about these secrets.

Looking back on that crisp fall day in 2001 when my flight was forced to land in Omaha for four days while the national airspace system shut down, it becomes clear how fragile America's aviation industry really is. Although the industry may be pretty good at managing routine operations, getting planes and passengers from departure to destination, when confronted with an abnormal situation the fractures widen and the system breaks down. Awareness about this fragility may be coming to each of us at different times in varying ways. Yet one thing seems certain: post-9/11 short-term profit seeking continues to trump safety in aviation and, like Wall Street before 2008, few measures are currently in place to significantly change this pattern anytime soon. Airline executives' fixation on maximizing short-term profits at the expense of long-term safety—and government regulators' inability to stop them—has created a period of increased risk to the flying public as well as airline employees. As one airline captain confessed, "I don't want to see an accident happen. But part of me thinks that maybe that's the only thing that will convince people where we are at. . . . It's just too complex a system for something not to fail."

Like Wall Street, airlines have counted on the fog of war in the post-9/11 period to keep the government supportive, citizens sympathetic, bankruptcy courts lenient, employees desperate, unions befuddled, and customers in muppet-like pacification. However, at some point, awareness about what is really happening in the airline industry will come to all of us, and if passengers do not trust an airline, they will eventually stop flying. The only question that remains is will the airline industry follow Wall Street as the next crash on America's horizon?

ACKNOWLEDGMENTS

First, I would like to thank US aviation industry employees, the dedicated professionals who work hard every day to keep our skies safe. In particular, I owe an immense debt of gratitude to the several hundred pilots, flight attendants, mechanics, FAA aviation safety inspectors, whistleblowers, and other professionals who had the courage to be interviewed for this book. I wish I could thank you by name, but I prefer to protect your anonymity. Second, I thank my Cornell University Press editor Frances Benson and her team, Ange Romeo-Hall, Katherine Hue-Tsung Liu, and Katy Meigs. Third, I would like to thank my family, friends, and colleagues for their understanding, encouragement, and support over the past three years. And finally, I thank Kathy for, well, everything.

Appendix A

AIRLINE PILOT QUESTIONNAIRE RESULTS

1. **What percentage of pay reduction do you estimate that you have you experienced since pre-9/11 levels?** Average: 56%
2. **Since September 11th 2001 (9/11), have you pursued supplemental sources of income while employed as an airline pilot because of airline pay cuts and/or the need for additional income?** Yes: 68%; No: 32%
3. **Since 9/11, have you pursued employment outside of aviation because of an airline pilot job loss (Furlough, voluntary leave, etc.)?** Yes: 70%; No: 30%
4. **If recalled by your airline, will you return to work?** Yes, definitely: 38%; Unsure: 50%; No, definitely not: 12%
5. **Have you applied for employment at another airline?** Yes: 48%; No: 52%
6. **If hired as a pilot for another airline, would you quit your former airline to fly for them even if it meant a significant reduction in pay and seniority?** Yes, definitely: 8%; Unsure: 47%; No, definitely not: 45%

7. **Compared to pre-9/11, how safe do you feel US airlines are in general today?** Very unsafe: 1%; Unsafe: 21%; Neutral: 30%; Safe: 34%; Very safe: 14%

8. **Many airlines have explored merging in the post-9/11 period. How safe do you feel US airlines are during the merger process?** Very unsafe: 1%; Unsafe: 15%; Neutral: 39%; Safe: 32%; Very safe: 13%

9. **Many airlines have been in bankruptcy in the post-9/11 period. How safe do you feel US airlines are during the bankruptcy process?** Very unsafe: 8%; Unsafe: 30%; Neutral: 28%; Safe: 27%; Very safe: 8%

10. **How likely do you feel it is that a major airline accident will occur in the coming years due to post-9/11 airline cost cutting?** Very likely: 24%; Somewhat likely: 46%; Neutral: 17%; Unlikely: 11%; Very unlikely: 2%

11. **While flying at your airline, how often did you witness increased stress on the pilot workforce due to post-9/11 company cost cutting measures?** Never: 1%; Very rarely: 3%; Monthly: 8%; Weekly: 17%; Daily: 71%

12. **How often did you witness questionable safety practices at your airline due to post-9/11 company cost cutting measures?** Never: 4%; Very rarely: 22%; Monthly: 22%; Weekly: 22%; Daily: 29%

13. **How often did you witness mistakes and/or distractions on the flight deck because of post-9/11 cost cutting and work-rule changes?** Never: 2%; Very rarely: 21%; Monthly: 16%; Weekly: 27%; Daily: 33%

14. **How competent are decision makers at leading your airline?** Very competent: 1%; Competent: 2%; Neutral: 14%; Incompetent: 47%; Very incompetent: 36%

15. **How competent are regulators at supervising safety in the US commercial airline industry?** Very competent: 0%; Competent: 5%; Neutral: 29%; Incompetent: 41%; Very incompetent: 25%

16. **Would you recommend an airline career to a young person today?** Yes: 8%; No: 92%

Appendix B

AIRLINE PILOT INTERVIEW GUIDE

I am interested in what it's like working in the post-9/11 airline industry, in particular, how things have changed from pre-9/11. I have about ten questions to ask, if you're ready to get started.

1. Can you please describe a timeline of your airline career—date hired at your airline, furloughed, recalled, etc. If on furlough, will you go back when recalled?
2. Can you describe how, in your experience, work conditions have changed at your airline since Sept 11th 2001 (9/11)?
3. How has this affected your job performance and the work of others?
4. While flying at your airline, did you witness increased stress on the pilot workforce due to company cost-cutting measures? If so, can you provide some examples?
5. While flying at your airline, did you witness questionable safety practices due to company cost-cutting measures? If so, can you provide some examples?

6. Do you feel that airlines are less safe now than they were before 9/11? Can you provide some examples?

7. Do you feel that airline mergers impact safety? Can you provide some examples?

8. Airline executives would like the public to believe that 9/11 caused the latest industry downturn, requiring the drastic cost-cutting measures that ensued. Do you think that's true or were there other causes?

9. Do you have confidence in the decision makers leading your airline—why/why not?

10. Do you have confidence in the aviation industry regulators to monitor safety—why/why not?

11. What are the biggest challenges facing the future of commercial aviation—what worries you most?

12. Is there anything else you'd like to add?

13. Who else would you recommend that I talk with? [snowball sampling]

14. Is there anything in particular I should ask them?

ABBREVIATIONS

ALPA   Air Line Pilots Association
ATC   air traffic control
BAC   Bureau of Air Commerce
BET   Business Education Training
CAA   Civil Aeronautics Authority (1938–40)
CAA   Civil Aeronautics Administration (after 1940)
CAB   Civil Aeronautics Board
CFTC   Commodity Futures Trading Commission
CRM   crew resource management
DOT   Department of Transportation
EAS   Essential Air Service
FAA   Federal Aviation Administration
FCC   Federal Communications Commission
GAO   Government Accounting Office
IPO   initial public offering
NASA   National Aeronautics and Space Administration

NAOMS	National Aviation Operations Monitoring System
NTSB	National Transportation Safety Board
PBGC	Pension Benefit Guarantee Corporation
RJ	regional jet
SEC	Securities Exchange Commission
TARP	Troubled Asset Relief Program
TIA	Texas International Airlines
TSA	Transportation Security Agency
TWA	Trans World Airways
WASP	Women Airforce Service Pilots
WAE	Western Air and Express

NOTES

Prologue: Falling

1. See, for example, T. A. Heppenheimer, *Turbulent Skies: The History of Commercial Aviation* (New York: John Wiley & Sons, 1995); James Ott and Raymond E. Neidl, *Airline Odyssey: The Airline Industry's Turbulent Flight into the Future* (New York: McGraw-Hill, 1995); Barbara Sturken Peterson and James Glab, *Rapid Descent: Deregulation and the Shakeout in the Airlines* (New York: Simon & Schuster, 1994); and Thomas Petzinger, Jr., *Hard Landing: The Epic Contest for Power and Profits That Plunged the Airlines into Chaos* (New York: Random House, 1995).

2. See, for example, Stephen Lippmann, "Rethinking Risk in the New Economy: Age and Cohort Effects on Unemployment and Re-Employment," *Human Relations* 61 (2008): 1259–92; Ruby Mendenhall, Ariel Kalil, Laurel J. Spindel, and Cassandra M. D. Hart, "Job Loss at Mid-Life: Managers and Executives Face the 'New Risk Economy,'" *Social Forces* 87 (2008): 185–209; Richard Sennett, *The Corrosion of Character: The Personal Consequences of Work in the New Capitalism* (New York: W. W. Norton, 1998); and Richard Sennett, *The Culture of the New Capitalism* (New Haven: Yale University Press, 2006).

3. See, for example, Amy L. Fraher, "When Profit-Seeking Trumps Safety: The Risks and Opportunities of Liminality in Commercial Aviation in Post-9/11 America," in *Towards a Socioanalysis of Money, Finance, and Capitalism: Beneath the Surface of the Financial Industry*, ed. Susan Long and Burkard Sievers (New York: Routledge, 2012); Miguel Martinez Lucio and Robert Perrett, "Meanings and Dilemmas in Community Unionism: Trade Union Community Initiatives and Black and Minority Ethnic Groups in the UK," *Work, Employment and Society* 23 (2009): 693–710; Miguel Martinez Lucio and Mark Stuart, "'Partnership' and New Industrial Relations

in a Risk Society: An Age of Shotgun Weddings and Marriages of Convenience?" *Work, Employment and Society* 19 (2005): 797–817; Jeffrey J. Sallaz, "Manufacturing Concessions: Attritionary Outsourcing at General Motor's Lordstown, USA Assembly Plant," *Work, Employment and Society* 18 (2004): 687–708; and Paul Stewart and Miguel Martinez Lucio, "Collective Narratives and Politics in the Contemporary Study of Work: The New Management Practices Debate," *Work, Employment and Society* 25 (2011): 327–41.

4. See, for example, Peter Cappelli, *The New Deal at Work: Managing the Market-Driven Workforce* (Boston: Harvard Business School Press, 1999); Cliff Hakim, *We Are All Self-Employed: The New Social Contract for Working in a Changed World* (San Francisco, CA: Berrett-Koehler, 1994); Carrie M. Lane, *A Company of One: Insecurity, Independence, and the New World of White-Collar Unemployment* (Ithaca: ILR Press/Cornell University Press, 2011); and Louis Uchitelle, *The Disposable American: Layoffs and Their Consequences,* (New York: Alfred A. Knopf, 2006).

5. See, for example, Christopher Grey and Amanda Sinclair, "Writing Differently," *Organization* 13 (2006): 443–53; Ajnesh Prasad and Albert J. Mills, "Critical Management Studies and Business Ethics: A Synthesis and Three Research Trajectories for the Coming Decade," *Journal of Business Ethics* 94 (2010): 227–37; Rasmus Koss Rasmussen, "Encouraging Cases: Exploring the Potential of Critical Realist Case Studies of 'What Could Be' for a Critically Performative CMS," Copenhagen Business School, accessed July 10, 2013, http://openarchive.cbs.dk/bitstream/handle/10398/8298/Encouraging_cases_Working_paper_2_.pdf; Andre Spicer, Mats Alvesson, and Dan Karreman, "Critical Performativity: The Unfinished Business of Critical Management Studies," *Human Relations* 62 (2009): 537–60; and Mayer N. Zald, "Spinning Disciplines: Critical Management Studies in the Context of the Transformation of Management Education," *Organization* 9 (2002): 365–86.

6. William Lazonick and Mary O'Sullivan, "Maximising Shareholder Value: A New Ideology for Corporate Governance," *Economy and Society* 29 (2000): 13–35; Julie Froud, Johal Sukhdev, Adam Leaver, and Karel Williams, *Financialization and Strategy: Narratives and Numbers* (London: Routledge, 2006).

7. Michael Foucault and Colin Gordon, *Power/Knowledge: Selected Interviews and Other Writings, 1972–1977* (Brighton, UK: Harvester Press, 1980), 82.

1. The (Not So) Secret Secrets

1. Joe Sharkey, "Fees on Top of Fees Obscure Cost of Flying," *New York Times,* July 23, 2012, accessed July 24, 2012, http://www.nytimes.com/2012/07/24/business/revenue-from-extra-fees-adds-up-for-airlines.html.

2. Jad Mouawad, "Airline Unions Seek a Share of the Industry Gains," *New York Times,* October 27, 2010, accessed on June 23, 2013, http://www.nytimes.com/2010/10/28/business/28labor.html.

3. "Operating Revenue—All US Carriers," Research and Innovative Technology Administration, Bureau of Transportation Statistics, accessed June 23, 2013, http://www.transtats.bts.gov/Data_Elements_Financial.aspx?Data=7.

4. Nathaniel Popper, "CEO Pay, Rising Despite the Din," *New York Times,* June 17, 2012, accessed June 23, 2013, http://www.nytimes.com/2012/06/17/business/executive-pay-still-climbing-despite-a-shareholder-din.html and see also http://www.nytimes.com/interactive/2012/04/08/business/executive-compensation.html?ref=business.

5. Andrew Ross Sorkin, "American Airlines and US Airways Dance around a Merger," *New York Times,* July 9, 2012, accessed July 10, 2012, http://dealbook.nytimes.com/2012/07/09/american-and-us-airways-dance-around-a-merger/.

6. Ibid.

7. Ibid.

8. Gretchen Morgenson, "Gee Bankruptcy Never Looked so Good," *New York Times,* January 15, 2006, accessed June 23, 2013, http://query.nytimes.com/gst/fullpage.html.

9. Primary data in this study included hundreds of informal conversations with aviation professionals, 127 in-depth pilot survey responses (appendix A), and 43 semistructured commercial pilot interviews (appendix B) of one to two hours in length. Informants' anonymity is protected through pseudonyms. Pilots interviewed ranged in age from thirty-two to sixty-three, were predominately male (96%), and averaged 23 years of total aviation experience with 13.5 years flying at a major commercial airline and an average of 10,271 flight hours. In sum, they were all established professionals with significant aviation experience and years invested in their airline career. Interviews were conducted between September 2010 and July 2011via telephone or Skype and were digitally recorded and transcribed. In addition, dozens of e-mails were exchanged with respondents over time to clarify discrepancies, expand discussion, and amplify points of interest as I deepened my analysis. An interview guide was used, however interviews were mainly nondirective. Informants were encouraged to talk about their life, feelings, family, and work. In response, a broad spectrum of material was produced.

10. Matthew L. Wald, "Fatal Airplane Crashes Drop 65," *New York Times,* October 1, 2007, accessed June 23, 2013, http://www.nytimes.com/2007/10/01/business/01safety.html.

11. Chesley B. Sullenberger, Statement before the Subcommittee on Aviation Committee on Transportation and Infrastructure United States House of Representatives, Washington, DC, February 24, 2009, accessed July 3, 2013, http://www.gpo.gov/fdsys/pkg/CHRG-111hhrg47866/html/CHRG-111hhrg47866.htm.

12. Ibid.

13. See, for example, US Government Accountability Office (GAO), "Commercial Aviation: Air Service Trends at Small Communities since October 2000," GAO-05-834T, Testimony before the Committee on Commerce, Science, and Transportation Subcommittee on Aviation, US Senate, March 2002, accessed December 18, 2009, http://www.gao.gov/new.items/d05834t.pdf; GAO, "Commercial Aviation: Structural Costs Continue to Challenge Legacy Airlines' Financial Performance," GAO-02–432, Report to Congressional Requesters, July 2002, accessed December 18, 2009, http://www.gao.gov/new.items/d02432.pdf; GAO, "Commercial Aviation: Legacy Airlines Must Further Reduce Costs to Restore Profitability," GAO-04–836, Report to Congressional Committees, August 2004, accessed December 18, 2009, http://www.gao.gov/new.items/d04836.pdf; GAO, "Commercial Aviation: Structural Costs Continue to Challenge Legacy Airlines' Financial Performance," GAO-05-834T, Testimony before the Committee on Commerce, Science, and Transportation, Subcommittee on Aviation, US Senate, July 2005, accessed January 30, 2010, www.gao.gov/new.items/d05834t.pdf; GAO, "Commercial Aviation: Bankruptcy and Pension Problems Are Symptoms of Underlying Structural Issue," GAO-05–945, Report to Congressional Committees, September 2005, accessed December 18, 2009, http://www.gao.gov/new.items/d05945.pdf; GAO, "Airline Deregulation: Reregulating the Airline Industry Would Likely Reverse Consumer Benefits and Not Save Airline Pensions Structural Costs Continue to Challenge Legacy Airlines' Financial Performance," GAO-06–630, Report to Congressional Committees, June 2006, accessed December 19, 2009, http://www.gao.gov/new.items/d06630.pdf; GAO, "Airline Industry: Potential Mergers and Acquisitions Driven by Financial and Competitive Pressures," GAO-08–845, Report to the Subcommittee on Aviation Operations, Safety, and Security, Committee on Commerce, Science, and Transportation, US Senate, July 2008, accessed December 13, 2009, http://www.gao.gov/new.items/d08845.pdf; and GAO, "Commercial Aviation: Airline Industry Contraction Due to Volatile Fuel Prices and Falling Demand Affects Airports, Passengers, and Federal Government Revenues," GAO-09–393, Report to Congressional Requesters, April 2009, accessed December 18, 2009, http://www.gao.gov/new.items/d09393.pdf.

14. GAO 2005, "Bankruptcy and Pension Problems," 19 and 27.

15. GAO 2005, "Structural Costs Continue to Challenge," 20.

16. Jonathan Levy, *Freaks of Fortune: The Emerging World of Capitalism and Risk in America* (Cambridge: Harvard University Press, 2013), 21–22.

17. Ibid., 295.

18. See, for example, cited in Levy, *Freaks of Fortune*, 281; J. B. Clark, "Insurance and Business Profit," *Quarterly Journal of Economics* 7 (1892), 40–54; and J. B. Clark, *The Distribution of Wealth: A Theory of Wages, Interest and Profit* (New York: Macmillan, 1902).

19. Mary Schiavo, *Flying Blind, Flying Safe* (New York: Avon Books, 1997), 65.

20. FAA, *Economic Values for FAA Investment And Regulatory Decisions: A Guide,* DTFA 01–02–C00200, prepared by FAA Office of Aviation Policy and Plans Data Base Products, 2004, accessed May 21, 2013, http://www.faa.gov/regulations_policies/policy_guidance/benefit_cost/media/050404%20Critical%20Values%20Dec%2031%20Report%2007Jan05.pdf.

21. FAA, "Economic Values," 2-2.

22. Mark Dowie, "Pinto Madness," *Mother Jones,* 1997, accessed May 21, 2013, http://www.motherjones.com/politics/1977/09/pinto-madness.

23. *Time,* "The 50 Worst Cars of All Time," 2007, accessed May 21, 2013, http://www.time.com/time/specials/2007/article/0,28804,1658545_1658498_1657866,00.html.

24. Dowie, "Pinto Madness."

25. Matthew T. Lee and M. David Ermann, "Pinto 'Madness' as a Flawed Landmark Narrative: An Organizational and Network Analysis," *Social Problems* 46 (1999): 30–47.

26. P. Greenberg, "Got Fear of Flying? Discover the Real Odds of a Travel Accident," *Bing Travel,* 2009, accessed January 6, 2011, http://www.bing.com/travel/content/search?q=Got+Fear+of+Flying%3f+Discover+the+Real+Odds+of+a+Travel+Accident&fc_idx=1.

27. The 2008 study reported only 564 aviation fatalities annually, while 37,261 people died in motor vehicles and 798 on railroads, accessed January 3, 2011, http://www.bts.gov/publications/national_transportation_statistics/html/table_02_01.html.

28. Scott Patterson, *The Quants: The Math Geniuses who Brought Down Wall Street* (London: Random House, 2010).

29. Arnold Barnett, MIT World Lecture, "Air Safety: Nothing But Blue Skies?," June 6, 2009, accessed September 1, 2011, http://video.mit.edu/watch/air-safety-nothing-but-blue-skies-9466.

30. Alan Levin, "Airways in USA Are the Safest Ever," *USA Today,* June 6, 2006, accessed July 3, 2013, http://usatoday30.usatoday.com/news/nation/2006-06-29-air-safety-cover_x.htm.

31. Barnett, "Air Safety."

32. Jad Mouawad and Christopher Drew, "Airline Industry at Its Safest since the Dawn of the Jet Age," *New York Times,* February 11, 2013, accessed May 19, 2013, http://www.nytimes.com/2013/02/12/business/2012-was-the-safest-year-for-airlines-globally-since-1945.html.

33. Ibid.

34. William Langewiesche, *Fly by Wire: The Geese, the Glide, the Miracle on the Hudson* (New York: Farrar, Straus and Giroux, 2009), 20–21.

35. J. A. Douglas, "Not Good Enough," *Aviation Safety World,* editorial page, August 2006, accessed January 20, 2009, http://www.flightsafety.org/asw/aug06/asw_aug06.pdf.

36. Schiavo, *Flying Blind,* 236.

37. Jad Mouawad, "When Flying 720 Miles Takes 12 Hours," *New York Times,* May 2, 2012, accessed May 19, 2013, http://www.nytimes.com/2012/05/03/business/regional-airlines-squeezed-by-flight-cutbacks-and-higher-fares.html.

38. Barnett, "Air Safety."

39. Jesse Eisinger, "Finding the Human Factor in Bank Risk," *New York Times,* April 3, 2013, accessed May 19, 2013, http://dealbook.nytimes.com/2013/04/03/uncovering-the-human-factor-in-risk-management-models.

40. Ibid.

41. See, for example, Max H. Bazerman and Michael D. Watkins, *Predictable Surprises: The Disasters You Should Have Seen Coming and How to Prevent Them* (Boston: Harvard Business School Press, 2004); Sidney W. A. Dekker, *Ten Questions about Human Error* (London: Lawrence Erlbaum Associates, 2005); Amy L. Fraher, *'Thinking through Crisis': Improving Teamwork and Leadership in High-Risk Fields* (New York: Cambridge University Press, 2011); Charles Perrow, *Normal Accidents: Living with High-Risk Technologies* (New York: Basic Books, 1984); James Reason, *Human Error* (Cambridge: Cambridge University Press, 1990); Mark Stein, "A Culture of Mania: A Psychoanalytic View of the Incubation of the 2008 Credit Crisis," *Organization* 19 (2011): 173–86; and Barry A. Turner, "The Organizational and Interorganizational Development of Disasters," *Administrative Science Quarterly* 21 (1976): 378–97.

42. Turner, "Development of Disasters," 381.

43. Dekker, *Ten Questions,* 18.

44. Reason, *Human Error,* 5.

45. Perrow, *Normal Accidents.*

46. Fraher, *Thinking through Crisis.*

47. See Bazerman and Watkins, 2004; and Max H. Bazerman and Michael D. Watkins, "Airline Security, the Failure of 9/11, and Predictable Surprises," *International Public Management Journal* 8 (2005): 365–76.

48. Bazerman and Watkins, *Predictable Surprises,* 5–7.

49. Al Gore, *White House Commission on Aviation Safety and Security: Final Report to President Clinton*, 1996, accessed November 23, 2008, http://www.fas.org/irp/threat/212fin~1.html.

50. Ibid., 7.

51. Ibid., 96–7.

52. Matthew L. Wald, "NASA Offers Airline Safety Data," *New York Times,* January 1, 2008, accessed July 10, 2013, http://www.nytimes.com/2008/01/01/us/01nasa.html.

53. "No Space for Aviation Safety at NASA," Union of Concerned Scientists, last modified February 11, 2008, accessed January 20, 2009, http://www.ucsusa.org/scientific_integrity/abuses_of_science/nasa-pilot-survey.html.

54. Wald, "NASA Offers Airline Safety Data."

55. CNN, "Report Containing Thousands of Pilot Complaints Is Released," December 31, 2007, accessed January 20, 2009, http://www.cnn.com/2007/TECH/space/12/31/nasa.airsafety/index.html.

56. Wald, "NASA Offers Airline Safety Data."

57. James L. Oberstar and John L. Mica, *Critical Lapses in FAA Safety Oversight of Airlines: Abuses of Regulatory "Partnership Programs,"* Summary of Subject Matter, US House of Representatives Committee on Transportation and Infrastructure (Washington, DC: US Government Printing Office, 2008), 7.

58. Oberstar and Mica, *Critical Lapses,* 4.

59. Ibid., 13.

60. Ibid., 5.

61. Ibid., 1.

62. Gore, *White House Commission,* 11.

63. Oberstar and Mica, *Critical Lapses,* 12.

64. Ibid., 12.

65. Matthew L. Wald and Micheline Maynard, "Behind Air Chaos, an FAA Pendulum Swing," *New York Times,* April 23, 2008, accessed July 3, 2013, http://www.nytimes.com/2008/04/13/business/13air.html.

66. Ibid.

67. Associated Press, "A Timeline of Boeing's 787 Dreamliner," *Komo News*, January 25, 2013, accessed May 21, 2013, http://www.komonews.com/news/boeing/A-timeline-of-Boeings-787-Dreamliner-188352651.html.

68. James Surowiecki, "Requiem for a Dreamliner?" *New Yorker,* February 4, 2013, accessed May 21, 2013, http://www.newyorker.com/talk/financial/2013/02/04/130204ta_talk_surowiecki.

69. Associated Press, "Timeline."

70. Associated Press, "Airlines Ground all Boeing 787s," *Boston Globe*, January 16, 2013, accessed May 23, 2013, http://www.bostonglobe.com/business/2013/01/16/japan-makes-emergency-landing-due-battery/Ne7TNT4Lrlqlx3HSfEqoIM/story.html.

71. James E. Hall, "A Back Seat for Safety at the FAA," *New York Times*, April 25, 2013, accessed May 21, 2013, http://www.nytimes.com/2013/04/26/opinion/a-back-seat-for-safety-at-the-faa.html.

72. Hiroko Tabuchi and Christopher Drew, "Japanese Pilots Worry about Repaired Boeing 787 Jets," *New York Times,* June 4, 2013, accessed June 10, 2013, http://www.nytimes.com/2013/06/05/business/japanese-pilots-worry-about-repaired-boeing-787-jets.html.

73. Joan Lowy, "Congress Quiet on Dreamliner Woes," *Post and Courier,* March 20, 2013, accessed May 21, 2013, http://www.postandcourier.com/article/20130320/PC05/130329981/1012/congress-quiet-on-dreamliner-woes.

2. The Roots of Turbulence

1. Tom D. Crouch, *Wings: A History of Aviation from Kites to the Space Age* (New York: W.W. Norton, 2003); R.G. Grant, *Flight: 100 Years of Aviation* (New York: Dorling Kindersley, 2002); Sherwood Harris, *The First to Fly: Aviation's Pioneer Days* (Summit, PA: Tab/Aero Books, 1991); Stephen Kirk, *First in Flight: The Wright Brothers in North Carolina* (Winston-Salem, NC: John F. Blair, 1995).

2. Grant, *Flight,* 15.

3. Ibid., 16 and 11.

4. Using the Consumer Price Index calculated at http://www.measuringworth.com/uscompare/result.php?use[]=DOLLAR&use[]=GDPDEFLATION&use[]=VCB&use[]=UNSKILLED&use[]=MANCOMP&use[]=NOMGDPCP&use[]=NOMINALGDP&year_source=1898&amount=1&year_result=2010#.

5. Crouch, *Wings,* 60–61 and 108.

6. For instance, in 1908 Lord Northcliffe offered £1,000 for a pilot to fly across the English Channel, and in 1911 William Randolph Hearst offered $50,000 for the first US coast-to-coast flight.

7. Kirk, *First in Flight,* 235–7.

8. Ibid., 239–40.

9. Ray Holanda, *A History of Aviation Safety Featuring the US Airline System* (Bloomington, IN: Authorhouse, 2009), 25.

10. Ibid., 24.

11. Crouch, *Wings*, 137–38 and 147.

12. Kirk, *First in Flight*.

13. Crouch, *Wings*, 146; Kirk, *First in Flight,* 241 and 258.

14. Frederick Lewis Allen, *Since Yesterday* (New York: Bantam Books, 1940).

15. Charles R. Geisst, *Wall Street: From Its Beginnings to the Fall of Enron* (Oxford: Oxford University Press, 2004), 10–11.

16. R.J. Teweles, E.S. Bradley, and T.M. Teweles, *The Stock Market* (New York: Wiley & Sons, 1992).

17. Geisst, *Wall Street*, 27.

18. Levy, *Freaks of Fortune,* 270–72.

19. Vernon M. Briggs, Jr., "The Mutual Aid Pact of the Airline Industry," *Industrial and Labor Relations Review* 19 (1965), 3–20, accessed July 4, 2013, http://works.bepress.com/vernon_briggs/3/.

20. Geisst, *Wall Street,* 31.

21. Ibid., 77.

22. Elisabeth S. Clemens, *The People's Lobby: Organizational Innovation and the Rise of Interest Group Politics in the United States, 1890–1925* (Chicago: Chicago University Press, 1997).

23. Christopher M. Loomis, "The Politics of Uncertainty: Lobbyists and Propaganda in Early Twentieth-Century America," *The Journal of Policy History* 21 (2009): 187–213.

24. "Lobbying Database," accessed October 2, 1023, http://www.opensecrets.org/lobby/.

25. Geisst, *Wall Street,* 68.

26. Louis Hyman, *Debtor Nation: The History of America in Red Ink* (Princeton: Princeton University Press, 2011).

27. Ibid., 32–34.

28. Alfred D. Chandler, Jr. "The Emergence of Managerial Capitalism," The Business History Review 58 (1984): 473–503.

29. Robinson, *Free Fall,* 13.

30. Crouch, *Wings*, 166; Grant, *Flight*, 83 and 91; Holanda, *History of Aviation Safety*, 26.

31. See, for example, P. M. Charles, *Women in Aeronautics* (New York: Thomas Nelson and Sons, 1962), 80; and Henry Holden, *Ladybirds: The Untold Story of Women Pilots in America.* (Freedom, NJ: Blackhawk 1992), 33–34.

32. Crouch, *Wings,* 156–58; Grant, *Flight,* 73.

33. "Centennial of Flight," accessed December 30, 2010, http://www.centennialofflight.gov/essay/Explorers_Record_Setters_and_Daredevils/barnstormers/EX12.htm.

34. Dean Jaros, *Heroes without Legacy: American Airwomen, 1912–1944* (Niwot: University Press of Colorado, 1993).

35. See, for example, R. E. G. Davies, *Airlines of the United States since 1914* (Washington, DC: Smithsonian Institution Press, 1972), 4; Grant, *Flight,* 108–9; and Crouch, *Wings.* 217.

36. T. A. Heppenheimer, *Turbulent Skies: The History of Commercial Aviation* (New York: John Wiley & Sons, 1995), 6–7.

37. Grant, *Flight,* 112–3.

38. Holanda, *History of Aviation Safety*, 28; "Air Mail Pioneers," accessed August 20, 2010, http://www.airmailpioneers.org/history/Sagahistory.htm.

39. Understandably, accidents do not occur this predictably. But for calculation purposes, 1.5 million airmail miles were flown between 1918–21 (Holanda, *History of Aviation Safety,* 32). At 200 miles per flight, 7,500 flights were flown, divided by 27 deaths, equals one death per 277 flights; 7,500 flights divided by three years, or 1,095 days, equals approximately 7 flights per day; 277 flights divided by 7 equals one death per 39 days.

40. Davies, *Airlines of the United States,* 23; Holanda, *History of Aviation Safety,* 28–32.

41. Between 1921 and 1927 (Holanda, *History of Aviation Safety*, 35).

42. Davies, *Airlines of the United States,* 14–15, and 582.

43. Ibid., 34.

44. Ibid., 33.

45. John T. Correll, "The Air Mail Fiasco," *Air Force Magazine,* March 2008, 60–65, accessed August 22, 2010, http://www.airforce-magazine.com/MagazineArchive/Pages/2008/March%202008/0308airmail.aspx.

46. Heppenheimer, *Turbulent Skies,* 33.

47. Hotel Lafayette and Brevoort Hotel in Greenwich Village.

48. From $21 to $71 million (Crouch, *Wings,* 268).

49. Davies, *Airlines of the United States,* 57.

50. A. Scott Berg, *Lindbergh* (New York: G. P. Putnam's Sons, 1998).

51. Davies, *Airlines of the United States,* 85; Holanda, *History of Aviation Safety,* 48.

52. Crouch, *Wings,* 270; Davies, *Airlines of the United States,* 83–84.

53. Holanda, *History of Aviation Safety,* 62.

54. Adam Cohen, *Nothing to Fear: FDR's Inner Circle and the Hundred Days that Created Modern America* (New York: Penguin, 2009), 276.

55. Heppenheimer, *Turbulent Skies,* 25.

56. Edward V. Rickenbacker, *Rickenbacker* (Englewood Cliffs, NJ: Prentice-Hall, 1967), 215.

57. Grant, *Flight,* 144–45.

58. Michelle Higgins, "63 Years Flying; from Glamour to Days of Gray," *New York Times,* March 17, 2012, accessed July 13, 2012, http://www.nytimes.com/2012/03/18/us/63-years-flying-from-glamour-to-days-of-gray.html.

59. Rogelio Saenz and Louwanda Evans, "The Changing Demography of US Flight Attendants," *Population Reference Bureau,* June 2009, accessed July 13, 2012, http://www.prb.org/Articles/2009/usflightattendants.aspx.

60. Saenz and Evans, "Changing Demography."

61. Holanda, *History of Aviation Safety,* 71–72.

62. Robert J. Serling, *Eagle: The Story of American Airlines* (New York: St Martin's Press, 1985), 65.

63. Correll, "Air Mail Fiasco," 61.

64. Holanda, *History of Aviation Safety,* 72.

65. Davies, *Airlines of the United States,* 155.

66. Ibid., 146.

67. Dominick A. Pisano, *To Fill the Skies with Pilots: The Civilian Pilot Training Program 1939–46* (Chicago: University of Illinois Press, 1993), 14–15.

68. Ibid.

69. Ibid.

70. Heppenheimer, *Turbulent Skies*, 57.

71. Correll, "Air Mail Fiasco," 61.

72. Rickenbacker, *Rickenbacker,* 185.

73. Davies, *Airlines of the United States,* 158; Heppenheimer, *Turbulent Skies*, 60–61.

74. Heppenheimer, *Turbulent Skies*, 62.

75. W. M. Emmons, "Private and Public Responses to Market Failure in the US Electric Power Industry, 1882–1942," *Journal of Economic History* 51 (1991): 452–54.

76. Cohen, *Nothing to Fear,* 147–9; W. M. Emmons, "Franklin D. Roosevelt, Electric Utilities, and the Power of Competition," *Journal of Economic History* 53 (1993): 880–907.

77. John G. Wensveen, *Air Transportation* (Burlington VT: Ashgate, 2007), 43.

78. Ibid., 38.

79. Crouch, *Wings,* 275.

80. Holanda, *History of Aviation Safety,* 81.

81. Ibid., 82.

82. Wensveen, *Air Transportation,* 52.

83. Emmons, "Private and Public Responses"; Emmons, "Power of Competition."

84. Pisano, *To Fill the Skies with Pilots,* 2.

85. Ibid., 43.

86. Ibid., 3.

87. Actually, the program first began in 1942 with the Women's Auxiliary Ferry Service (WAFS) and the Women's Flying Training Detachment (WFTD). In 1943, these merged into the WASPs (Holanda, *History of Aviation Safety,* 76–77).

88. Holden, *Ladybirds*, 88.

89. Sam Matthews, "Flashbacks Reveal Airport's Rich Heritage," *Tracy Press*, April 22, 2009, accessed August 20, 2011, http://www.tracypress.com/pages/full_story/push?article-Flashbacks+reveal+airport%E2%80%99s+rich+heritage%20&id=2423639.

90. Pisano, *To Fill the Skies with Pilots,* 115–19.

91. See for example, ATP flight school website, http://www.atpflightschool.com/.

92. Sixteen million passengers flew on US airlines in 1949 versus 1 million in 1939 (Holanda, *History of Aviation Safety,* 101–3).

93. Wensveen, *Air Transportation,* 41.

94. Civil Aeronautics Board, *Accident Investigation Report: Trans World Airlines, Inc., Lockheed 1049A, N6902C, and United Air Lines, Inc., Douglas DC-7, N6324C, Grand Canyon, Arizona,* April 17, 1957, accessed January 27, 2011, http://ntl1.specialcollection.net/scripts/ws.dll?websearch&site=dot_aircraftacc.

95. CAB, *TWA-United Accident Investigation Report,* 3.

96. "Maryland Plane Crash Stirs Need for Air Controls," *Fresno Bee,* May 21, 1956, 8-B.

3. Riding the Jet Stream

1. Holanda, *History of Aviation Safety,* 164.

2. Dwight D. Eisenhower, *Annual Budget Message to Congress,* January 16, 1961, accessed February 18, 2011, http://www.eisenhowermemorial.org/onepage/IKE%20&%20Transportation.EN.Nov08.FINAL.pdf.

3. See, for instance, Paul Stephen Dempsey and Andrew R. Goetz, *Airline Deregulation and Laissez-Faire Mythology* (Westport, CT: Quorum Books, 1992); and Jagdish N. Sheth, Fred C. Allvine, Can Uslay, and Ashutosh Dixit, *Deregulation and Competition: Lessons Learned from the Airline Industry* (Los Angeles: Sage, 2007).

4. Heppenheimer, *Turbulent Skies,* 315–16.

5. Richard H.K. Vietor, "Contrived Competition: Airline Regulation and Deregulation, 1925–1988," *Business History Review* 64 (1990): 69.

6. John E. Robson, "Airline Deregulation: Twenty Years of Success and Counting," *Regulation* (1998), 17–18, accessed July 5, 2013, http://www.cato.org/sites/cato.org/files/serials/files/regulation/1998/4/airline2-98.pdf.

7. Sheth, et al., *Deregulation and Competition,* 22; Thomas Petzinger, Jr., *Hard Landing: The Epic Contest for Power and Profits That Plunged the Airlines into Chaos* (New York: Random House, 1995), 17.

8. Robson, "Airline Deregulation," 17–18.

9. "Boeing History," accessed July 5, 2013, http://www.boeing.com/history/boeing/747.html.

10. See, for instance, Nick Bunkley, "Automakers Start Rush for New Models," *New York Times,* August 6, 2009, accessed May 17, 2012, http://www.nytimes.com/2009/08/07/business/07auto.html; and Nick Bunkley and Bill Vlasic, "Nearly the End of the Line for SUVs," *New York Times,* December 23, 2008, accessed May 17, 2012, http://www.nytimes.com/2008/12/24/business/24auto.html.

11. David M. Herszenhorn, "Deal to Rescue American Automakers Is Moving Ahead," *New York Times,* December 8, 2008, accessed June 23, 2012, http://www.nytimes.com/2008/12/09/business/09auto.html.

12. Sheth, et al., *Deregulation and Competition,* 24–25.

13. Petzinger, *Hard Landing,* 15.

14. Rickenbacker, *Rickenbacker,* 220.

15. Petzinger, *Hard Landing,* 15.

16. Petzinger, *Hard Landing,* 16; Vietor, "Contrived Competition," 67.

17. Vietor, "Contrived Competition," 66.

18. C.E. Woolman, *Business Week,* July 21, 1956, 170.

19. Rickenbacker, *Rickenbacker,* 223.

20. A. R. Sorkin, "Morgan Stanley's Mack: "We Cannot Control Ourselves," *New York Times*, November 19, 2009, accessed February 20, 2011, http://dealbook.nytimes.com/2009/11/19/morgan-stanleys-mack-we-cannot-control-ourselves/.

21. William Greider, *Secrets of the Temple: How the Federal Reserve Runs the Country* (New York: Simon & Schuster, 1987).

22. *Time*, "Transport: Ceiling Zero," May 13, 1935, accessed February 20, 2011, http://www.time.com/time/magazine/article/0,9171,754759,00.html.

23. Petzinger, *Hard Landing*, 16.

24. Vietor, "Contrived Competition," 68.

25. Geisst, *Wall Street*, 217 and 229.

26. S. James Snyder, "Clinton Says Don't Blame Him for the Economic Crisis," *Time*, February 16, 2009, accessed June 23, 2012, http://www.time.com/time/nation/article/0,8599,1879774,00.html.

27. Cyrus Sanati, "10 Years Later, Looking at Repeal of Glass-Steagall," *New York Times*, November 12, 2009, accessed May 19, 2012, http://dealbook.nytimes.com/2009/11/12/10-years-later-looking-at-repeal-of-glass-steagall/.

28. Petzinger, *Hard Landing*, XX.

29. John Helyar, "Why Is This Man Smiling? Continental's Gordon Bethune Turned the Airline Around, Guided It through 9/11, and Became a Great CEO" *Fortune,* October 18, 2004, accessed July 9, 2012, http://money.cnn.com/magazines/fortune/fortune_archive/2004/10/18/8188058/index.htm.

30. Mike Gordon, "William 'Pat' Patterson," *Honolulu Advertiser,* July 2, 2006, accessed February 11, 2011, http://the.honoluluadvertiser.com/150/sesq3patterson.

31. "American National Business Hall of Fame," accessed July 5, 2013, http://www.anbhf.org/laureates/patterson.php.

32. Ibid.

33. Ibid.

34. "Delta News Archive," accessed July 5, 2013, http://news.delta.com/index.php?s=43&item=458.

35. "Delta Flight Museum," accessed July 5, 2013, http://deltamuseum.org/M_Education_DeltaHistory_Facts_FounderQuotes.htm.

36. "Delta Flight Museum."

37. Rickenbacker, *Rickenbacker*, 178, 193, 191, and 182.

38. Ibid., 201, 209, 200.

39. American Aviation Historical Society, *Jack Frye—TWA's First President*, vol. 39 (1994), accessed February 12, 2011, http://www.reocities.com/nas51st/Jack-Frye.html.

40. Public Broadcasting Service (PBS), *Chasing the Sun: TWA*, accessed February 12, 2011, http://www.pbs.org/kcet/chasingthesun/companies/twa.html.

41. Esperison Martinez, Jr., "Trans World Airlines—Dawn to Dusk, Part 2," *Air Line Pilot,* October 2001, accessed February 13, 2011, http://www.alpa.org/portals/alpa/magazine/2001/Oct2001_TransWorldAirlinesII.htm.

42. *Star Citizen,* "Jack Frye Killed in Auto Accident," February 4, 1959, accessed February 12, 2011: http://www.reocities.com/nas51st/frye5.jpg.

43. *Time*, "Aviation: Jets across the US," November 17, 1958, accessed February 13, 2011, http://www.time.com/time/magazine/article/0,9171,810685-1,00.html.

44. Petzinger, *Hard Landing*, 12–3. Heppenheimer, *Turbulent Skies,* 64.

45. Time, "Jets across the US."

46. Robert J. Serling, *From the Captain to the Colonel: An Informal History of Eastern Airlines* (New York: Dial, 1980), 3–5.

47. "Strike Report: US Airlines," National Mediation Board, accessed July 5, 2013, http://www.nmb.gov/publicinfo/airline-strikes.html.

4. A New Solution: Deregulation

1. Public Broadcasting System (PBS), *First Measured Century*, Ben Wattenberg, host, "Interview with A. E. Kahn," accessed May 10, 2012, http://www.pbs.org/fmc/interviews/kahn.htm.

2. Vietor, "Contrived Competition."

3. Liesl Miller Orenic, *On the Ground: Labor Struggle in the American Airline Industry* (Chicago: University of Illinois Press, 209), 139.

4. Ibid., 137.

5. Ibid., 140.

6. Petzinger, *Hard Landing*, 17.

7. Mark Gillespie, "American Public Has Mixed Feelings on Airline Safety: Pilots Get Most Credit for Efforts to Maintain Safety Standards," Gallup News Service, February 2, 2000, accessed March 15, 2012, http://www.gallup.com/poll/3271/american-public-has-mixed-feelings-airline-safety.aspx.

8. Tim Murphy, "For Fear of Flying, Therapy Takes to the Skies," *New York Times,* July 24, 2007, accessed May 19, 2012, http://www.nytimes.com/2007/07/24/health/psychology/24fear.html.

9. See, for example, Richard E. Caves, *Air Transport and Its Regulators: An Industry Study* (Cambridge: Harvard University Press, 1962); William A. Jordon, *Airline Regulation in America: Effects and Imperfections* (Baltimore: Johns Hopkins University Press, 1970); Alfred E. Kahn, *The Economics of Regulation* (New York: John Wiley & Sons, 1970); and Samuel B. Richmond, *Regulation and Competition in Air Transportation* (New York: Columbia University Press, 1961).

10. John F. Stover, *American Railroads* (Chicago: University of Chicago Press, 1997).

11. Alfred E. Kahn, "Surprises of Airline Deregulation," *American Economic Review* 78 (1988): 316–22; and Alfred E. Kahn, *Lessons from Deregulation: Telecommunications and Airlines after the Crunch* (Washington, DC: AEI Brookings Joint Center for Regulatory Studies, 2003).

12. Alfred E. Kahn, "Reflections of an Unwitting 'Political Entrepreneur,'" *Review of Network Economics* 7 (2008): 619.

13. Robert D. Hershey, "Alfred E. Kahn Dies at 93; Prime Mover of Airline Deregulation," *New York Times,* December 28, 2010, accessed March 17, 2012, http://www.nytimes.com/2010/12/29/business/29kahn.html.

14. Hershey, "Kahn Dies at 93."

15. Vietor, "Contrived Competition," 61.

16. Anthony E. Brown, *The Politics of Airline Deregulation* (Knoxville: University of Tennessee Press, 1987), 108.

17. James Ott and Raymond E. Neidl, *Airline Odyssey* (New York: McGraw Hill, 1995).

18. Ibid., 1.

19. "Our Favourite Air Lines," *Economist*, December 22, 2011, accessed July 9, 2012, http://www.economist.com/blogs/gulliver/2011/12/business-quotations.

20. Robson, "Airline Deregulation."

21. James Lardner and Robert Kuttner, "Flying Blind: Airline Deregulation Reconsidered," Dēmos, accessed June 23, 2013, http://www.demos.org/sites/default/files/publications/Flying%20Blind.pdf.

22. GAO, "Airline Mergers: Issues Raised by the Proposed Merger of American Airlines and US Airways," GAO-13–403T, Testimony before the Subcommittee on Aviation Operations, Safety, and Security, Committee on Commerce, Science and Transportation, US Senate, June 2013, accessed June 20, 2013, http://www.gao.gov/assets/660/655314.pdf.

23. Dan Reed, "Wrath of Kahn Kept Airfares Low," *USA Today,* July 24, 2007, accessed March 18, 2012, http://www.usatoday.com/money/industries/travel/2007-07-23-alfred-kahn_N.htm.

24. "1966–1971: The Fight to Fly," SWAMedia, accessed July 5, 2013, http://www.swamedia.com/channels/By-Date/pages/1966-to-1971.

25. GAO, "Airline Mergers."

26. William A. Niskanen, "Reaganomics," *Concise Encyclopedia of Economics*, Library of Economics and Liberty, accessed September 10, 2010, http://www.econlib.org/library/Enc/Reaganomics.html.

27. Sheth, et al., *Deregulation and Competition,* 58–59.

28. Lou Gannon, "Actor, Governor, President, Icon," *Washington Post,* June 6, 2004, accessed September 10, 2010, http://www.washingtonpost.com/wp-dyn/articles/A18329-2004Jun5.html.

29. Joseph A. McCartin, "A Historian's Perspective on the PATCO Strike, Its Legacy, and Lessons," *Employee Responsibilities and Rights Journal* 18 (2006): 215–22.

30. Bruce Webber, "J. Lynn Helms, Who Led the FAA, Dies at 86," *New York Times,* December 13, 2011, accessed May 26, 2012, http://www.nytimes.com/2011/12/14/us/j-lynn-helms-who-led-the-faa-dies-at-86.html.

31. Joseph A. McCartin, *Collision Course: Ronald Reagan, the Air Traffic Controllers, and the Strike That Changed America* (Oxford: Oxford University Press, 2011).

32. Sandra L. Albrecht, "'We are on Strike!' The Development of Labor Militancy in the Airline Industry," *Labor History* 45 (2004): 101–17.

33. Alan Greenspan, "The Reagan Legacy," Remarks at the Ronald Reagan Library, Simi Valley, California, April 9, 2003, accessed July 23, 2012, http://www.federalreserve.gov/boarddocs/speeches/2003/200304092/default.htm.

34. McCartin, "Historian's Perspective."

35. GAO, "Air Traffic Control: FAA Needs to Better Prepare for Impending Wave of Controller Attrition," GAO-02–591, Report to the Chairman and Ranking Democratic Member of the Subcommittee on Aviation, House Committee on Transportation and Infrastructure, June 2002, accessed July 14, 2012, http://gns.gannettonline.com/misc/2002cs.pdf.

36. Matthew L. Wald, "Growing Old at Air Traffic Control," *New York Times,* April 3, 2001, accessed May 26, 2012, http://www.nytimes.com/2001/04/03/us/growing-old-at-air-traffic-control.html.

37. Elizabeth A. Harris, "FAA to Change Air Traffic Controllers' Schedules," *New York Times*, April 16, 2011, accessed May 26, 2012, http://www.nytimes.com/2011/04/17/us/17faa.html.

38. Michael J. Sniffen, "As US Air Traffic Controllers Retire, A Staffing 'Emergency' Arises, Union Says," *New York Times,* January 10, 2008, accessed July 14, 2012, http://www.nytimes.com/2008/01/10/business/worldbusiness/10iht-10control.9119299.html.

39. Heppenheimer, *Turbulent Skies*.

40. Vietor, "Contrived Competition," 90.

41. Heppenheimer, *Turbulent Skies,* 342–43.

42. Sheth, et al., *Deregulation and Competition*, 66.

43. R. E. G. Davies and I. E. Quastler, *Commuter Airlines of the United States* (Washington, DC: Smithsonian Institution Press, 1995), xiv.

44. Davies and Quastler, *Commuter Airlines,* 117.

45. FAA, Modernization and Reform Act of 2012, Conference Report to Accompany HR 658, House Of Representatives, 112th Congress, 2nd Session, 91, accessed May 25, 2012, http://www.gpo.gov/fdsys/pkg/CRPT-112hrpt381/pdf/CRPT-112hrpt381.pdf.

46. Dana Lowell, Tom Curry, Lily Hoffman-Andrews, and Lea Reynolds, *Comparison of Essential Air Service Program to Alternative Coach Bus Service* (Manchester, NH: M. J. Bradley & Associates, 2011), 1–4, accessed May 25, 2012, http://www.buses.org/files/Foundation/EAS%20Study%20Final%20Report%20FINALv2%20%2012sep11.pdf.

47. Ibid.

48. Davies and Quastler, *Commuter Airlines,* 121.

49. Ibid., 131.

50. GAO, "Airline Mergers."

51. "United's Pension Debacle," *New York Times*, May 12, 2005, accessed July 15, 2012, http://www.nytimes.com/2005/05/12/opinion/12thu1.html.

52. GAO, "FAA Needs to Better Prepare."

53. Marilyn Adams, "Airlines: Most Northwest, Delta Pension Plans Saved," *USA Today*, August 8, 2006, accessed July 13, 2012, http://www.usatoday.com/money/perfi/retirement/2006-08-07-air-pensions-usat_x.htm.

54. Alexei Barrionuevo, "Unions Threaten to Strike after Pension Default at United," *New York Times,* May 12, 2005, accessed July 15, 2012, http://www.nytimes.com/2005/05/12/business/12union.html.

55. GAO, "Bankruptcy and Pension Problems."

56. Mary Williams Walsh, "How Wall Street Wrecked United's Pension," *New York Times,* July 31, 2005, accessed July 14, 2012, http://www.nytimes.com/2005/07/31/business/yourmoney/31pension.html.

57. Mary Williams Walsh and Jad Mouawad, "US Pension Agency Pressures American Airlines," *New York Times,* January 31, 2012, accessed July 13, 2012, http://www.nytimes.com/2012/02/01/business/pension-agency-pressures-american-airlines.html.

58. Mary Williams Walsh, "At Airline, a Pensions Compromise," *New York Times,* March 7, 2012, accessed July 13, 2012, http://www.nytimes.com/2012/03/08/business/american-airlines-parent-says-it-will-freeze-most-pension-plans.html.

59. Ibid.

60. Walsh and Mouawad, "Pension Agency Pressures American Airlines."

61. Hershey, "Kahn Dies at 93."

62. George E. Hopkins, *Flying the Line*, vol. 2, *The Line Pilot in Crisis: ALPA Battles Airline Deregulation and Other Forces* (Washington, DC: Air Line Pilots Association, 2000), 111.

63. Hershey, "Kahn Dies at 93."

64. Hopkins, *Line Pilot in Crisis,* 112.

65. George E. Hopkins, *Flying the Line: The First Half Century of the Airline Pilots Association* (Washington, DC: Air Line Pilots Association, 1982).

66. "Strike Report: US Airlines."

67. Hopkins, *Line Pilot in Crisis,* 54.

68. Ibid., 57.

69. Ibid., 55.

70. Ibid., 53–54.

71. Dempsey and Goetz, *Airline Deregulation and Laissez-Faire Mythology*, 25.

72. Gordon Bethune, *From Worst to First: Behind the Scenes of Continental's Remarkable Comeback* (New York: John Wiley & Sons, 1998), 13.

73. Cohen, *Nothing to Fear,* 308.

74. Dempsey and Goetz, *Airline Deregulation and Laissez-Faire Mythology*, 25.

75. Aaron Bernstein, *Grounded: Frank Lorenzo and the Destruction of Eastern Airlines.* (New York: Simon & Schuster, 1990), 18.

76. Dempsey and Goetz, *Airline Deregulation and Laissez-Faire Mythology*, 25.

77. Cohen, *Nothing to Fear,* 311.

78. Bernstein, *Grounded*, 13.

79. Cohen, *Nothing to Fear,* 312; Jack E. Robinson, *Free Fall: The Needless Destruction of Eastern Airlines and the Valiant Struggle to Save It* (New York: Harper Collins, 1992), 20.

80. Cohen, *Nothing to Fear,* 312.

81. Pamela G. Hollie, "Continental without Its Chief," *New York Times,* August 11, 1981, accessed June 24, 2012, http://www.nytimes.com/1981/08/11/business/continental-without-its-chief.html.

82. Hopkins, *Line Pilot in Crisis,* 154.

83. "Strike Report: US Airlines."

84. Bernstein, *Grounded,* 15.

85. Hopkins, *Line Pilot in Crisis,* 163–64.

86. Bernstein, *Grounded,* 16 and 17.

87. Robinson, *Free Fall,* 17.

88. Ibid., 138.

89. Ibid., 13, 17, and 3.

90. Agis Salpukas, "Allegis Corp. Replaces Chairman and Plans to Sell Hertz and Hotels," *New York Times,* June 10, 1987, accessed May 29, 2012, http://www.nytimes.com/1987/06/10/business/allegis-corp-replaces-chairman-and-plans-to-sell-hertz-and-hotels.html.

91. Hopkins, *Line Pilot in Crisis,* 113.

92. Ibid., 180.

93. Kenneth Labich and Patricia A. Langan, "How Dick Ferris Blew It: The Boss of Allegis Corp. Lost His Job—and His Dreams of a Diversified Travel Empire—by Angering the Unions and Trying to Sell Pie in the Sky to Wall Street," *CNNMoney,* July 6, 1987, accessed May 29, 2012, http://money.cnn.com/magazines/fortune/fortune_archive/1987/07/06/69232/index.htm.

94. Ibid.

95. Joe Nocera, "The Sinatra of Southwest Feels the Love," *New York Times,* May 24, 2008, accessed June 29, 2012, http://www.nytimes.com/2008/05/24/business/24nocera.html.

96. Kevin Freiberg and Jackie Freiberg, *Nuts! Southwest Airlines Crazy Recipe for Business and Personal Success* (New York: Broadway Books, 1996).

97. Kenneth Labich and Ari Hadjian, "Is Herb Kelleher America's Best CEO?" *Fortune,* May 2 1994, accessed July 5, 2013, http://money.cnn.com/magazines/fortune/fortune_archive/1994/05/02/79246/.

98. Jeff Bailey, "On Some Flights, Millionaires Serve the Drinks," *New York Times,* May 15, 2006, accessed June 29, 2012, http://www.nytimes.com/2006/05/15/business/15millionaires.html.

99. Jeff Bailey, "Co-Founder of Southwest Airlines to Retire as Chairman Next Year," *New York Times,* July 20, 2007, accessed June 29, 2012, http://www.nytimes.com/2007/07/20/business/20southwest.html.

100. Katrina Brooker and Alynda Wheat, "The Chairman of the Board Looks Back," *Fortune,* May 28, 2001, accessed June 23, 2013, http://money.cnn.com/magazines/fortune/fortune_archive/2001/05/28/303852/.

101. Nocera, "Sinatra of Southwest."

102. Brooker and Wheat, "Chairman of the Board Looks Back."

103. Ibid.

104. Jody Hoffer Gittell, *The Southwest Airlines Way: Using the Power of Relationships to Achieve High Performance* (New York: McGraw-Hill, 2003).

105. PBS, "Interview with A. E. Kahn."

5. Escalating Risks

1. Dennis Overbye, "They Tried to Outsmart Wall Street," *New York Times,* March 10, 2009, accessed June 30, 2012, http://www.nytimes.com/2009/03/10/science/10quant.html.

2. Scott Patterson, "The Minds behind the Meltdown," *Wall Street Journal,* January 22, 2010, accessed June 30, 2012, http://online.wsj.com/article/SB10001424052748704509704575019032416477138.html.

3. Saul Hansell, "How Wall Street Lied to Its Computers," *New York Times,* September 18, 2008, accessed June 30, 2012, http://bits.blogs.nytimes.com/2008/09/18/how-wall-streets-quants-lied-to-their-computers/.

4. Scott Patterson, *The Quants: The Math Geniuses Who Brought Down Wall Street* (London: Random House, 2010).

5. Hansell, "How Wall Street Lied."

6. Harry Hurt III, "In Practice, Stock Formulas Weren't Perfect," *New York Times,* February 20, 2010, accessed June 30, 2012, http://www.nytimes.com/2010/02/21/business/21shelf.html.

7. Landon Thomas, Jr., "Once-Stodgy World of London Banking Losing Its Old-School Ways," *New York Times,* July 13, 2012, accessed July 14, 2012, http://dealbook.nytimes.com/2012/07/13/once-stodgy-world-of-london-banking-losing-its-old-school-ways/.

8. Simon Johnson and James Kwak, *13 Bankers: The Wall Street Takeover and the Next Financial Meltdown* (New York: Pantheon, 2010), 7–8.

9. Suzanne McGee, *Chasing Goldman Sachs: How the Masters of the Universe Melted Wall Street Down . . . and Why They'll Take Us to the Brink Again* (New York: Crown, 2010), 45–9.

10. Ibid., 55.

11. Kevin Roose and Susanne Craig, "It's Goldman Bonus Day," *New York Times,* January 19, 2012, accessed August 14, 2012, http://dealbook.nytimes.com/2012/01/19/its-goldman-sachs-bonus-day/.

12. Evelyn M. Rusli and Michael J. De La Merced, "Facebook IPO Raises Regulatory Concerns," *New York Times,* May 22, 2012, accessed June 30, 2012, http://dealbook.nytimes.com/2012/05/22/facebook-i-p-o-raises-regulatory-concerns/; and Somni Sengupta, "Facebook Shares Plummet in an Earnings Letdown," *New York Times,* July 26, 2012, accessed July 27, 2012, http://www.nytimes.com/2012/07/27/technology/facebook-reports-a-loss-but-its-revenue-beats-expectations.html.

13. Nathaniel Popper, "Flood of Errant Trades Is a Black Eye for Wall Street," *New York Times,* August 1, 2012, accessed August 2, 2012, http://www.nytimes.com/2012/08/02/business/unusual-volume-roils-early-trading-in-some-stocks.html.

14. Nathaniel Popper, "Nasdaq Is Fined $10 Million over Mishandled Facebook Public Offering," *New York Times,* May 29, 2013, accessed June 10, 2013, http://dealbook.nytimes.com/2013/05/29/nasdaq-to-pay-10-million-fine-over-facebook-i-p-o/.

15. Gina Chon, Aaron Lucchetti, and Ryan Dezember, "Morgan Stanley, Other Underwriters Make $100 Million Profit on Facebook IPO," *Wall Street Journal*, May 23, 2012, accessed July 5, 2013, http://blogs.wsj.com/deals/2012/05/23/morgan-stanley-other-underwriters-make-100-million-profit-on-facebook-ipo/.

16. Popper, "Nasdaq Is Fined."

17. Ibid.

18. Popper, "Flood of Errant Trades."

19. Dawn Kawamoto, "TheGlobe.com's IPO One for the Books," *CNET*, November 13, 1998, accessed July 6, 2013: http://news.cnet.com/2100-1023-217913.html.

20. Ianthe Jeanne Dugan and Aaron Lucchetti, "After Becoming Stars of the Dot-Com Boom, Theglobe.com Founders Find Fame Fleeting," *Wall Street Journal*, May 2, 2001, accessed July 6, 2013, http://online.wsj.com/article/SB988750097459636.html; Edward Helmore, "So Who's Crying over Spilt Milk?," *Guardian*, May 10, 2001, accessed July 6, 2013, http://www.guardian.co.uk/technology/2001/may/10/internet.onlinesupplement.

21. Greg Ip, Susan Pulliam, Scott Thurm, and Ruth Simon, "How the Internet Bubble Broke Records, Rules, Bank Accounts," *Wall Street Journal,* July 14, 2000, accessed October 3, 2013, http://online.wsj.com/article/SB963527415634796028.html.

22. Ibid.

23. Ibid.

24. Greg Smith, "Why I Am Leaving Goldman Sachs," *New York Times,* March 14, 2012, accessed July 15, 2012, http://www.nytimes.com/2012/03/14/opinion/why-i-am-leaving-goldman-sachs.html.

25. Frank Partnoy, *F.I.A.S.C.O. Blood in the Water on Wall Street* (New York: W. W. Norton, 1997), 48, 14–5, 212, 90, 3, and 52.

26. Nomi Prins, *It Takes a Pillage: Behind the Bailouts, Bonuses, and Backroom Deals from Washington to Wall Street* (New York: John Wiley & Sons, 2009), 137–8.

27. "Senator Phil Gramm's Statement at Signing Ceremony for Gramm-Leach-Bliley Act," press release, November 12, 1999, accessed September 8, 2010, http://banking.senate.gov/prel99/1112gbl.htm.

28. Cyrus Sanati, "10 Years Later, Looking at Repeal of Glass-Steagall," *New York Times*, November 12, 2009, accessed May 19, 2012, http://dealbook.nytimes.com/2009/11/12/10-years-later-looking-at-repeal-of-glass-steagall/.

29. Stephen Labaton, "Congress Passes Wide-Ranging Bill Easing Bank Laws," *New York Times*, November 5, 1999, accessed September 9, 2010, http://www.nytimes.com/1999/11/05/business/congress-passes-wide-ranging-bill-easing-bank-laws.html.

30. Labaton, "Congress Eases Bank Laws."

31. Sanati, "10 Years Later."

32. Partnoy, *F.I.A.S.C.O.,* 97.

33. Peter S. Goodman, "Taking Hard New Look at a Greenspan Legacy," *New York Times,* October 8, 2008, accessed July 1, 2012, http://www.nytimes.com/2008/10/09/business/economy/09greenspan.html.

34. Stephen Mihm, "Dr. Doom," *New York Times,* August 15, 2008, accessed July 1, 2012, http://www.nytimes.com/2008/08/17/magazine/17pessimist-t.html.

35. Raghuram G. Rajan, *Fault Lines: How Hidden Fractures Still Threaten the World Economy* (Princeton: Princeton University Press, 2010), 1.

36. "Niall Ferguson at the 2010 Aspen Ideas Festival," video, accessed September 17, 2010, http://www.realclearpolitics.com/video/2010/07/08/niall_ferguson_on_the_future_of_americas_economy.html.

37. McGee, *Chasing Goldman Sachs,* 279; Johnson and Kwak, *13 Bankers,* 7.

38. Goodman, "Hard New Look."

39. Ibid.

40. "Barons of Wall St. Concede Failures; No Apology," January 13, 2010, accessed July 6, 2013, http://www.reuters.com/article/idUSTRE60C1Y520100113.

41. Ibid.

42. McGee, *Chasing Goldman Sachs,* 58.

43. Matt Taibbi, "The Great American Bubble Machine," *Rolling Stone*, April 5, 2010, accessed July 15, 2012, http://www.rollingstone.com/politics/news/the-great-american-bubble-machine-20100405.

44. Michael J. De La Merced and Ben Protess, "New York Fed Knew of False Barclays Reports on Rates," *New York Times,* July 13, 2012, accessed July 14, 2012, http://dealbook.nytimes.com/2012/07/13/barclays-informed-new-york-fed-of-problems-with-libor-in-2007/.

45. Thomas, "Banking Losing Its Old-School Ways."

46. De La Merced and Protess, "New York Fed Knew of False Rates."

47. Ibid.

48. Associated Press, "FAA Begins Review of Standards for Pilots," *New York Times,* November 22, 1987, accessed July 6, 2013: http://www.nytimes.com/1987/11/22/us/faa-begins-review-of-standards-for-pilots.html.

49. Ibid.

50. Carl H. Lavin, "Pilots Scarce, Airlines See 30-Year-Olds as Captains," *New York Times*, January 11, 1989, accessed July 6, 2013: http://www.nytimes.com/1989/01/11/us/pilots-scarce-airlines-see-30-year-olds-as-captains.html.

51. NTSB, *Aircraft Accident Report: Continental Airlines Flight 1713,* NTSB/AAR-88/09, 1987, accessed March 25, 2010, http://libraryonline.erau.edu/online-full-text/ntsb/aircraft-accident-reports/AAR88-09.pdf.

52. Ibid., 10 and 11.

53. Ibid., 38.

54. NTSB, *Aircraft Accident Report: GP Express Airlines Flight 861*, NTSB/AAR-93/03, 1993, accessed March 25, 2010, http://libraryonline.erau.edu/online-full-text/ntsb/aircraft-accident-reports/AAR93-03.pdf.

55. Ibid., 31.

56. NTSB, *Aircraft Accident Report: Scenic Air Tours Flight 22,* NTSB/AAR-93/01, 1993, accessed March 25, 2010, http://libraryonline.erau.edu/online-full-text/ntsb/aircraft-accident-reports/AAR93-01.pdf.

57. Ibid., 51.

58. Schiavo, *Flying Blind*.

59. NTSB, *Aircraft Accident Report: GP Express Airlines N115GP*, NTSB/AAR-94/01, 1994, accessed March 25, 2010, http://libraryonline.erau.edu/online-full-text/ntsb/aircraft-accident-summaries/AAR94-01S.pdf.

60. Ibid., 12.

61. Carl Rochelle, "FAA Study Raises New Questions about ValuJet's Safety Record," *CNN*, May 16, 1996, accessed July 5, 2012, http://www.cnn.com/US/9605/16/faa.safety.records/index.html.

62. NTSB, *Aircraft Accident Report: Valujet Airlines Flight 592*, NTSB/AAR-97/06, 1996, accessed June 26, 2012, http://www.airdisaster.com/reports/ntsb/AAR97-06.pdf.

63. Schiavo, *Flying Blind*, 6.

64. Ibid., 6, 14, and 12.

65. Ibid., 16.

66. Ibid., 19.

67. Adam Bryant, "FAA Chief Admits Mistakes on Valujet," *New York Times,* June 26, 1996, accessed July 5, 2012, http://www.nytimes.com/1996/06/26/us/faa-chief-admits-mistakes-on-valujet.html.

68. Schiavo, *Flying Blind,* 3.

69. Ibid., 8.

70. Adam Bryant, "The Nation; Lessons of Flying in a Free Market," *New York Times,* May 19, 1996, accessed July 5, 2012, http://www.nytimes.com/1996/05/19/weekinreview/the-nation-lessons-of-flying-in-a-free-market.html.

71. Schiavo, *Flying Blind*, 7.

72. Bryant, "Lessons of Flying in a Free Market."

73. Schiavo, *Flying Blind*, 12.

74. Ibid., 73.

75. Ibid., 19.

76. "Valujet timeline," accessed July 7, 2013, http://www.cnn.com/US/9606/17/valujet.timeline/.

77. Bryant, "Lessons of Flying in a Free Market."

78. Ibid.

79. Ibid.

80. Adam Bryant, "Presto! Valujet Lives," *New York Times,* September 29, 1996, accessed July 5, 2012, http://www.nytimes.com/1996/09/29/weekinreview/presto-valujet-lives.html.

81. Dan Reed and Charisse Jones, "Low-Fare King Southwest to Buy AirTran for $1.4 billion," *USA Today*, September 28, 2010, accessed June 20 2013, http://usatoday30.usatoday.com/money/industries/travel/2010-09-27-southwest-airtran-merger_N.htm.

82. Bryant, "Lessons of Flying in a Free Market."

83. Bryant, "FAA Chief Admits Mistakes."

6. Strapped In for the Ride

1. Air Line Pilots Association (ALPA), "Producing a Professional Airline Pilot: Candidate Screening, Hiring, Training, and Mentoring," Air Line Pilots Association white paper, September 2009, accessed January 1, 2010, http://www.alpa.org/portals/alpa/pressroom/inthecockpit/ProducingProfessionalPilot_9-2009.pdf.

2. Caroline Salas, "Fatal Flying on Airlines No Accident in Pilot Complaints to FAA," *Bloomberg Markets* magazine, December 29, 2009, accessed September 2, 2011, http://www.bloomberg.com/news/2009-12-30/fatal-flying-on-airlines-no-accident-in-pilot-complaints-to-faa.html.

3. "Delta Airlines Aircraft," accessed January 5, 2010, http://www.delta.com/planning_reservations/plan_flight/aircraft_types_layout/index.jsp.

4. US Department of Transportation (DOT), *Profile: Regional Jets and Their Emerging Roles in the US Aviation Market*, Office of the Assistant Secretary for Aviation and International Affairs, June 1998, 5, accessed July 7, 2013, http://adg.stanford.edu/aa241/supplement/regjets.pdf.

5. "Airline Pilot Salaries," accessed May 15, 2010, www.glassdoor.com.

6. Civil Aviation Authority (CAA), *Global Fatal Accident Review, 1997–2006,* Gatwick Airport, UK Safety Regulation Group, July 21, 2008, 1, accessed January 6, 2010, http://www.caa.co.uk/docs/33/CAP776.pdf.

7. DOT, *Profile: Regional Jets*, 5.

8. S. T. Gaal and A. Husain, *Large Regional Jets—The Next Battleground*, May 2006, accessed July 7, 2013, http://65.110.70.37/pointofview/regional.php.

9. Elisabeth Bumiller, "A Day Job Waiting for a Kill Shot a World Away," *New York Times,* July 29, 2012, accessed July 30, 2012, http://www.nytimes.com/2012/07/30/us/drone-pilots-waiting-for-a-kill-shot-7000-miles-away.html.

10. Ibid.

11. ALPA, *Producing a Professional Airline Pilot.*

12. Ibid., 4.

13. Aaron Smith, "Help Wanted: Boeing Says Airlines Need 1 million Workers," *CNNMoney,* September 16, 2010, accessed December 21, 2010, http://money.cnn.com/2010/09/16/news/international/boeing_jobs_airline/index.htm.

14. Federal Register, *Rules and Regulations*, FAA 14 CFR Parts 61 and 121, July 15, 2009, accessed December 27, 2010, http://www.nbaa.org/admin/personnel/age-60/20090715-finalrule.pdf.

15. "Aviation Accident Database," National Transportation Safety Board, accessed July 7, 2013, http://www.ntsb.gov/aviationquery/index.aspx.

16. National Transportation Safety Board (NTSB), *Colgan Air, Inc. Operating as Continental Connection Flight 3407,* NTSB/AAR-10/01 (Washington, DC, 2009), 82, accessed March 31 2010, http://www.ntsb.gov/doclib/reports/2010/aar1001.pdf.

17. Ibid., 12–13.

18. Caroline Salas, "The Hidden Risks of Flying," *Bloomberg Markets* magazine, March 2010, http://newsodrome.com/aviation_news/the-hidden-risks-of-flying-14500328.

19. NTSB, *Colgan Air*, 10.

20. Salas, "Hidden Risks of Flying," 69.

21. NTSB, *Colgan Air*, 278 and 291.

22. NTSB, *Aircraft Accident Report: Attempted Takeoff from Wrong Runway: Comair Flight 5191,* NTSB/AAR-07/05, 2007, 105, accessed September 4, 2011, http://www.ntsb.gov/doclib/reports/2007/AAR0705.pdf.

23. NTSB, *Aircraft Accident Report: Collision with Trees and Crash Short of Runway: Corporate Airlines Flight 5966,* NTSB/AAR-06/01, 2004, 6, accessed September 10, 2011, http://libraryonline.erau.edu/online-full-text/ntsb/aircraft-accident-reports/AAR06-01.pdf.

24. Ibid.

25. NTSB, *Aviation Accident Report: Crash of Pinnacle Airlines Flight 3701,* NTSB/AAR-07/01, 2007, accessed June 24, 2013, http://www.ntsb.gov/doclib/reports/2007/aar0701.pdf.

26. Ibid., 3.

27. Ibid., 108 and 73.

28. Ibid., 60.

29. NTSB, *Aircraft Accident Report: In-Flight Separation of Vertical Stabilizer: American Airlines Flight 587,* NTSB/AAR-04/04. 2004, accessed June 24, 2013, http://www.ntsb.gov/doclib/reports/2004/AAR0404.pdf.

30. Ibid., 4.

31. Ibid., 160.

32. Fraher, *Thinking through Crisis.*

33. Andy Pasztor and Susan Carey, "FAA Probes Trainer of Commuter Pilots," *Wall Street Journal,* May 25, 2009, accessed September 2, 2011, http://online.wsj.com/article/SB12429389 1324544689.html.

34. "Whistle-Blowing Ex-Pilot Prompted Gulfstream International Airlines' $1.3 Million FAA Fine," *Tampa Bay Times,* May 23, 2009, accessed September 5, 2011, http://www.tampabay.com/news/business/airlines/article1003561.ece.

35. Jaclyn Giovis, "Gulfstream Settles Federal Safety Complaint, Agrees to Pay $550,000," *Sun Sentinel* (Fort Lauderdale), July 13, 2010, accessed September 5, 2011, http://articles.sun-sentinel.com/2010-07-13/business/fl-gulfstream-fine-20100713_1_faa-times-for-pilot-scheduling-record-keeping.

36. Alan Levin, "Airline That Trained Buffalo Crash Pilot Fined $1.3M," *USA Today,* May 22, 2009, accessed September 5, 2011, http://abcnews.go.com/Politics/story?id=7649829&page=1.

37. Salas, "Hidden Risks of Flying."

38. NTSB, *American Airlines Flight 587,* 239.

39. FAA, *Answering the Call to Action on Airline Safety and Pilot Training* (Oklahoma City, 2010), accessed October 4, 2013, http://www.skybrary.aero/bookshelf/books/1013.pdf.

40. FAA, *Answering the Call to Action,* 22.

41. Calvin L. Scovel III, *Progress and Challenges with FAA's Call to Action for Airline Safety,* CC-2010–028, Statement before the Committee on Transportation and Infrastructure, Subcommittee on Aviation, US House of Representatives, February 4, 2010, 1, accessed July 8, 2013, http://www.oig.dot.gov/sites/dot/files/WEB%20FILE_Call%20to%20Action%20Testimony.pdf.

42. Ibid., 5.

43. Ibid., 11.

44. Jeffrey B. Guzzetti, *FAA's Progress and Challenges in Advancing Safety Oversight Initiatives,* Statement before the Committee on Commerce, Science, and Transportation, US Senate, April 16, 2013, accessed July 9, 2013, http://www.oig.dot.gov/sites/dot/files/Aviation%20Safety%20Testimony_4-16-13.pdf.

45. See, for example, Michael P. Huerta, *FAA's Progress on Key Safety Initiatives,* Statement before the Committee on Commerce, Science and Transportation, US Senate, April 16, 2013, accessed July 9, 2013, http://testimony.ost.dot.gov/test/huerta2.htm; and Michael P. Huerta, *A Lookback on Reauthorization—One Year Later,* Statement before the Committee on Transportation and Infrastructure, Subcommittee on Aviation, February 27, 2013, accessed July 9, 2013, http://testimony.ost.dot.gov/test/huerta1.htm.

46. FAA, *Pilot Certification and Qualification Requirements for Air Carrier Operations*, 14 CFR Part(s) 61, 121, 135, 141, and 142, accessed July 11, 2013, http://www.faa.gov/regulations_policies/rulemaking/recently_published/media/2120-AJ67.pdf.

47. Ibid., 17.

48. "Pinnacle Airlines, Inc. Releases November Performance Data," accessed December 27, 2010, http://phx.corporate-ir.net/phoenix.zhtml?c=131072&p=irol-newsArticle&ID=1505593&highlight=.

49. Public Broadcasting Service (PBS), *Frontline,* "Flying Cheap, the Cozy Relations," February 9, 2010, accessed February 1, 2011, http://www.pbs.org/wgbh/pages/frontline/flyingcheap/safety/cosy.html.

50. Mike M. Ahler, "Airliner Crew Flies 150 Miles Past Airport," *CNN*, October 22, 2009, accessed January 30, 2010, http://www.cnn.com/2009/TRAVEL/10/22/airliner.fly.by/index.html.

51. Marylynn Ryan, "FAA Probes Plane's Landing on Atlanta Airport's Taxiway," *CNN*, October 21, 2009, accessed January 30, 2010, http://www.cnn.com/2009/US/10/21/georgia.taxiway.incursion/index.html.

52. Scovel, *Challenges with FAA's Call to Action,* 7.

53. NTSB, *SEA08IA080: History of Flight* (Mesa Airlines as Go! Flight 1002), February 13, 2008, accessed July 8, 2013, http://www.ntsb.gov/aviationquery/brief2.aspx?ev_id=20080222X00229&ntsbno=SEA08IA080&akey=1.

54. Roger Yu, "United Flight Canceled When Pilot Says He's Too Upset to Fly," *USA Today*, June 23, 2008, accessed July 8, 2013, http://usatoday30.usatoday.com/travel/flights/2008-06-22-united-pilot_N.htm.

55. Oskar Garcia and Betsy Blaney, "Passengers Tackle Airline Pilot after Mental Breakdown," *San Diego Union Tribune*, March 28, 2012, accessed July 8, 2013, http://www.utsandiego.com/news/2012/Mar/28/tp-passengers-tackle-airline-pilot-after-mental/.

56. Jad Mouawad, "Fracas on JetBlue Shows Gap in Screening," *New York Times,* March 28, 2012, accessed July 8, 2013, http://www.nytimes.com/2012/03/29/business/jetblue-incident-raises-questions-about-screening-pilots.html.

57. Paul J. Weber and Russ Bynum, "JetBlue Captain's Unraveling Baffles Friends," *Bloomsburg Business Week,* March 29, 2012, accessed July 8, 2013, http://www.businessweek.com/ap/2012-03/D9TQ9QBG1.htm.

58. Mouawad, "Fracas on JetBlue."

59. Associated Press, "Texas: Disruptive Pilot Is Acquitted," *New York Times,* July 3, 2012, accessed July 4, 2012, http://www.nytimes.com/2012/07/04/us/disruptive-jetblue-pilot-is-acquitted-in-texas.html.

60. NTSB, *Group Chairman's Factual Report of Investigation Cockpit Voice Recorder, DCA09MA026* (US Airways Flight 1549), 2009, 22, accessed January 30, 2010, http://ntsb.gov/dockets/aviation/dca09ma026/420526.pdf.

61. Joseph Berger and Duff Wilson, "Hole in Southwest Jet Attributed to Cracks," *New York Times,* April 3, 2011, accessed October 4, 2013, http://www.nytimes.com/2011/04/04/business/04plane.html?_r=0.

7. Airlines Today

1. FAA, press release, "FAA to Propose Pilot Retirement Age Change," January 30, 2007, accessed July 8, 2013, http://www.faa.gov/news/press_releases/news_story.cfm?newsId=8027.

2. Susan Carey, Bruce Stanley and John Larkin, "US Pilots Fly to Better Pay in Asia, Middle East," *Wall Street Journal,* May 5, 2006, accessed May 23, 2013, http://www.post-gazette.com/stories/business/news/us-pilots-fly-to-better-pay-in-asia-middle-east-432690/.

3. Ibid.

4. Micheline Maynard and Jeremy W. Peters, "Strike Is Called by Mechanics for Northwest," *New York Times,* August 20, 2005, accessed July 13, 2012, http://www.nytimes.com/2005/08/20/business/20northwest.html.

5. Micheline Maynard, "Well-Laid Plan Kept Northwest Flying in Strike," *New York Times,* August 22, 2005, accessed July 13, 2012, http://www.nytimes.com/2005/08/22/business/22northwest.html.

6. ALPA, *ALPA Newsletter,* "Strength in Unity: Airline Pilots Securing Their Future through ALPA," October 2005, accessed July 24, 2012, http://www.alpa.org/portals/alpa/magazine/2005/Oct2005_StrengthInUnity.pdf.

7. Ibid.

8. Ibid.

9. Chris Serres, "Steenland: Odd Man Out?" *Star Tribune,* February 24, 2008, accessed July 15, 2012, http://www.startribune.com/business/15887132.html.

10. Alison Grant, "Airline Executives Get Millions of Dollars in Mergers," *Plain Dealer,* March 5, 2011, accessed July 15, 2012, http://www.cleveland.com/business/index.ssf/2011/03/airline_executives_get_millions_of_dollars_in_mergers.html.

11. Associated Press, "Richard Anderson, Delta CEO, Gets Huge Pay Boost as Company's Stock Price Plunges," *Huffington Post,* April 27, 2012, accessed July 21, 2012, http://www.huffingtonpost.com/2012/04/28/richard-anderson-delta-ceo_n_1461273.html.

12. Dan Reed, "Executive Suite: Delta Chief Takes Unlikely Flight Path," *USA Today,* February 14, 2008, accessed July 21, 2012, http://www.usatoday.com/travel/flights/2007-10-21-delta-ceo-anderson_N.htm.

13. Micheline Maynard, "How to Succeed in Business, without Really Succeeding," *New York Times,* May 15, 2005, accessed July 15, 2002, http://www.nytimes.com/2005/05/15/business/yourmoney/15air.html.

14. Jeff Bailey, "The Cycle Turns, and Airline Shares Have Fans Again," *New York Times,* April 3, 2007, accessed July 8, 2013, http://www.nytimes.com/2007/04/03/business/03airline.html; and Gretchen Morgenson, "Gee Bankruptcy Never Looked so Good," *New York Times,* January 15, 2006, accessed July 8, 2013, http://query.nytimes.com/gst/fullpage.html.

15. Ibid.

16. Ibid.

17. *Economist,* "The Oil Man in the Jump Seat: How Glenn Tilton Is Struggling to Stop United Airlines Crashing," September 30, 2004, accessed July 15, 2012, http://www.economist.com/node/3242961?story_id=3242961.

18. Maynard, "How to Succeed in Business."

19. Micheline Maynard, "United Said to Restart Talks with US Airways," *New York Times,* April 29, 2008, accessed July 15, 2012, http://www.nytimes.com/2008/04/29/business/29air.html.

20. Shira Ovide and Matthias Rieker, "J P Morgan Hires New Rainmaker: Ex-UAL CEO Glenn Tilton," *Wall Street Journal,* June 6, 2011, accessed July 15, 2012, http://blogs.wsj.com/deals/2011/06/06/j-p-morgan-hires-new-rainmaker-ex-ual-ceo-glenn-tilton/.

21. Amy L. Fraher, "Airline Downsizing and Its Impact on Team Performance," *Team Performance Management* 1 (2013): 109–26.

22. For more on organizational "toxicity," see, for example, Sally Maitlis and Hakan Ozcelik, "Toxic Decision Processes: A Study of Emotion and Organizational Decision Making," *Organization Science* 15 (2004): 375–93; Aneil K. Mishra and Gretchen M. Spreitzer, "Explaining How Survivors Respond to Downsizing: The Roles of Trust, Empowerment, Justice, and Work Redesign," *Academy of Management Review* 23 (1998): 567–87; Lynn R. Offermann, "When Followers Become Toxic," *Harvard Business Review* 81 (2004): 54–60; and Mark Stein, "Toxicity and the Unconscious Experience of the Body at the Employee-Customer Interface," *Organization Studies* 28 (2007): 1223–41.

23. Fraher, "Airline Downsizing."

24. Sheth et al., *Deregulation and Competition*, 78.

25. Based on United and Continental 2012 salary schedules.

26. Scott McCartney, "Pilot Pay: Want To Know How Much Your Captain Earns?" *Wall Street Journal*, June 16, 2009, accessed July 10, 2012, http://blogs.wsj.com/middleseat/2009/06/16/pilot-pay-want-to-know-how-much-your-captain-earns/.

27. NTSB, press release, "NTSB Chairman Offers Support for National Sleep Awareness Week," March 5, 2012, accessed July 25, 2012, http://www.ntsb.gov/news/2012/120305.html.

Epilogue

1. See, for example, Adam M. Pilarski, *Why Can't We Make Money in Aviation?* (Burlington, VT: Ashgate, 2007); Severin Borenstein, "Why Can't US Airlines Make Money?" *American Economic Review* 101 (2011): 233–37; and Joshua Freed and Scott Mayerowitz, "Why's It So Hard to Make Money Running an Airline?" *USA Today,* December 4, 2011, accessed July 21, 2012, http://travel.usatoday.com/flights/story/2011-12-04/Whys-it-so-hard-to-make-money-running-an-airline/51646890/1.

2. Oliver Wright, "You Thought Ryanair's Attendants Had It Bad? Wait 'Til You Hear about Their Pilots," *Independent,* May 17, 2013, accessed July 11, 2103, http://www.independent.co.uk/news/uk/home-news/you-thought-ryanairs-attendants-had-it-bad-wait-til-you-hear-about-their-pilots-8621681.html.

3. See, for example, Mary Scott and Howard Rotham, *Companies with a Conscience: In-Depth Profiles of Businesses That Are Making a Difference* (Franklin Lakes, NJ: Career Press, 2002); Mark Benioff and Karen Southwick, *Compassionate Capitalism: How Corporations Can Make Doing Good an Integral Part of Doing Well* (Franklin Lakes, NJ: Career Press, 2004); Marc Gunther, *Faith and Fortune: How Compassionate Capitalism Is Transforming American Business* (London: Crown, 2005); Fred Kofman, *Conscious Business: How to Build Value through Values* (Boulder, CO: Sounds True, 2006); Rajendra S. Sisodia, David B. Wolfe, and Jagdish N. Sheth, *Firms of Endearment: How World-Class Companies Profit from Passion and Purpose* (Philadelphia: Wharton School Publishing, 2007); and Michael Strong and John Mackey, *Be the Solution: How Entrepreneurs and Conscious Capitalists Can Solve All the World's Problems* (Hoboken, NJ: John Wiley & Sons, 2009).

4. David Vogel and James O'Toole, "Two and a Half Cheers for Conscious Capitalism," *California Management Review* 53 (2011): 60–76.

5. Robert K. Greenleaf, *Servant Leadership: A Journey into the Nature of Legitimate Power and Greatness* (Mahwah, NJ: Paulist Press, 1977).

6. Greg J. Bamber, Jody Hoffer Gittell, Thomas A. Kochan, and Andrew Von Nordenflycht, *Up in the Air: How Airlines Can Improve Performance by Engaging Their Employees* (Ithaca: Cornell University Press, 2009), 308.

7. Michelle Conlin, "Where Layoffs Are a Last Resort," *Business Week,* October 8, 2001, accessed July 9, 2013, http://www.businessweek.com/stories/2001-10-07/where-layoffs-are-a-last-resort.

8. Brooker and Wheat, "Chairman of the Board Looks Back."

9. Bamber et al., *Up in the Air,* 188.

10. Ibid., 4.

11. "TSA passenger security fee," accessed July 11, 2013, http://www.tsa.gov/stakeholders/september-11-security-fee-passenger-fee.

12. "Passengers Carried—All US Airports," accessed July 11, 2013, http://www.transtats.bts.gov/Data_Elements.aspx?Data=1.

13. NBC News, "Number of Air Passengers Increased in 2011," March 22, 2012, accessed July 11, 2013, http://www.nbcnews.com/travel/number-air-passengers-increased-2011-523879.

14. Jad Mouawad, "Airline Unions Seek a Share of the Industry Gains," *New York Times,* October 27, 2010, accessed July 9, 2013, http://www.nytimes.com/2010/10/28/business/28labor.html.

Index

Note: Page references followed by a *t* indicate tables.